THE CYBERNETICS OF KENYAN RUNNING

Nashville
Public Library
Foundation

*This book
made possible
through generous gifts
to the
Nashville Public Library
Foundation Book Fund*

The Cybernetics of Kenyan Running

Hurry, Hurry Has No Blessing

Randall E. Mayes

Carolina Academic Press

Durham, North Carolina

Library of Congress Cataloging-in-Publication Data

Mayes, Randall E.
 The cybernetics of Kenyan running: hurry, hurry has no blessing / by
Randall E. Mayes.
  p. cm.
 Includes bibliographical references.
 ISBN 1-59460-058-9
 1. Runners (Sports)--Kenya. 2. Running--Social aspects--Kenya.
3. National characteristics, Kenyan. I. Title.

GV1061.23.K4M39 2004
796.42'096762--dc22

                                                          2004027979

Carolina Academic Press
700 Kent Street
Durham, NC 27701
Telephone (919) 489-7486
Fax (919) 493-5668
www.cap-press.com

Printed in the United States of America
Cover Design: Erin M. Ehman

Dedicated to Syed Shariq, Valentin Mudimbe, and George Brooks

CONTENTS

PART III   CULTURAL FACTORS: HOW THEY DO THINGS

PART V   ANALYSIS: CYBERNETICS AND REVERSE ENGINEERING

FOREWORD

After graduating from the University of Southern Indiana in 1998, my life changed: I decided to become a full-time runner. Initially, things did not go as expected, as I was going from one city to another in search of paid road races. That led me to Washington DC for a race. There I met Randy Mayes who later became interested in writing a book about Kenyan runners. Since then he has been a friend to me.

In running, focusing is the most important ingredient; most people like to refer to this as the sports psychology. My self motivation has enabled me to accomplish what I have. My running ability may have also come naturally because running is such a big part of the Kenyan culture. Compared to other sports, however, runners do make that much money—so, it is more of an interest in running that has kept me devoted.

For now, my goal is to run faster times. I'm hoping that everything will be good on my side. I have realized that running sub 2:10 is not an easy thing to do, but with speed work, long runs, hill work, tempo runs, and planning, this will be an easy goal.

Randy has been a very helpful person to me several times during my running career. More than one time I stayed in his house in Washington D.C. waiting for a race. We drove to different cities together—Baltimore, twice to Pennsylvania, and a number of road races in the Washington area. For all these activities, Randy was a huge help to me and other Kenyan runners. For someone to be doing all this without any pay in the U.S., I know he has to be great friend who loves running.

We have had many discussions about sport psychology and the mental preparation that runners need to succeed. I personally find it to be the most effective part of my success in running marathons. I have made all kinds of changes in training from when I started pro running. When I was making a critical decision to adopt new training methods, Randy was one of the people who helped me.

Elly Rono, professional runner from Nandi

Acknowledgments

I am extremely grateful to the Duke community for its support—Alumni affairs, Carson Holloway, Richenel Ansano, and the East Campus Trinity Café which was equipped with a generator and free gourmet coffee during the 2002 ice storms and power outages. My special thanks go to Professor Mudimbe, one of Duke's most respected and decorated intellectuals, for reviewing my manuscript.

I am also grateful to the following people for their insight: Syed Shariq, Ph.D., introduced me to the esoteric field of cybernetics. Stuart Umpleby, Ph.D., taught me the intricacies of second and third order cybernetics. Valentin Helou advised me on categories of intelligence to gather and modeling techniques. Brian Cantwell Smith, Ph.D., helped categorize intelligence. Richard Moon, MD, led me to George A. Brooks, Ph.D, who was gracious enough to review the biology section of my manuscript. Brian Bergemann and Rafael Escamillia, Ph.D., provided technical analysis of preliminary physiological testing. Naomi Quinn, Ph.D. and Claudia Strauss, Ph.D. walked me through the basics of their book on cognitive anthropology. Wayne Hurr, Ph.D. and Gregory Dale, Ph.D. provided insights into Western sport psychology theory and practice. Susana Zabala de Utreras, Ph.D., provided insight into the concept of self and consciousness. Robert Daniels, Ph.D. and John Jackson, Ph.D. provided a balance of old school/new school ethnography. Hiram Kibui and runner Ben Kapsoiya assisted with Initiation. Manager Konstantin Selenivich and his Russian runners in Rockville, MD provided their cultural perspective. Kwasi Wiredu. Ph.D., Grant Farred, Ph.D., and Alphonse Mutima all provided an African perspective to view the African psyche. Road racing rankings were provided by Lucas Meyer, an intern at Running Times magazine. Track and Field News granted permission to use their track rankings.

Thanks also to Frank Gagliano, the Reebok Enclave, and the many Kenyan runners allowed me to interview them and offered their friendship: Eliud Barngetuny (Nandi), Joshua Chelanga (Kipsigis), Simon Cheregony (Saboat),

Kibet Cherop (Tugen), Reuben Cheruiyot (Nandi), Reuben Chesang (Tugen), Peter Githuka (Kikuyu), Milka Jipchirchir (Nandi), Margaret Kagiri (Kikuyu), Ben Kapsoiya (Marakwet), Joseph Kariuki (Kikuyu), Simon Karori (Kisii), Kefah Keraro (Kisii), Daniel Kihara (Kikuyu), Joseph Kimani (Kikuyu), Julius Kimtai (Kipsigis), Amos Kipyegen (Tugen), Paul Koech (Nandi), Daniel Komen (Keiyo), John Korir (Kipsigis), Shem Kororia (Saboat), Augustus Kuvutu (Kamba), Hillary Lelei (Nandi), Felix Limo (Nandi), David Maritim (Kipsigis), Andrew Masaii (Saboat), Leonard Mucheru (Kikuyu), Josephat Muchuka (Kisii), Jimmy Muindi (Kamba), Paul Mwangi (Kikuyu), Joseph Nderitu (Kikuyu), John Ngugi (Kikuyu), Nelson Njeru (Kikuyu), Sammy Nyamongo (Kisii), Elly Rono (Nandi), Peter Rono (Nandi), Emily Samoei (Nandi), Vincent Temu (Kisii), Paul Tergat (Tugen), and Daniel Too (Nandi).

THE CYBERNETICS OF KENYAN RUNNING

PART I

BACKGROUND

INTRODUCTION

It may be in our nature or genes to seek simple linear explanations rather than circular causations.[1]

Matt Ridley, *Nature via Nurture*

You must empty your cup (mind) so that it may be filled.

Bruce Lee, *The Tao of Jeet Kune Do*

Followers of professional running may recall prior eras dominated by Scandinavians, Eastern and Western Europeans, New Zealanders, and Americans. Today, it is rare for someone from these regions to place high in international endurance events. There has been speculation, but no definitive answer, as to why many of the fastest middle and long distance runners are Kenyan. An overwhelming majority of the fastest Kenyan runners are from four of over forty ethnic groups—the Kikuyu, the Kamba, the Kalenjin, and the Kisii. For the past decade, the Kalenjins have been the dominant ethnic group. Curiously, only several Kalenjin sub-tribes account for a majority of the runners. These runners are not sure if they are gifted. All they know is they train hard. Is the secret to their success simply that they are suited for endurance running and work hard to develop their gift?

I argue that the current superiority of Kenyan runners is the result of a complex interaction of variables and historical forces. Kenya is not unique—the U.S. has experienced similar historical forces. These essential factors responsible for the Kenyans' success will change over time. A trio of factors—biological, cultural, and psychological—are crucial to peak performance and manifest themselves in both ethnic variations and individual motivations and circumstances. I will try to answer the question: What advantages do these differences present to world class running? I exhibit Western ways of thinking by providing numerous insights into these factors while simultaneously providing blinders and dogmas. I will unpack a historical point of view through models with perspectives from scholars in specialized fields, and will discuss and analyze proposed theories.

What We Know

Since Kenyan domination in running is a relatively new phenomenon, few significant academic or professional studies devoted to the topic have been published. From 1995–97, several works significantly raised our level of understanding. Hard training, genetics, globalization, and culture have been the major theories discussed.

Toby Tanser's *Train Hard, Win Easy*, published in 1997, documents the ascetic lifestyle and training of Kenyan runners and chronicles the first detailed insights into the mysterious tribesmen who are winning the major road races and track meets. Tanser proposes that hard training is the key to their success.

In 1995, Bengt Saltin performed physiological testing on Swedish and Kenyan sedentary teenagers and elite runners, concluding that Kenyan runners have physiological traits more favorable to endurance running. His findings were published in the *Scandinavian Journal of Medicine and Science in Sports*.

In 1996, John Bale and Joe Sang authored *Kenyan Running*, the second book dedicated specifically to understanding Kenyan runners. They propose that colonialism, globalization, Westernization, and modernization are responsible for the Kenyans' success, and venture into the Kenyan psyche, that they assert is not well understood.

In 1997, John Manners presented a paper, *The Running Tribe*, to the British Society of Sports History. A pioneer effort to document the magnitude of Kenyan domination in professional running, the paper was later published in the society's journal, *The Sports Historian*.

Gray Areas and Missing Pieces

We have barely scratched the surface of understanding Kenyan runners. Genetics, culture, ascetic lifestyle, and training have drawn considerable attention from journalists, while psychology, philosophy, world view, belief and knowledge systems, ethnography, and sociology have been discussed to a lesser extent. Eager for new insights, I draw freely from many disciplines; any new ideas are regarded not as determinisms, but as data for interactions in a collaborative model.

Committing the Imagination to Attending the Essential Knowledge

Kenyan running is not a discipline itself, but a complex integration of disciplines and sub-disciplines. If one is going to undertake an interdisciplinary project, where is the logical or perhaps intuitive place to start? After reviewing my cybernetics notes from graduate school, I sought advice from my former professor and mentor. Within forty-eight hours, I had received a coherent road map from a person who knows little about running or Kenya.

Subj: Re: Cybernetic project

Date: Sun, 24 Feb 2002 11:35:48 Eastern Standard

From: "S. shariq" sshariq@stanford.edu

To: mayesrandy@aol.com

Randy:

It is pleasant surprise to hear from you and learn about your journey since 1982. The question you are seeking an answer to may not have an easy answer. It may require further research and exploration. There does not seem to be much insightful work on the significance of beliefs or imagination.

Work on culture, shared cognition to get to issues of support, information processing and brain, embracing the incentives, selection based on intuitive process, and committing the imagination to attending the essential knowledge.

However, we know so little about these factors and their interactions, though you may begin the process with what we know.

Hope this would get you started.

Shariq

Cybernetics (First Order)

Cybernetics is not easily defined. Common threads are cognitive power and interactions among variables in a system. Norbert Weiner, who earned a Harvard Ph.D. at age eighteen, revived the word once used by Aristotle in politics and governing. Greek for steersman, cybernetics refers to a system with built in correction mechanisms (self-steering). An early application of self-regulating systems was for guided missiles whose trajectories had to be corrected in flight in order to hit a target. The additional data used for the correction is called feedback.

In the 1940s, before mainframe computers and computer modeling, pioneers like Weiner used their minds rather than microchips and software. Work with feedback mechanisms in biological systems led to an exponential growth in knowledge, from which evolved the General Systems Theory. The Macy Conferences, funded by the Macy Foundation, established leaders of the new cybernetics field.

The 1950s and 1960s was the engineering period when feedback loops, control systems, artificial intelligence, reverse engineering, and robotics proliferated. Management science flourished with applied operations research, systems analysis, and flow charts. Other applications included government intelligence, military analysis, game theory, and Club of Rome forecasting. In the 1970s, systems science and computer programs succeeded cybernetics as a discipline; its focus was transformed into second order cybernetics. In the 1980s and 1990s, then, applications of cybernetics included data mining, cognitive engineering, and increased use in management.

I use cybernetics as a means of identifying and improving understanding of gray areas (what we do not know). I have found the following cybernetics concepts useful, and applied them in this study.

1. Cybernetics is by nature meta. Analyzing multidisciplinary viewpoints is a discipline in itself. A Meta-ethnography is a research methodology that can be used to integrate the findings of multiple sources and research methods. Considered a complete study in itself, it compares and analyzes texts, creating new interpretations (Noblit 1988, 9).

2. Systems science and cybernetics are sometimes used by analysts to maximize the reduction and preservation of complexity among disciplines. When a model is separated into subsystems, the tendency is to simplify by throwing away interrelationships of non-linear systems. I integrate linkages and interactions among disciplines in non-linear models. An additional layer of analysis discusses interrelationships between biology, culture, and psychology:

   a. Biology——The Endless loop——Environment

   b. Biology——Sociobiology——Psychology (behavior)

   c. Psychology——Psychological Anthropology——Culture

3. The assumption is a group of individuals are working together for a common purpose. A system, therefore, is designed by building a model and leading a group discussion. What is designed in the process are tactics to carry out strategies for removing obstacles (Umpleby 1994, 643).

4. Cybernetics is amorphous and flexible, a dynamic model allowing for updated information such as traditional to modern society and new science.

5. Multiple layers of complexity require multiple layers of analysis. Cognitive analysis requires obtaining the knowledge required to perform the task at each layer by consulting appropriate specialists.

6. A regard for logic and intuition. While humans are subjective, emotional, and slower than computers, cognitive power remains useful. As Nicholas Negroponte, Chairman of the MIT Media Lab, points out, computers are also limited. He is currently working with ways of using common sense and multiple perspectives in computing. The dual approach of acquiring intelligence is used for analyzing stocks by incorporating input from technical (statistics) and fundamental (common sense) analysts.

Second Order Cybernetics

In the 1970 and 1980s, the shift from observed to observer took place—a new era named second order cybernetics by Heinz von Foerster. Also known as Constructivism, it is an alternative to Realism or scientific reasoning and may involve single or multiple observers. Similar to the philosophy of social science, second order cybernetics addresses the relationships, issues, and interactions between the observed and observer. Further, it provides a theory of accountability by embracing self-reference rather than trying to ignore or control it.[2]

Second order cybernetics offers the Law of Requisite Variety, that variety in the observer must be greater than the observed system. For example, incorporating African epistemology or the non-Western equivalent to psychology requires the modeler to use appropriate methods to understand their perspective. The applied focus of this esoteric field is the complex relationship between the observer (author, researcher, or ethnographer) and the observed system. What differentiates the professions that act as observers? They all investigate a topic, collect information, and write about it. What does each bring to a project? In a recent graduate cultural anthropology class, this question was not easily answered.

The media, especially sports journalists and the popular press, often cite living at altitude, genetics, training, and motivation as the primary reasons for Kenyan runners' success. Unarguably, these are all contributing variables. Unfortunately, they do not explain why similar countries and other Kenyan ethnic groups who live at altitude and have ascetic lifestyles do not produce the same quantity of world class runners.

While the anatomy and physiology of Ethiopian, Russian, and Moroccan runners differs from that of the Kenyans, they nevertheless break world records and win Olympic gold medals.

Ethnography combines science and literature based on participant observation. There have been three distinct eras in writing ethnography:

1. In the 1800s and early 1900s, travelers, missionaries, and later Peace Corps workers were collectors of information that was later interpreted and written up by British anthropologists. These first ethnographers enjoyed the illusion that their work was scientific and non-rhetorical, and intended to uncover the emic (the observed) meaning in their discourse.[3]

2. In the early 1900s, American ethnographers (Realists), notably Margaret Mead, performed their own field work and wrote about it. Mead was not only a pioneer in cultural anthropology, but also cybernetics. After attending the Macy Conferences, she applied cybernetics to the social sciences.

3. Ethnographic writings after the mid-1900s are placed in the Self-Reflective Era. Anthropologists inject their own backgrounds, experiences, theories, politics, and perspectives into the narrative (Layton 1997, 215).

Ethnographers' authority stems from their specialized training and skilled understanding of culture (Clifford: 30), acquired through the study of languages, behavior, institutions, rituals, and symbols. The self-reflective writing style seen in literature, philosophy, and ethnography includes such genres as experimental, post-modern, Meta, critical, post-structuralism, performative, and confessional. Each positions itself from a particular perspective. Appropriately, authors are more playful with writing styles and the use of visuals that do not follow the traditional style.

Up to the Mau Mau Rebellion in the 1950s, Kenya's ethnic groups were referred to as tribes. Early Eurocentric ethnographic writings portrayed them as primitive. Still, ethnic affiliation remains extremely important; runners proudly refer to their ethnic groups as tribes and sub-tribes.

I have found the following second order cybernetics concepts useful:

1. Embrace using multiple perspectives and methodologies rather than the univocal approach (Nicholas Negroponte and Brian Cantwell Smith).

2. Proactively avoid pitfalls of logic and shifting levels of analysis.

   a) Language. Problems with ambiguity.

   b) Errors in thought and circular reasoning. For example, as languages may be used to understand cognitive processes, semiotics and hermeneutics or symbols are used to explain social processes. Some critics argue that circular reasoning, a hermeneutic circle between the parts and the whole, is involved. For example, with the survival of the fittest, the fittest are the ones who survive.

c) Feelings: emotional considerations (Umpleby 1989, 113)

3. How the system is being observed. Ways of defining and describing the systems/disciplines involved.

a) Variables: engineering, physics, economics

b) Events: political science, psychology, history, computers

c) Groups: sociology, game theory

d) Ideas: cultural anthropology, sociology (Umpleby 1994, 641)

My Perspective

The Cybernetics of Kenyan Running is a result of my experiences as a journalist, researcher, and observer. My first experience with Kenyan running was in 1996 as a volunteer at the Sallie Mae 10K road race in Washington, DC. Following the race, I spent several hours with Jimmy Muindi, from the Kamba tribe, discussing his training and culture. His humility inspired me to become a part-time running journalist. I cannot imagine a similar experience with an American football or basketball star. Consequently, I had the opportunity to meet and live with many Kenyan runners.

While writing feature articles on the Reebok Enclave, groups of professional Kalenjin, Kikuyu, and Russian runners, and numerous professional runners, I noticed a diverse range of perspectives. That inspired more research into the mental aspects of running. Coach Frank Gagliano, former Reebok Enclave and current Nike Farm Team coach, encouraged me to write an article with sport psychologist Dr. Wayne Hurr.

My appreciation of interdisciplinary studies began upon hearing the comments of a cultural anthropology professor: "The more knowledge he acquired, the more he noticed how everything is related." A Systems Science (Cybernetics) course, intended to help in managing ecosystem projects and environmental impact statements by integrating multiple disciplines, changed how I process information and analyze problems. My training with a secret service agent who taught Bruce Lee's martial arts and philosophy also left me with a unique source of knowledge. All of these experiences developed my perspective as a journalist and researcher, and my interpretation of Kenyan running.

Bruce Lee's Cybernetic Precedent

It is doubtful that any martial arts student is not influenced by Lee's philosophy. Never a professional fighter, Lee paid his bills by making movies and teaching martial arts. Transcending the customs of his time and place, Lee suggested all ways and means should be used to accomplish goals, stating, "Conformers are second hand artists."[4] A philosophy major at the University of Washington, Lee was a visionary; his curiosity and interest in interdisciplinary studies resulted in his collecting over two thousand books.

Lee was careful not to call his way a "system" or "style" like other martial arts that by definition have limitations. He preferred a dynamic model of no-way or adaptability (that mirrors cybernetics), saying, "Freedom of expression occurs when one is beyond systems."[5]

By breaking thousands of years of tradition, Lee revolutionized the way we know martial arts. He was controversial at a time when China was closed to the West, he married an American and shared ancient martial arts secrets. In contrast, Jhoon Rhee's *Tae Kwon Do* cookie cutter franchise approach placed Rhee on the Forbes's wealthiest list. Rhee's affiliated studios are teaching self esteem through *katas* and discipline in almost every medium to large city in the United States. Traditional Eastern martial arts are practiced barefooted with loose fitting clothing and color coded belts or sashes for rank. Each student, regardless of size or age, memorizes the same system of movements.

In the introduction to his book, Lee conveys the concept: "*The Tao of Jeet Kune Do*, you see, has no lines or boundaries-only those you make for yourself (Lee 1975, 5)." From Zen, he learned the importance of opening and expanding one's mind by clearing everything that obscures reality. When searching for advanced footwork, for example, he learned from fencing experts. Lee sought the strengths from over thirty martial arts disciplines, continually refining his fighting techniques. He discarded bowing and rank (as they were inconsistent with his philosophy), and practiced in street clothes and shoes to better simulate real fighting conditions. His students became acquainted with different styles and techniques that were useful at different ranges. Each student could select what was appropriate based both on their own and their opponent's strengths and weaknesses. A former student, Joe Lewis, combined Okinowan karate with boxing to start what became American kickboxing. Lee's hand-picked instructors at his three schools, Ted Wong, Taky Kimura, and Dan Inosanto, each taught based on their interpretations and strengths. Lee's students share his legacy and sports cybernetics model.

The Cybernetic Model

This book includes perspectives from numerous disciplines. Part I focuses on Kenya, from casual tribal to formal international competitions. I discuss globalization, political forces, the business vs. sport aspect of professional running, Olympics and national pride, and its effects on American road racing.

Parts II and III present both sides of the nature vs. nurture debate. I discuss the biologist's perspective, the endless loop of linked environmental factors, and examine why we have no definitive biological answer, physiological models, or institutional and scientific dogma. Based on research by Dr. George Brooks, I discuss the enigmatic role of lactate.

Part III examines how the runners do things, the perspectives of sociologists and ethnographers. Social forces covered include support systems, life stages, socialization processes, institutions, and different routes to the U.S. I chronicle the life of professional Kenyan runner in the U.S., unpacking the theories and examining conflicting schemas. I discuss ethnocentrisms, ethnic variations, and how those variations are unique in their relationship to success in running.

John Bale's observation that the Kenyan mindset is not well understood is understandable given that psychological factors have received less attention and analysis. The Swahili phrase *haraka haraka haina baraka* (hurry, hurry has no blessing) conveys a mental concept, ironically reflecting part of the Kenyan world view.

Part IV offers the perspective of psychologists and philosophers in understanding individual and collective thought and their relationship to running. Do essential differences exist in humans? I compare four approaches to understanding African Belief and Knowledge Systems, and attempt to answer what is the Kenyan equivalent to Western sport psychology.

In Part V, I present a cybernetic analysis of the model, and the theories proposed by various disciplines and perspectives. Based on merit, they are placed in hierarchy—necessary, contributing, and possible factors or no merits. Chapter 12 covers social Darwinism and the controversial sociobiology that provides alternative views to socialization for understanding behavior. As Kenya is changing rapidly, how much longer will the culture be conducive to their domination in running?

Finally, in Third Order Cybernetics, I discuss the reader's perspective and role in the conversation. Institutional and scientific dogma, ethnocentrism, and political correctness create barriers to finding answers. Thinking outside the box, evolving Western schemas, new science and social science, and constructive dialogue assist in obtaining answers. Each discipline and each perspective are influenced by these factors.

1

TIME: HISTORICAL CONSIDERATIONS

New Zealand used to be the best, then Finland. Kenya will not always be on top. Someday someone else will be number one.[1]

Kipchoge Keino

Clues from the Historical Evidence

Kenny Moore's fascination with Kenyan runners resulted in the 1990 publication of *Out of Africa: Sons of the Wind*, perhaps the earliest linkage of Kenyan running with culture. An Olympic marathoner and writer for *Sport's Illustrated*, Moore makes the reader feel as though he is in the Rift Valley. With references to Kalenjins and circumcision, speculation soon began that cattle raiding and socialization were somehow linked to running success, and the Initiation Theory hit the national media.

Moore's research reveals that the pastoralist Cushites migrated from Ethiopia to Kenya around 1000 B.C. In the first 1000 A.D., the Nilotic people migrated from the north, and the Bantus arrived.[2] Because Kenyans vary ethnically, it is risky to generalize about them. The Kalenjin people have a distinct language, culture, identity, and agricultural-pastoral economy (their lifestyle is linked with milking and bleeding cattle). The Tugens still practice the custom of chipping or removing a tooth to allow for food, milk, and water in the event of lockjaw, fainting, or comas.[3] While the Rift Valley preserves archeological artifacts remarkably well, it is unclear what took place in pre-colonial centuries. Warring tribes were pastoral, tending cattle and searching for water and food.

In 1498, Portuguese explorer Vasco de Gama arrived on the East African coast in search of China. The Portuguese established trading posts and stayed for two hundred years. "Portuguese rule was harsh, unpopular, and economically debilitating for the local people (July 1970, 85)." To establish dominance, Oman and other Arab nations confronted the Portuguese. Oman prevailed, and took control in 1698. By 1720, the last remaining Portuguese had left the East African coastal region. The Moslem influence has magnified the regional and ethnic differences throughout Kenya.

Around 1800, Christian missionaries and explorers came to Africa in the Great Trek (July 1970, 237). The British occupation of inland Kenya led to the establishment of a British Protectorate in 1895. British rule, culture, and religion were resisted, eventually leading to bloodshed. Hillary Lelei, a Kenyan runner who began racing in the U.S. in 2003, recalls how British soldiers forced his father to carry messages over twenty miles. The letters were attached to a stick to avoid being damaged. If he delivered the message late, he was beaten.

The Mau Mau Rebellion, led by the Kikuyu tribe, began in 1952, and resulted in Kenya winning independence in 1963. The British cultural influence, however, still remains—language, tea, Christianity, cash economy, currency, metric system, driving habits, private schools, and organized running.

Who Owns the Cattle?

Little was known about the enigmatic Kenyan runners before several 1996 publications—for example, *The Running Tribe* by John Manners. Manner's father, an anthropologist and himself a Peace Corps volunteer in Kenya, theorized that cattle raiding and initiation were possible reasons for the Kenyan's (specifically the Kalenjin) success in running. Danish researcher Dirk Lund Christiansen also proposes the Cattle Raiding Theory. "Euphemistically known as cattle raiding, cattle theft was a common practice among some Kenyan tribes. The cattle rustlers felt by divine right they owned the cattle."[4] The night runners covered between fifty and sixty km, risking their lives; those who could round up the most cows garnered more wives, in turn producing more children.[5] Logically it follows that these warriors would make great endurance runners.

"Raiders who were caught were jailed, and prisoners were sent out as laborers on public works projects; among these were the leveling and marking out of running tracks."[6] Manners also investigates the connection between social control and the Kalenjin. "The British suggested, show your valor in sports and games, not in war. So it seemed that the Kalenjin fondness for raiding earned them an extra push from the colonial administration to take up track instead. But try as I may, I haven't been able to find any evidence in colonial records that my correspondent's approach was ever applied throughout Kalenjin country. There are lots of references to Kalenjin cattle raiding, some with a detectable note of admiration, but none that mention the promotion of sport as a surrogate. I've looked through some of the literature on sport as a mechanism of social control, and there's certainly evidence that sport was used this way among another Kenyan tribe, the Kikuyu, after the Mau Mau rebellion in the 1950s. But I've found nothing about the Kalenjin. Another possible reason for Kalenjin success that has to do with a British colonial law is enforcement policy. I once had high hopes for this idea, but up to now I haven't had much luck finding evidence to support it."[7]

Tribal to World Class Status and Domination

Before modernization, tribal status served as a motivation for amateur athletes. The Maasai were the great runners—competitions included running, sometimes over hurdles (Bale 1996, 51). In 1950, The Jeanes School at Kabete was equipped with modern track facilities (Bale 1996, 94). Arthur 'Archie' Evans, the first (British) Kenyan Sports Officer, kept sports records and initiated the local and national track meets that form the basis of Kenya's track program today (Amin 1972, 16).

The transition from folk (traditional) to modern running occurred as Sir Derek Erskine established Athletics Kenya (AK), the Kenyan sports federation, in 1952—the first year the Kenyan team was allowed to participate in competitions outside East Africa. Increasing numbers of runners from the Kamba, Kisii, Kikuyu, and Kalenjin ethnic groups competed at the international level. The national team participated in the Indian Ocean Games in Madagascar. In 1966 and 1967, Naftali Temu, a Kisii, topped the world rankings in the 10,000m; in 1967 and 1968, he also made the top ten for the 5,000m. Kip Keino, a Kalenjin, was ranked first in the 5,000m in 1966, and second in 1967.

In the 1950s and 1960s, the U.S. Department of State/U.S. Information Agency was involved in developing athletes, sports programs, and scholarships in Africa. American Olympic gold medalist Mal Whitfield spent seventeen years in Kenya as an officer of the program, conducting clinics and preparing training guides. In 1967, he authored *Learning to Run,* published by the East African Publishing House in Nairobi.

At the 1968 Mexico City Olympic Games, Kip Keino defeated American world record holder Jim Ryun in one of the greatest 1,500m races in the history of the Games. The East Africans (especially the Kenyans), received attention, as did the effects of altitude on training and competition. A new era in scientific research began; remarkable advances in sports medicine and science followed.

For political reasons, Kenya did not participate in the 1976 or 1980 Olympics. The International Olympic Committee (IOC) suspended South Africa from 1964–88 for its apartheid system under which blacks were denied equal rights with whites. Approximately thirty African nations boycotted the 1976 Montreal Olympics after the IOC allowed New Zealand to compete (New Zealand's rugby team had recently played in South Africa). When the former Soviet Union invaded Afghanistan, the U.S. and sixty-five other countries (e.g., Kenya, Canada, Japan, China, the Federal Republic of Germany, and Norway) protested by boycotting the 1980 Moscow Olympics.

In 1978, when Europeans and Scandinavians were dominating track and road racing, Henry Rono (a Nandi) set four world records (3,000m, 3,000m steeplechase, 5,000m, and 10,000m) in eighty days. He was a student athlete at Washington State, a university that continues its relationship with Kenyan runners today. Even as early as the 1960s, when Kenya placed several athletes in the record books, their talent was evident; the extent of their talent, however, remained unclear.

World Cross Country

From 1981–85, Ethiopia swept the team title. But for the next eighteen years, the Kenyan squad won the team title at the World Cross Country Championships. Kenyan runners emerged on the scene when John Ngugi won the individual 12K World Cross Championship from 1986–89 and again in 1992. William Sigei followed, winning in 1993–94. Paul Tergat, then, won the last individual Kenyan long course titles from 1995–99. He then began focusing on other surfaces and events. Since 1999, East African runners have won all the individual titles. In 2000, Kenyans went one through five in the short course led by John Kibowen. Enock Koech won the short course in 2001.

Commenting not just on Kenya dominance, but more specifically Kalenjin dominance, Manners wrote, "Kalenjin runners have made up fully three-quarters of the scoring runners on those twelve winning Kenyan teams. In fact, in eight of the twelve winning years, if only the Kalenjin runners had competed,

Figure 1.1   Reuben Cheruiyot, 2000 road racer of the year; the author; and Felix
Limo, former 25km world record holder. Photo by Milka Jipchirchir.

they'd still have taken the team title. I contend that this record marks the greatest geographical concentration of achievement in the annals of sport."[8]

In 2004, the Ethiopian team won the 12km and 4km events. This dramatic
shift may be due to a number of reasons. There has been a shift in emphasis

to the marathon which results in managers and national team coaches competing for athletes. Kenyan newspapers report that Kenyan athletes are increasingly more frustrated with the demands required for making and training on the national teams. In addition, the defection to other countries has resulted in Kenya losing top athletes.

Road Racing: What Happened in 1992?

Before 1992, no more than two Kenyan men were in the top ten of the World Road Racing Rankings. After 1992, no less than five were in the top ten. Several events contributed to this shift. "In 1990, Kenya's Commissioner of Sports lifted restrictions on athletes' travel and access to agents, a hugely significant move that led directly to the spiral of opportunities and incentives that have driven recent performances (Tanser 1997, 18)." In addition, manager Kim McDonald began working with Kenyan athletes in 1990 at the request of Kenyan Commissioner of Sports Mike Boit. At the time, most Kenyan runners competing internationally had been filtered through American colleges; for the rest, opportunities were scarce.[9] According to Tom Ratcliffe of KIM Management (that represented seven of the top ten road racers in 1992), Kenyans assumed dominance on the roads because Boston hosted the World Cross Country Championships, and several runners stayed in the U.S. to compete.

In 1982, when *Running Times Magazine* began publishing rankings, two of the top ten runners were from Kenya—a Kamba and a Kikuyu. In 1991, Kenya also placed two runners in the top ten—a Kamba and a Kalenjin (see Table 1.1).

In 1992, nine of ten runners were Kenyan—five Kalenjin, three Kisii, and one Kamba (see Table 1.2). Of those nine, only Mutwol, Akonay, and Masya were not KIM Management athletes. Originally, the majority of top Kenyan runners in the international men's road racing rankings were from the Kamba, Kikuyu, or Kisii ethnic groups. After 1992, the Kalenjin became dominant.

In 1992, five of the top nine Kenyans were Kalenjin (see Table 1.3). In 2001, five of the top men were from Kenya and all were Kalenjin (see appendix C). "The Kalenjin tribe has three million people, that is about ten percent of Kenya's population. But this group has earned about seventy-five percent of Kenya's distance running honors and has won close to forty percent of all the top international honors available in men's distance running disciplines; cross country, road racing and track. The Nandi, a Kalenjin sub-tribe, with roughly five hundred thousand people, account for 1/12,000 of the world's population. They account for twenty percent of the top international distance medals."[12]

Table 1.1   Men's World Road Racing Rankings[10]

1982	1991
1. Alberto Salazar	1. Steve Spence
2. Michael Musyoki (Kamba)	2. Alejandro Cruz
3. Jon Sinclair	3. Frank O'Mara
4. Greg Meyer	4. Steve Kogo (Kalenjin-Nandi)
5. Rodolfo Gomez	5. Dionicio Ceron
6. Rod Dixon	6. John Halvorsen
7. Nick Rose	7. Ed Eyestone
8. Gabriel Kamau (Kikuyu)	8. Mark Plaatjes
9. Benji Durden	9. William Musyoki (Kamba)
10. Dick Beardsley, Bill Rodgers (tie)	10. Bill Reifsnyder

In 2000, six of the top ten runners were Kenyan—four Kalenjin, one Kikuyu, and one Kisii. In 2001, five of the top ten were Kalenjin, led by Paul Tergat. In 2002, five of the top ten were Kenyans—four Kalenjins, and one Kikuyu (see Table 1.4).

In 1991, the first Kenyan women appeared in the top ten. In 1995, three Kenyan women were in the top ten, in 2001, five, and in 2002, four (see Table 1.5).

Marathon

Before 1998, no more than three Kenyan marathoners ranked in the top ten (see appendix I). Runners shifted to this event largely because of financial incentives— cash prizes, time bonuses, and appearance fees to obtain fast times and world records. Kenyan runners began dominating the marathon later than they did track and road races. In 1998, Kenya placed fifth in the top

Table 1.2   1992 Men's World Road Racing Rankings[11]

1. William Mutwol (Kalenjin-Marakwet)
2. Benson Masya (Kamba)
3. Dominic Kirui (Kalenjin-Kipsigis)
4. William Sigei (Kalenjin-Kipsigis)
5. Simon Karori (Kisii)
6. Sammy Lelei (Kalenjin-Nandi)
7. Lameck Aguta (Kisii)
8. Ondoro Osoro (Kisii)
9. Boay Akonay (Tanzania)
10. Godfrey Kiprotich (Kalenjin-Keiyo)

ten marathon rankings, with Ondoro Osoro at number one. In 2002, six of the top ten marathon runners were Kenyan (see Table 1.6).

The U.S. had one marathoner, Rod DeHaven, competing in the 2000 Olympics. According to the IOC rules, if certain times were not met at the trials, only one athlete would be eligible to compete. In 1999, 106 Kenyan marathoners ran sub 2:14 (see Table 1.7). Two Americans qualified, out of a population of approximately two hundred million more people.[16] In 2003, Kenyans Paul Tergat and Sammy Korir broke the world record and became the first to run sub-2:05 marathons.

Track

The Track and Field News World Rankings have documented Kenya's increasing dominance in distances from 1,500m to 10,000m (see appendix I). The quantity of Kenyan runners in the Grand Prix track competitions (that have limited entrants based on talent and manager negotiating skills), reflect their obvious dominance. In the 1990s, Kenyan runners began their domination in the middle distances (see Table 1.8).

Table 1.3   Kenyan Ethnic Representation of World Top Ten Male Road Racers by Year

A = Kamba, B = Kikuyu, C = Kalenjin, D = Kisii

82	83	84	85	86	87	88	89	90	91	92	93	94	95	96	97	98	99	00	01	02	03
									A												
									C						B	B	B				
									C		A		B	B	B	B					
									C		B	B	B	C	C	C	B				C
										C	C	C	B	B	C	C	C	C	C	B	C
	A									C	C	C	C	C	D	C	C	C	C	C	C
	A			A						D	C	D	D	C	D	D	C	C	C	C	C
A	A	B	A	A		C	C		A	D	D	D	D	D	D	D	D	C	C	C	C
B	A	C	C	C	C	C	D		C	D	D	D	D	D	D	D	D	D	C	C	D

Table 1.4   Men's World Road Racing Rankings[13]

2000	2002
1. Reuben Cheruiyot (Kalenjin-Nandi)	1. Paul Kosgei (Kalenjin-Nandi)
2. Joseph Kimani (Kikuyu)	2. Haile Gebrselassie
3. Khalid Khannouchi	3. Chales Kamathi (Kikuyu)
4. Mark Yatich (Kalenjin-Nandi)	4. James Koskei (Kalenjin-Nandi)
5. Faustin Baha	5. Paul Tergat (Kalenjin-Tugen)
6. David Makori (Kisii)	6. Khalid Khannouchi
7. Antonio Pinto	7. John Yuda
8. Hendrick Ramaala	8. Tesfaye Jifar
9. John Korir (Kalenjin-Kipsigis)	9. Hendrick Ramaala
10. David Chelule (Kalenjin-Nandi)	10. Jackson Koech (Kalenjin-Nandi)

Table 1.5   Women's World Road Racing Rankings[14]

1991	1995	2002
1. Liz McColgan	1. Delilah Asiago (Kisii)	1. Paula Radcliffe
2. Lynn Jennings	2. Rose Cheruiyot (Kalenjin)	2. Lornah Kiplagat (Kalenjin)
3. Jill Hunter	3. Tegla Loroupe (Kalenjin)	3. Birhane Adere
4. Wanda Panfil	4. Uta Pippig	4. Susan Chepkemei (Kalenjin)
5. Francie Larrieu-Smith	5. Lynn Jennings	5. Catherine Ndereba (Kikuyu)
6. Delilah Asiago (Kisii)	6. Joan Nesbit	6. Sonia O'Sullivan
7. Judi St. Hilaire	7. Olga Appell	7. Deena Drossin
8. Susan Sirma (Kalenjin)	8. Collette Murphy	8. Asmae Leghzaoui
9. Kim Jones	9. Kamila Gradus	9. Isabella Ochichi (Kisii)
10. Shelly Steely	10. Colleen De Reuck	10. Mizuki Noguchi

In 1988, Kenyans began placing runners at the top of the rankings in the 3,000m steeplechase. In 1992, six of the top ten were Kenyans (see Table 1.9). This event has since become dominated by Kenyans.

In 1991, Kenya placed four runners in the top ten of the 5,000m world rankings—two more than ever before. From 1992–2002, Kenyans earned fifty-two of the 110 available spots. In 2001 and 2002, seven of the top ten were Kenyan (see appendix I) (see Table 1.10).

In 1991, Kenya placed five runners in the top ten of the 10,000m world rankings—like the 5,000m, two more than ever before. From 1992–2002, Kenyans earned fifty-one of the 110 available spots. From 2000–02, Kenyans held seventeen of the thirty available spots (see appendix I). The World Cham-

Table 1.6   Men's World Marathon Rankings[15]

1998	2002
1. Ondoro Osoro (Ken)	1. Khalid Khannouchi (US)
2. Ronaldo da Costa (Bra)	2. Paul Tergat (Ken)
3. Moses Tanui (Ken)	3. Daniel Njenga (Ken)
4. Joseph Chebet (Ken)	4. Toshinari Takaoka (Jpn)
5. Fabiän Roncero (Spa)	5. Abdelkader El Mouaziz (Mor)
6. John Kagwe (Ken)	6. Rodgers Rop (Ken)
7. Gert Thys (SA)	7. Haile Gebrselassie (Eth)
8. Khalid Khannouchi (Mor)	8. Raymond Kipkoech (Ken)
9. Jackson Kabiga (Ken)	9. Simon Biwott (Ken)
10. Abel Anton (Spa)	10. Christopher Cheboiboch (Ken)

pionships and the Olympics do not reflect the same domination by Kenya in the 5,000 and 10,000m events (see appendices E, F, and G).

National Teams: The Paradox of Talent and Achievement

Why don't Kenyans dominate the World Championships and the Olympics as they do track, cross country, and road races? A coach's frustration captured

Table 1.7   Sub 2:20 Marathons[17]

	United States	Great Britain	Kenya
1989	64	54	18
1999	34	7	222

Table 1.8   1,500m / Mile and 3,000m World Rankings[18]

1998 1,500m / mile	1992 3,000m
1. Hicham El Guerrouj (Mor)	1. Moses Kiptanui (Ken)
2. Laban Rotich (Ken)	2. Paul Bitok (Ken)
3. John Kibowen (Ken)	3. Yobes Ondieki (Ken)
4. Noureddine Morceli (Alg)	4. Dieter Baumann (Ger)
5. Daniel Komen (Ken)	5. William Sigei (Ken)
6. Noah Ngeny (Ken)	
7. Reyes Estevez (Spa)	
8. William Tanui (Ken)	
9. Rui Silva (Por)	
10. Andres Diaz (Spa)	

by journalist Tom Kennedy's coverage of a Kenyan training camp before the 1996 Atlanta Olympics might offer a clue. The majority of athletes did not show up at the training camp, but went directly to Atlanta several days before the Olympics. "For one surreal week Kip Keino waited in Hattiesburg, MS for the runners who seem to defy the laws of biology. They unfortunately couldn't defy the laws of physics being in Europe collecting appearance fees and prize money."[22]

Immannel Wallerstein's 1970s World Systems Theory is a global economic model with three geographic economic regions—core states with economic power exploiting the periphery (colonial states), and semi-peripheral (buffer) states. He claims that globalization has resulted in the underdevelopment and dependency of peripheral states.

The cost of losing resources and runners to Westernization and modernization appears accurate. American road racing and European Grand Prix Track have drawn resources from AK to the point where a paradox of talent and achievement is required to win Olympic medals. Agents and race directors have prevailed.

Table 1.9   3,000m Steeplechase World Rankings[19]

1988	1992
1. Julius Kariuki (Ken)	1. Moses Kiptanui (Ken)
2. Peter Koech (Ken)	2. Matthew Birir (Ken)
3. Mark Rowland (GB)	3. Patrick Sang (Ken)
4. Patrick Sang (Ken)	4. Philip Barkutwo (Ken)
5. Francesco Panetta (Ita)	5. William Mutwol (Ken)
6. Alessandro Lambruschini (Ita)	6. Micah Boinett (Ken)
7. William van Dijck (Bel)	7. Alessandro Lambruschini (Ita)
8. Henry Marsh (US)	8. Steffen Brand (Ger)
9. Boguslaw Maminski (Pol)	9. Tom Hanlon (GB)
10. Hagen Melzer (EG)	10. Brian Diemer (US)

Since 1988, when Kenyans claimed four gold medals, results have been inconsistent with their free market results—two in 1992, one in 1996, and two in 2000 (see appendix G). Olympic marathon gold medalist Frank Shorter notes, "Prior to the Kenyans, it was industrialized nations who had access to technology and the financial incentives. The Africans finally got a level playing field. Then, the game was over."[23] The rivalry between the AK and national coaches, and athletes and agents is both political and economical. According to Keino, athletes got away as the Kenyan Amateur Athletics Federation (KAAA) officials had no jurisdiction.[24]

An attempt to reverse their mediocre results for the 2003 World Championships placed the athletes and mangers at odds with the AK. Prior to the 2003 World Junior Championships, AK Secretary General David Okeyo warned the managers against scouting underage runners. In 2003, an article in *The East African Standard* reported that Kenyan National Coach Mike Kosgei wanted athletic officials to ban managers who interfered with his work by giving the runners different instructions. In addition, he blamed the mushrooming shoe

Table 1.10   5,000m World Rankings[20]

1991	2002
1. Yobes Ondieki (Ken)	1. Benjamin Limo (Ken)
2. Fita Bayissa (Eth)	2. Sammy Kipketer (Ken)
3. Salvatore Antibo (Ita)	3. Richard Limo (Ken)
4. Brahim Boutaib (Mor)	4. Abraham Chebii (Ken)
5. Khalid Skah (Mor)	5. Salah Hissou (Mor)
6. Ibrahim Kinuthia (Ken)	6. John Kibowen (Ken)
7. Richard Chelimo (Ken)	7. Paul Bitok (Ken)
8. Julius Korir II (Ken)	8. Abderrahim Goumri (Mor)
9. Mathias Ntawulikura (Rwa)	9. Mohammed Amyn (Mor)
10. Mikhail Dasko (SU)	10. Mark Bett (Ken)

company camps for initiating conflicting loyalties.[25] Kosgei continues to salvage his national teams despite defectors pursuing financial gain. As far back as 1996, Keino preached that there is more to running than money, saying, "Talent opens doors to college scholarships and team medals."[26]

According to Kenyan journalists, the respect and financial incentives at home are less than runners can command abroad. Over ten Kenyans, therefore, represented other countries in the 2003 Paris World Championships—Wilson Kipketer (gained Danish citizenship), Lornah Kiplagat (Holland), Elly Rono (applied for U.S. citizenship), Albert Chepkurui and Stephen Chereno (Qatar), and Abel Cheruiyot and Leonard Mucheru (Bahrain) (the AK questioned their status because they were on Kenyan national teams). The controversy stems from a question concerning time period allowance and eligibility to represent another country in international meets. The IOC and IAAF rulings will determine their eligibility at international events.

Some Kenyan runners say the process of competing in the Division, District, Province, Nationals, and Trials competitions, followed by a government-

Table 1.11   10,000m World Rankings[21]

1991	2002
1. Moses Tanui (Ken)	1. Sammy Kipketer (Ken)
2. Richard Chelimo (Ken)	2. Assefa Mezgebu (Eth)
3. Khalid Skah (Mor)	3. Richard Limo (Ken)
4. Thomas Osano (Ken)	4. Albert Chepkurui (Ken)
5. John Ngugi (Ken)	5. Paul Kosgei (Ken)
6. Salvatore Antibo (Ita)	6. Wilberforce Talel (Ken)
7. Julius Korir II (Ken)	7. John Cheruiyot Korir (Ken)
8. Arturo Barrios (Mex)	8. John Yuda (Tan)
9. Richard Nerurkar (GB)	9. Meb Keflezighi (US)
10. Hammou Boutayeb (Mor)	10. Jose Martinez (Spa)

sponsored month-long training camp, is arduous and extremely competitive. Only established runners are able to bypass these steps. Further frustrating athletes is the fact that placing in the top three in the Trials has not guaranteed making the national team.

Historically, the national steeplechase and cross country teams have been extremely successful (see Table 1.12). In 2002, the rivalry with neighbor Ethiopia intensified; the increased depth of Ethiopian runners, especially in track, resulted in new world records and a challenge to Kenya's cross-country dominance. It was no longer a given that Kenyan runners would control any given event. Since the loss of Kim McDonald and Dr. Gabriela Rosa's shift to cross country and road racing, track performances have declined.[27]

Ethnic clashes existed in Kenya until 1990. With the transition from Moi to Mwai Kabaki, the KAAA reverted back to AK and, concerned with restoring national pride, espoused a new philosophy. At a banquet, monetary awards were given to medal winners from past international competitions—a gesture well-received by the runners.

Table 1.12   When Kenyan Men's Domination Began

Cross Country Team Championships	1986
3,000m Steeplechase	1988
Road Racing	1992
Track	
1,500m / mile	1998
3,000m	1992
5,000m / 10,000m	1991
Marathon	1998

Implications for U.S. Runners and Road Racing

Whether road racing is a sport, business, or entertainment depends on who you talk to. The percentage of participants running a six-minute-mile pace or better in road races is small. In 2004, when commentator Toni Reavis asked a gathering of industry leaders if they could name a contender in the Arizona Rock and Roll Marathon competition, not one of them could. He claimed that marathon coverage aimed at quantity (tens of thousands of runners) over quality. "All those runners and we get slower and fatter, the mind reels."[28]

National and international sports federations have influenced running competitions. The amateur/professional status of the Olympics remains controversial. "The construction of the concept of amateurism only truly began in the nineteenth century in England. The fact that there were professionals in the ancient games was overlooked by the founders of the modern games."[29]

Joggers fueled the first American running boom in the 1970s. The second running boom in the 1990s has taken road racing to a new level. The affiliation of charities and marathon training groups such as Jeff Galloway's have offered masses of people healthy ways to promote causes. Some, however, have voiced the elitist position that the charities and Gallowalkers are dumbing down the sport.

While track follows regulations from federations and by-laws, road racing events and agents work in a free market environment in which individuality and creativity are rewarded. Race committees, composed of race directors, sponsors, and charities, decide how prize money is to be distributed. By far, the overwhelming majority of prize money is open to citizens of all nationalities. Some events have restructured prize money and perks. The Ocean City Ten Miler, Bix, and Gaspirilla eliminated prize money altogether, then the Gaspirilla Distance Run reinstated it in 2004. The Sallie Mae 10K has reduced prize money, and gives more to charities.

Colorado's Bolder Boulder, to ensure that no one country dominates their event, employed cybernetic skills and demonstrated that the modeler can be more sophisticated than the model. In 1997, when six of the top eight finishers were Kenyan, corporate sponsors called the Kenyan runners "marketing liabilities." To ensure that more Americans finished among the leaders, officials passed a rule limiting the number of runners from any foreign country to three. "We hope to level the playing field," said race director Mr. Reef. Then he enunciated what could have become the Monroe Doctrine for the sports world: "It's our country, our event, our money. American sponsors want American winners, or at least Americans among the top finishers." To "level the playing field" even more, sponsors have promised to double the prize money for American athletes finishing in the top five.[30]

The Chicago, Boston, London, Berlin, and New York Marathons, on the other hand, spend hundreds of thousands of dollars attracting top runners to break course and world records. At the 1999 Suntrust Marathon, Julius Rotich said that the limousine that picked him up at the airport was larger than the one belonging to the President of Kenya. Rotich led most of the race, however became dehydrated and finished in second. He said later, "I felt like I let down the race director."

The Kenyan dominance is unsettling to struggling American elite and sub-elite runners; increasing numbers are not showing up to road races, favoring American prize money races, or focusing on races with separate prize money for Americans. While foreign professional baseball and hockey players have multi-million dollar annual contracts, some American sub-elites have expressed resentment of the Kenyan runners. In a live NPR debate with Jon Entine, Dr. Grant Farred of Duke University said that the domination by certain ethnic groups has created "white anxiety."[31] To be sure, some sub-elite American runners speak with envious tones. With so many Kenyan runners breaking world records, accusations of their using performance enhancement drugs have become common. Kenyans runners with families, jobs, businesses, and farms in Kenya are occasionally called 'B' Kenyans or "road whores."

Coach and former elite runner Alberto Salazar recommends dealing with the situation. "Instead of limiting Kenyan participation in races, we should try to learn from the Kenyans. Bob Kennedy, who consistently ranks in the

PART II

BIOLOGICAL FACTORS

2

PLACE: ENVIRONMENT AND ADAPTATIONS

In their daily lives a lot of Kenyans are training
completely unbeknownst to themselves.[1]

  Brother Colm O'Connell, Headmaster of St. Patrick's School in Kenya

Training Hard vs. the Ability to Train Hard

In *Train Hard, Win Easy*, Toby Tanser points out no one trains harder than the Kenyans. Are they currently the best because they train harder or because they train at a higher intensity? Why is it that they can train faster and harder? What evidence do we have they train at a higher intensity?

Some argue that Kenyan athletes, like American athletes, are a product of their environment. What environmental and historical factors, if any, might impact the quantity of world class runners? According to Tanser, their training environment—the soft red soil, moderate climate, healthy diet, and the elevation in the Rift Valley—supports the notion that such factors are essential. It seems to be the mix of factors rather than each factor on its own that impacts the runners. Other countries with similar circumstances, for example, produce few or no world class runners.

Other researchers claim that inherited traits are the essential determining factors. According to Bengt Saltin, Director of the Institute of Sports Science in Copenhagen, very many in sports physiology would like to believe that it is training, the environment, what you eat that plays the most important role. But, based on the data it is in your genes whether or not you are talented or whether you will become talented.[2]

Is There Genetic Evidence?

Elite athletes in the U.S. have joked that Kenyan athletes have a "different engine." Scientific studies show that there is some truth to this idea; so, Kenyan running ability may be the result of genes and anatomy. Physiologists have considered a high VO$_{2max}$ reading the best indicator of distance running—a belief that has been questioned as other physiological attributes have become linked to world class runners, especially Kenyans.

In Darwinist theory, two topics are of biological interest: environmental factors that shape humans and the redesign of the body for greater endurance. Over time, the body is amazingly adaptable to environmental conditions. In addition to being pastoral, climate, and altitude acclimatization have been major environmental determinants of Kenyan physiology. But could Kenyan runners have developed a genetic advantage?

Most organisms share an enormous amount of genetic coding information. What separates humans from each other and from other animals is gene regulation, how and when a gene is expressed. Athletes train to improve performance; during the recovery period, the muscles modify their structure and oxygen usage increases. Gene expression, known as the central dogma of molecular biology, involves two steps. First, gene transcription of DNA to messenger RNA (mRNA) occurs in the cell nucleus. Some genes are activated, some repressed. Second, the mRNA (that carries information in an amino acid sequence in the ribosomes) is translated to proteins, the building blocks of cells.

Although no specific running gene has been identified, research does support certain genetic advantages (see Table 2.1).

Table 2.1   Genetic Factors and Theories

1. Geographic distribution of talent	Statistical analysis of population genetics
2. Out of Africa theory	Allan Wilson, Rebecca Cann
3. Mitochondria inherited from mother	Owen Anderson
4. Trainability	Bengt Saltin, Claude Bouchard
5. Higher levels of testosterone and human growth hormone	John Hoberman

Statistical analysis of population genetics reveals that superior athletic performances in track and road racing events are geographically based: West
African athletes dominate distances from sixty to 400m, East, North, and
South African athletes dominate distances ranging between 5K and the
marathon, and European runners (especially Russians), are increasingly dominant at distances longer than the marathon.

In *The Journey of Man*, Spencer Wells explains how genetic markers were
used to trace human origins. Rebecca Cann, as part of her PhD work at the
University of California at Berkeley, studied patterns of mitochondrial DNA
(mtDNA) in humans around the world to better understand human origins.
Since mtDNA does not recombine, we can define a single ancestral mito-
chondrion from which all mitochondria are descended (Wells 2002, 31). Mitochondria, that help provide energy for endurance, have their own genes that
carry the DNA code. The mitochondria are derived exclusively from the
mother's DNA.[3]

The greatest divergence between mtDNA sequences were found among
Africans. According to the Principle of Variability (genetic variety results over
time), this result indicates that Africans have been diverging for a longer time
(Wells 2002, 30). Dr. Kenneth Kidd, Professor of Psychiatry and Genetics at
Yale Medical School, says one African ethnic group has more genetic variation
than the rest of the world combined.[4] Accordingly, one would expect to find
some excellent, some terrible, and some average runners.

Bengt Saltin's findings do suggest the possibility that the Kalenjin have an
uncommon capacity to increase aerobic efficiency with training. Research by
Canadian geneticist Claude Bouchard has shown this trait to be largely hereditary. Further, in research undertaken to account for African Americans having double the rate of prostate cancer than Caucasian American men, higher
levels of testosterone and human growth hormones were found. Higher circulatory levels of testosterone promote the growth of lean muscle mass and
the production of hemoglobin, while the human growth hormone increases
muscle mass and bone density (Hoberman 1997, 228).

Medium Altitude and Hypoxia

Many Kenyan world class runners grow up and train in medium to high altitudes (2,000–2,500m). As Manners observes, a large number are Kalenjin
highlanders from military training camps. Given the complexity of the many

variables causing the human body to adapt, altitude has raised as many questions as it has answered.

Hypoxemia refers to a deficient oxygenation of the blood. Oxygen enters the body through the lungs, binds to hemoglobin in the blood, and is transported to the tissues where it is released into the cells of working muscles to sustain aerobic metabolism. Altitude affects the body's ability to deliver oxygen to the tissues. Hypoxia results from a decreased oxygen supply to tissues, particularly as a direct response to lower atmospheric pressures at altitude.

Oxygen at Altitude

At altitude, there is a reduction in barometric pressure and an accompanying decrease in the density of oxygen molecules in the air.[5] The decrease in the partial pressure of oxygen (PO_2) has a direct effect on the saturation of hemoglobin and, consequently, on oxygen transport.

There is conflicting information concerning atmospheric composition at 2000-2500m where many world class runners train. A quote from *Exercise Physiology*, a respected medical textbook, states that "The percentage of oxygen remains fixed at 20.93 percent regardless of altitude" (McArdle 2001, 605). The earth's atmosphere is composed of particles with different densities: seventy-eight percent nitrogen (N_2), twenty-one percent oxygen (O_2), and half a percent water vapor (H_2O), along with much smaller amounts of argon, carbon dioxide, neon, helium, krypton, xenon, hydrogen, methane, and other trace gases.[6]

Humans depend on atmospheric pressure (the force exerted by gas molecules in the air on any surface area) to breathe. Atmospheric pressure pushes air through the trachea (windpipe) and into the lungs, while the air in the lungs exerts a pulmonary pressure that pushes air back out.

The mixture of gases in the air may vary depending on the temperature, altitude, pressure, density, and humidity level. Unlike water, air is a compressible fluid; pressure decreases higher in the atmosphere. The density and kinetic energy (how fast molecules are moving) of gas molecules in the air affects the level of pressure in the atmosphere. Gravity causes molecular density and a greater number of collisions closer to the earth. With more collisions, the pressure and temperature increase. Atmospheric pressure, therefore, decreases with height. Air density decreases at a rate of three percent per 1,000 feet of elevation.

Air density also decreases at higher temperatures; and increasing the pressure increases the density. Cold air can be less dense than warm if pressure is

Table 2.2   **Physiological Factors**

Cardiovascular system changes	Increased red blood cells, EPO, and mitochondria. Vascularization of capillaries surrounding the muscle fibers. Mitochondria closer to the capillaries enhancing oxygen diffusion. Increased myoglobin and hemoglobin, increased blood circulation.
Metabolic changes	Decreased hormonal sympathetic nervous system responses. Pathways shift to fat for fuel. Increased oxidative enzyme activity. Reduced glycolytic activity.
Pulmonary changes	Increased capillary density in lungs. Larger lung capacities. Ventilation altered to assist in exhaling carbon dioxide and modifications in buffering system.

lower (higher elevation). In mathematical terms, this relationship is expressed in Charles' Law ($V1/V2=T1/T2$), Boyle's Law ($P1V1=P2V2$), and the Ideal Gas Law (pressure = density x gas constant x temperature).

According to Duke University Physics Professor Emeritus Dr. Lawrence Evans, while there is a slight difference in the atmospheric composition where the Kalenjin live, it is insignificant. Because nitrogen is lighter than oxygen (nitrogen's atomic mass is fourteen ($N_2 =28$), and oxygen's is sixteen ($O_2 =32$)), the effects of gravity will result in more nitrogen rising and slightly less oxygen being available.

To minimize the effects of reduced oxygen delivery in medium altitude, the human body adapts at the pulmonary, cardiovascular, and metabolic levels (see Table 2.2).

Cardiovascular System Changes

1. In cases of hypoxia, the sympathetic nervous system triggers the release of catecholamines. This increases blood pressure, heart rate, and car-

diac output. Blood circulation increases, in turn increasing the rate at which the muscles unload oxygen and pick up carbon dioxide.

2. The erythrocyte-stimulating hormone erythropoietin (EPO) produced in the kidneys increases hemoglobin, iron-containing respiratory pigment in red blood cells, and initiates red blood cell formation (McArdle 2001, 613). The increased concentration of red blood cells (hemocrit level) results in an increased oxygen carrying capacity along with increased blood viscosity.

3. At the tissue and cellular level, changes favor oxygen delivery from the blood to the skeletal muscle cells where it can be used to make energy. Quadriceps muscle tissues have shown increased vascularization of capillaries surrounding the muscle fibers. Additionally, these fibers contain more mitochondria and a lower cross-sectional area, bringing the mitochondria closer to the capillaries for improved oxygen diffusion.[7]

4. The concentration of myoglobin (a molecule similar to hemoglobin that is located in the muscles) increases.

Pulmonary System Changes

1. Lung capillaries acquire increased density, similar to muscle tissues.
2. Whereas carbon dioxide accumulation dictates normal ventilation (the movement of air into and out of the lungs), the Hypoxic Ventilatory Response (HVR) (rate and volume of breaths) is controlled by a depleted oxygen supply.[8] Carbonic acid and bicarbonate act as buffers, keeping the blood pH near 7.4. The loss of bicarbonate means a lower buffering capacity for lactic acid.
3. Hypoxia causes vasodilation in most blood vessels. In many pulmonary vessels it causes vasoconstriction because of reduced oxygen levels.

Metabolic Changes and Fuel Sources

1. At altitude, the sympathetic drive through catecholamines increases the basal metabolism rate. Unless food intake is increased, the body mass lowers. Unless water intake is increased, the body becomes dehydrated.
2. More efficient pathways and enzymatic changes necessary for aerobic energy transfer are used at altitude. Lipids appear to be the preferred fuel for exercise, because of a dramatic decrease in carbohydrate metabolism.

Table 2.3   Sources of Fuel During Exercise[9]

Carbohydrates (CHO)
Blood glucose (40 kcal)
Liver glycogen (240 kcal)
Muscle glycogen (1,400 kcal)

Fat
Adipocytes (100,000 + kcal) (3,500 kcal in one pound of adipose tissue)
Plasma FFA (from adipose tissue lipolysis)
Intramuscular triglycerides (3,850 kcal)
Muscle and liver (450 kcal)

Protein
Small contribution from muscle and liver (24,000 kcal available)

There is a higher occurrence of muscle enzymes that metabolize fat rather than glycogen or protein (see Table 2.3).

During exercise, carbohydrates come from blood glucose, and muscle and liver glycogen. At low intensity, more blood glucose is used. At high intensity, more muscle glycogen is used. In prolonged exercise (between one and two hours), carbohydrates shift from muscle glycogen to blood glucose.

One gram of fat contains approximately nine kcal of energy; protein and carbohydrates have four. Fatty acids are stored in the body as triglycerides, which are then stored in fat cells and skeletal muscle cells (Powers 1997, 27). Fatty acid stores are placed near mitochondria to facilitate energy production. At low intensity, plasma-free fatty acids are the primary source of energy production; at higher intensity, triglycerides increase (Powers 1997, 57). Fats can only be metabolized aerobically. Lower carbohydrate stores result in a reduced ability to use fats as fuel.

It is estimated that only two percent of total energy production is derived from protein. According to Dr. Brooks, it has the potential to play a larger role in certain situations:

Other fuels can provide alternative energy sources which allow for muscle glycogen-sparing and an increased potential for prolonged high metabolic rates. Blood-borne glucose and intra-muscular lipids and plasma free fatty acids derived from adipose tissue provide the main energy alternatives to muscle glycogen. Several amino acids, in-

Table 2.4   Heat Stress Adaptations

Small body mass with maximum surface area for heat dissipation and less metabolic heat.	Fournier's Law of Heat Conduction, Carl Bergmann
Thin, long appendages with maximum surface area for heat dissipation.	Joel Allen
Vasodilation of blood vessels and more cutaneous blood flow.	Hormonal response

cluding the essential amino acid leucine, are also used directly as oxidizable fuels during exercise. Depending on the duration and intensity of exercise and other factors such as glycogen stores and energy intake, amino acids can provide from a few to approximately 10% of the total energy for sustained exercise. Additionally, many amino acids can be converted to glutamate and then to alanine. Alanine, along with lactate and pyruvate, are recognized as the major carbohydrate precursors.[10]

3. In studies performed at both sea level and 2000m, Bengt Saltin found that Kenyan runners have extremely low ammonia accumulations in the blood even at high exercise intensities.[11] Ammonia, the result of the breakdown of proteins, contributes to fatigue.

Heat Stress Adaptations

Anatomical and physiological changes accompany mechanisms for heat regulation (see Table 2.4). Genetic variations in the amount of body hair (minimizes heat loss) and specialized eccrine or sweat glands (maximize heat loss) are seen in different climates.

Anatomical Adaptations

In running, especially long distances, body size is an important factor in cooling off. Metabolic heat is generated when food is burned, releasing energy; it is estimated that sixty percent of the energy released during catabolism is heat (Hochachka & Somero 2002, 382).

In the nineteenth century, Carl Bergmann observed that humans living near the equator are smaller. Because larger mass bodies have more cells producing heat (a byproduct of metabolism) and smaller surface areas relative to their body mass, they are less efficient at radiating body heat. Fournier's Law of Heat Conduction states that the rate of heat loss from the core of an animal is directly proportional to the surface area available for heat conduction to the environment and inversely proportional to the distance that is needed to be traveled from the core to the surface.

Also in the nineteenth century, Joel Allen observed that the length of appendages varies with climate. Species living in warmer climates tend to have longer limbs, which have a greater surface area.

Elite Kenyan marathoners are typically small (approximately 5'6" and 115 pounds), and have thin, long appendages—both anatomical designs for maximum heat loss in an equatorial climate.

Physiological Adaptations

Thermal regulation uses heat conservation and dissipation. Heat can be transferred to other tissues, or to the environment. When more blood is needed elsewhere, the sympathetic nervous system constricts vessels and redirects the blood. The temperature of the blood surrounding the hypothalamus regulates body warmth. Input to the hypothalamus temperature receptors comes from both the skin and the body core. Vasodilatation of the blood vessels and sweating prevent brain damage by increasing the amount of heat moving from the body core to the skin. Heat loss is reduced when the skin is wet, or in humid conditions.

Heat can also be transferred from the environment to other human tissues. Runners from colder climates like the Soviet Republic have blood vessel vasoconstriction to limit heat dissipation.

Heat stress can cause profuse sweating and dehydration. The more stressful the exercise, the more surface blood flow and the less blood flow to the muscles; less blood flow means less oxygen, less substrate, and less removal of metabolic waste products. Blood must be directed to working muscles to meet their demand for oxygen and energy substrates. If too much strain is placed on the heart, a person might experience the following sensations: heavy limbs, extreme fatigue, dizziness, nausea, and tunnel vision. Finally, the person might fall into a comatose state.

Pastoral Lifestyle Adaptations

At one time, humans were primarily hunter gathers. A speed gene might have evolved out of the necessity to hunt wild animals or flee enemies—currently, however, there is no genetic proof.

The introduction of carbohydrates increased plasma insulin levels. The Thrifty Gene Hypothesis, proposed by geneticist James Neel in 1962, suggests that increased energy storage (as fat) occurs in periods of fasting.[12] This results in the reduction of muscle mass and alters metabolic processes.

In 1991, Wendorf and Goldfine proposed that insulin resistance in muscle would limit hypoglycemia during periods of starvation by limiting muscle glucose use. Insulin resistance in muscle would have the effect of blunting the hypoglycemia that occurs during fasting, but would allow energy storage in the form of fat.

Muscle Fibers

Two major types of muscle fibers make up skeletal muscle: Type I (slow twitch) and Type II (fast twitch) (see Table 2.5). Humans are born with a certain ratio of muscle fiber types. Those passed down in genes can be partially modified with exercise, training, and lifestyle. Type II fibers are subdivided into IIA (oxidative, glycolytic) and IIB (glycolytic). Type IIB can become IIA, and vice versa. In muscle fibers, the nuclei can stop expressing the IIB gene and begin expressing the IIA gene. Fibers can increase their production of proteins, becoming thicker (hypertrophy).

Space research of microgravity exposure to muscle tissue has shown significant muscle fiber atrophy; this is more pronounced in oxidative muscle fibers (Type I and IIA) than in glycolytic muscle fibers (Type IIB). Spinal cord injury patients have also shown similar results. A ten percent loss in thigh muscle can occur after a mountaineering expedition in Himalayas (Hoppeler & Fluck 2003, 98). White fibers are not converted to red during aerobic training, implying that there are advantages to retaining different fiber types (Hochachka & Somero 2002, 75).

Specific muscle types favor different running events. In 1990, Bengt Saltin conducted elaborate treadmill tests and muscle biopsies on several dozen Kalenjin runners, and found that Kenyans are born with a high number of slow twitch fibers (approximately sixty to seventy percent). Fast twitch IIA fibers readings ranged from thirty to forty percent, and fast twitch IIB fiber

Table 2.5   Comparison of Muscle Fibers

Fiber Type	I	IIA	IIB
Muscle fiber recruitment and event	5K – Marathon	400m – mile	Sprinting 100m – 400m
Speed of contraction and energy type	Oxidative or aerobic slow twitch	Oxidative and glycolytic fast twitch	Anaerobic fast twitch, glycolytic
Enzyme activity	Oxidative	Oxidative and glycolytic	Glycolytic
Fuel source	Fat and carbohydrate, consumes lactate	Glycogen, glucose	Glycogen, produces lactate
Fiber diameter	Small	Medium	Large
Fatigue resistance	High	Medium	Low
Color of fiber	Red	Light red	White
Glycolytic capacity 1. Glycogen content 2. ATP	Low	Medium	High
Oxidative capacity 1. Capillary density 2. Mitochondrial density 3. Myoglobin content	High	Medium	Low

readings were less than six percent.[13] A study conducted on South African elite runners revealed that they have a lower percentage (seventeen percent mean difference) of Type I fibers than Caucasian elite runners.[14] West African runners have a higher percentage of fast twitch fibers.

Type IIB fibers contract approximately ten times faster that Type I fibers; Type IIA fiber contraction speed falls somewhere between the two. Slow fibers rely on efficient aerobic metabolism, such as cardiovascular exercise. Fast fibers rely on anaerobic metabolism, such as weight training. The differences in the contraction speeds can be explained by the rates of release of calcium by the sarcoplasmic reticulum (the muscle's storage site for calcium) and by the activity of the enzyme myosin-ATPase that breaks down ATP inside the myosin head of the contractile proteins.[15] Myosin ATPase splits ATP to ADP, providing energy for muscle contraction. Type IIB fibers are high in intramuscular stores of ATP.

The oxidative capacity is determined by the number of mitochondria, the number of capillaries surrounding the fiber, and the amount of myoglobin in the fiber. A large number of mitochondria provide a greater capacity to produce ATP aerobically. High levels of mitochondria and myosin, a contractile protein of muscle, give slow twitch fibers their red appearance. A high number of capillaries surrounding a muscle fiber insure that the fiber will receive adequate oxygen during periods of contractile activity. Myoglobin is more prominent in Type I fibers, and adds to the oxidative capacity, binding and shuttling oxygen between the cell membrane and the mitochondria. A high myoglobin concentration improves the oxygen delivery from the capillary to the mitochondria, where it is used.

Each muscle type has specific enzyme activities and metabolic processes. In soft twitch fibers, the myosin ATPase levels are low, the glycolytic capacity is less developed, the oxidative enzyme levels are high, and there is a high concentration of mitochondrial enzymes. Type I fibers have a higher citrate synthase (CS) activity, a marker of the oxidative capacity of muscle. A study revealed that South Africans elite runners have fifty percent greater CS activity than do elite Caucasian runners (Weston 1999, 10). Slow twitch muscles generate energy from fats and carbohydrates via aerobic metabolism, while fast twitch muscles are dependent on glycogen for fuel. Type II fibers have low mitochondria, a high concentration of ATP, glycolytic enzymes, and are rich in glycolytic enzymes to allow instantaneous release of intramuscular glycogen.

Type IIB produces large amounts of lactic acid, that can enter Type I or IIA mitochondria.

Table 2.6   Pastoral Lifestyle Factors and Theories

Ectomorphic frame	Pastoral heritage and genetic diversity
The Thrifty Gene Hypothesis	Muscle mass and metabolic processes were altered
Speed gene	Flee from enemies, hunt wild animals
Insulin resistance	Energy storage of fat blunting hypoglycemia

3

PHYSIOLOGICAL MODELS AND LIMITATIONS TO ENDURANCE

Rather than simply continuing to accept inconsistencies among research findings, modern exercise physiologists should challenge old dogmas to attain the truth.

Timothy Noakes

Physiological Models: Institutional Scientific Dogma vs. New Science

According to Dr. Timothy Noakes, current physiological models resist new science, resulting in a number of unanswered questions and inconsistencies among research findings. Noakes contends that because A.V. Hill (whose ideas served as a basis for current physiological models) did not empirically test the plateau phenomenon, his research methodology would not be accepted by today's standards of scientific inquiry.

An unusual feature of the exercise sciences is that certain core beliefs are based on an historical physiological model that, it will be argued, has somehow escaped modern, disinterested intellectual scrutiny.

This particular model holds that the cardiovascular system has a limited capacity to supply oxygen to the active muscles, especially during maximal exercise. As a result, skeletal muscle oxygen demand outstrips supply causing the development of skeletal muscle hypoxia or even anaerobiosis during vigorous exercise. This hypoxia stimulates the onset of lactate production at the *"anaerobic," "lactate,"* or ventilation thresholds and initiates biochemical processes that terminate maximal exercise. The model further predicts that the important effect of training is to increase oxygen delivery to and oxygen utilization by the active muscles during exercise. Thus, adaptations that reduce skeletal muscle anaerobiosis during exercise explain all the physiological, biochemical, and functional changes that develop with training. The historical basis for this model is the original research of Nobel Laureate A. V. Hill which was interpreted as evidence that oxygen consumption "plateaus" during progressive exercise to exhaustion, indicating the development of skeletal muscle anaerobiosis (Anaerobic respiration, respiration that's occurs in the absence of oxygen).

Hill's research failed to establish the existence of the plateau phenomenon during exercise and it is argued that this core component of the historical model remains unproven. Furthermore, definitive evidence that skeletal muscle anaerobiosis develops during sub maximal exercise at the anaerobic threshold initiating lactate production by muscle and its accumulation in blood is not currently available. The finding that exercise performance can improve and metabolism alter before there are measurable skeletal muscle mitochondrial adaptations could indicate that variables unrelated to oxygen use by muscle might explain some, if not all, training-induced changes.[1]

The Cardiovascular/Anaerobic Model

Once considered a definitive indicator of endurance fitness, the meaning of VO_{2max} readings has been revised by new science. When elite marathoner coach Dr. Gabrielle Rosa first began to train Moses Tanui and other Kenyan athletes, he observed that the workouts were not improving times as expected. He soon realized that the workouts were not taking physiological differences into account, as Kenyan runners are able to train at a higher percentage of maximal heart rate and VO_{2max}.

Among elite male long distance runners and cross country skiers, a champion Norwegian cross country skier recorded the highest VO_{2max} value (ninety-four ml/kg/min). A Russian cross country skier recorded the highest value for a female (seventy-four ml/kg/min). In contrast, adults in poor physical condition can have values below twenty ml/kg/min.

A superior capacity for oxygen consumption, however, does not explain Kenyan runners' endurance capacity—some mechanism must exist that prevents their hearts from becoming anaerobic during maximal exercise. Their superior fatigue resistance has been credited to their endurance rather than aerobic capacity. The percentage of VO_{2max}, therefore, is a valid measure of fatigue resistance. Noakes' VO_{2max} testing of elite South African runners at a 10K race pace revealed readings of 92.2 percent for black runners compared

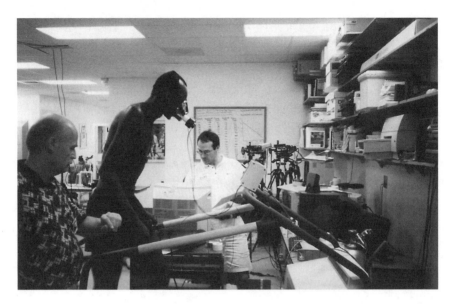

Figure 3.1   Elly Rono VO2max testing at the Nike Coach K Human Performance Lab.

to eighty-six percent for white runners.[2] Thirty-two year old Kenyan marathoner Elly Rono had a VO2max test performed shortly after running a 2:10 marathon in 2002. His sixty-seven ml/kg/min reading, while relatively low, was Olympic-class for his age (see appendix B). When I told him that Steve Prefontaine's reading was in the mid-eighties, he wanted a retest. I explained that a VO2max test does not measure all physiological variables determining success—altitude, age, heat stress, and a lower fitness level will affect the results. Indeed, VO2max readings are less effective than lactate-threshold readings at predicting distance running performance.

The Energy Supply/Energy Depletion Model

In the traditional model of fatigue, demand outstrips supply. Noakes' paradigm contradicts this model, stating that energy demand is regulated so that it cannot outstrip supply. So, ATP is maintained. According to Noakes, the energy supply model predicts that performance in events of varying duration is determined by the capacity to produce energy, measured by a chemical unit (ATP), by separate metabolic pathways including the phosphagens, oxygen-independent glycolysis, aerobic glycolysis, and aerobic lipolysis.[3] A sprinter has a greater capacity to generate ATP from intramuscular phosphagen stores and oxygen-independent glycolysis. Marathoners and ultramarathoners have a greater capacity to oxidize fat through aerobic lipolysis.Muscle and liver glycogen depletion occurs with fatigue. A direct relationship is therefore assumed between muscle glycogen depletion and fatigue in prolonged exercise. Any energy depletion model predicts that exercise must cease upon the occurrence of muscle ATP depletion. A popular explanation for reserving carbohydrate is that the body's ability to oxidize fats improves with training; performance can be extended and improved without requiring higher carbohydrate utilization. This explanation, however, proposes that ATP depletion limits exercise—which is false.[4] This model and the cardiovascular/anaerobic model are both based on the assumption that the delivery of substrate either in blood (oxygen) or via the glycolytic and oxidative pathways (ATP) limits exercise performance. While the validity of either of these models remains difficult to prove, both continue to dominate research and teaching in the exercise sciences.[5]

The Muscle Recruitment (Central Fatigue)/Muscle Power Model

This alternate physiological model proposes that performance is not limited by the rate of supply of substrate, oxygen, or ATP to muscle, but rather by the processes involved in skeletal muscle recruitment, excitation, and contraction. Professor Noakes argues that a reduced central activation of exercising muscles is a protective mechanism. Research indicates that peripheral muscles are linked to sub-maximal work. According to Duke University Medical Center physiologist Brian Duscha, peak VO_2 and the percentage of VO_{2max} are linked to the heart muscle. The central nervous system, through central and peripheral chemical receptors, regulate skeletal muscle contractile activity to prevent a number of unwelcome scenarios including organ damage or even death during exercise, myocardial ischaemia, muscle ATP depletion, a fall in blood pressure, heatstroke, and brain damage during hypoglycemia.[6]

The central nervous system protects the heart and brain from inadequate oxygen supply by limiting skeletal muscle recruitment and activation. Constraints are put on cardiac output by regulating the skeletal mass that can be activated during exercise in hypoxia. This muscle inactivation can occur at high altitude, when liver glycogen stores are depleted, and from heat induced fatigue.[7]

Running Economy: The Biomechanical Model

This model, in contrast to the cardiovascular/anaerobic model, predicts that increased oxygen delivery to muscle and an increased rate of energy results in superior performance during prolonged exercise, and increased heat production. Efficiency results from slowing the rate of metabolite accumulation and the rise in body temperature.[8]

Two factors that reduce heat production are small size and superior running economy—the more economical the athlete, the faster they will be able to run before reaching a limiting body temperature. Studies show that practice produces improvements. According to Georgia State University exercise physiologist David Martin, "Whether you lift weights, run hills, or run from childhood, I would think those would be the three likely contributors to running economy."

Kenyan runner biomechanics include a lean ectomorphic frame, a small muscle mass, minimal subcutaneous fat, long heel bones and Achilles tendons from large amounts of walking, long and light calf muscles, narrow and high hips, and long levers for legs to shift with each stride. Reducing the rate of oxygen consumption and heat production by increasing the economy of movement, therefore, seems a more logical explanation for enhanced endurance performance than having a high VO_{2max}.[9]

Research on Kenyan women carrying weight on their head revealed superior running economy. They have less breaking action, light legs acting as levers with forward momentum, gait efficiency, and body masses centered over their legs. Treadmill testing revealed no increase in oxygen consumption. Most humans transfer sixty-five percent of their potential energy forward at the height of the step. They could transfer over eighty percent, rather than stepping down through an unconscious altered gait.[10] Consequently, they are able to use less energy.

The Psychological/Mental Model

While physiology usually ignores the effect of the mind on the body, sports psychology and the placebo effect of carbohydrate loading studies have lent this concept credibility.[11] This model is discussed in Part IV.

Table 3.1   **Physiological Limitations Models: Theories and Factors**

Cardiovascular/anaerobic model	Higher percentage VO2max, fatigue resistance.
Energy supply model	Oxidize fat, aerobic lipolysis, questions correlation of ATP depletion and fatigue.
Muscle recruitment/neural fatigue model	Medium altitude and heat adaptations.
Running economy model	Reduced metabolites, reduced oxygen consumption, biomechanical efficiency, running from childhood, adjustments to prevent rising body temperature.

4

LACTATE

The finding that lactate can be formed in and released from diverse tissues such as skeletal muscle and liver under resting conditions of CHO loading and epinephrine stimulation, counters the long-held belief that lactate is formed as the result of oxygen-limited metabolism.[1]

George Brooks

Troublemaker or Secret Weapon?

Popular literature on endurance training all seems based on Arthur Lydiard's basics of interval training, tempo runs, lactate threshold runs, and long runs. Recent research has questioned the physiological principles behind these training methods—VO_{2max}, oxygen debt, lactic acid, and anaerobic threshold. Articles on lactate and lactic acid, incorrectly used as interchangeable terms, have left readers wondering what to believe. Lactic acid, a cation or positively-charged ion, dissociates to lactate. Lactate is an anion or negatively-charged particle, and includes a proton (H+). In metabolic pathways, lactate takes a different course—it is the proton rather than the lactate ion that causes ph to decrease (Brooks 2000, 805). Old theories link lactate production with metabolic acidosis, muscle fatigue and soreness, oxygen debt, and anaerobic glycolysis. These ideas have been perpetuated by journalists and commentators; as a result, many non-scientific articles describe lactate as a chemical with only negative side effects. Studies are now linking metabolic acidosis and skeletal muscle fatigue to phosphate, hydrogen ions, and ATP hydrolysis. Dr. Richard Moon MD, an anesthesiologist and hyperbaric chamber specialist at Duke University, says lactate is produced all day long, even when at rest. It does not necessarily cause fatigue or come from working muscles. Dr. George A. Brooks, Professor of Integrative Biology at the University of California at Berkeley, claims that lactate explains some of the inconsistencies in physiological models. Based on his findings, Dr. Brooks attributes Kenyan running success to bioenergetics or cellular metabolism, and gene expression.

Lactate as a Fuel Source

Despite the claims of traditional physiological models, lactate plays a crucial role in metabolism as a fuel source. As running pace increases, more fast twitch muscles and carbohydrates are used, and more lactic acid is produced. In times of increased demand, lactate is a useful carbohydrate. Highly oxidative tissues, the heart, slow twitch muscle fibers, and breathing muscles prefer lactate as fuel during exercise.[2] Compared to glucose and other fuels, lactate is smaller and better exchanged between tissues in a process called facilitated transport. Other fuels need slower carrier systems such as insulin, made in large quantities in muscle and released into circulation. Muscle cells with large glycogen reserves, however, cannot release significant amounts of this energy source as glucose.[3] Lactate is a key chemical, used to dispose of dietary carbohydrate (CHO) and prevent weight gain without increasing insulin or stimulating fat synthesis. Without lactate, it would be difficult to maintain normal blood-sugar levels or keep the liver and muscles stockpiled with carbohydrates.

During exercise, an increase in insulin is not desired, as this decreases the availability of carbohydrates. During a hard training session, muscles use lactate to form glucose that in turn provides energy. Studies indicate that seventy-five to eighty percent of lactate is disposed of through oxidation. The remaining twenty to twenty-five percent is used by the liver to make glucose for the brain and heart.[4] Free fatty acids are the major energy substrate for the heart while at rest. During exercise, when arterial lactate rises, exogenous arterial lactate becomes the heart's major fuel.[5]

Because muscle can use carbohydrates faster than lipids, more energy is available, and muscles contract more forcefully. Carbohydrates enter the circulation mainly in the form of glucose (blood sugar). Most glucose from dietary carbohydrate bypasses the liver, enters the circulatory system, and converts into lactic acid upon reaching the muscles. Lactic acid then returns to the liver where it is used as a substrate for liver glycogen synthesis—a process called the Glucose Paradox.[6]

The Lactate Shuttle

Bengt Saltin found that plasma lactate concentration levels were substantially lower in Kenyan runners after a workout than before.[7] According to George Brooks, "If one is to interpret these results as the Kenyan runners are not producing lactate or similar reports that Lance Armstrong is not producing lactate during the Tour de France, this is not correct."[8] The amount of lactate in the blood is not an indication of how much anaerobic work has been completed; rather, it is the result of the processes that produce and catabolize it after its removal from the blood. The blood concentration of lactate, therefore, shows only that there has been an increased metabolic rate and glycolytic carbon flow.[9]

According to the lactate shuttle concept, lactate is a means of distributing carbohydrate energy for oxidation and gluconeogenesis.[10] Whenever carbohydrates are used as fuel, a significant portion is converted to lactate, which is then made available for energy production in oxidative muscles fibers. Lactate is produced in active skeletal muscle and other sites not directly involved with physical exercise. It can also be transported by the blood to other tissues, and used for energy. According to Brooks, the Cell-Cell concept involves a deposit of lactate from one muscle cell into another (uptake by Type I fibers (lactate oxidation cells) and release by Type II fibers (lactate producing cells)), where it can be oxidized.

Mitochondria are structures within cells that process fuels, consume oxygen, and produce large amounts of ATP. Mitochondria oxidize lactate directly within a cell via the intracellular lactate shuttle. This exchange occurs through the mitochondrial reticulum, located just outside blood vessels.[11] Red skeletal muscle, cardiac muscle, and the liver have high mitochondrial densities.

During endurance races, blood lactic acid levels stabilize even though production increases. This occurs because the body's capacity to produce lactic acid is matched by its ability to use it as fuel. Early in a race, there is a tremendous increase in the rate of lactate uptake by muscles, the use of glucose, and the breakdown of glycogen. The increased rate of carbohydrate metabolism steps up the production of muscle lactic acid, which causes an increase in blood lactic acid. As the body directs blood to working muscles, lactate is shuttled to other tissues and used as fuel. The lactate never leaves the working muscle, but is eventually depleted because it is dependent on carbohydrates as a substrate. This reduces lactic acid levels in the muscles and blood, even though the body continues to produce it in great quantities. This relief is sometimes called the 'second wind'.[12]

The Lactate Paradox

It was often found in high-altitude natives that the higher the altitude, the greater the degree of hypoxia, and the lower the blood lactate concentration post-exercise. This observation, first noted over fifty years ago, has perplexed physiologists, because theoretically, arterial hypoxemia should increase lactate formation.

The phenomenon became known as the lactate paradox. There are two aspects to its definition: 1) lower than expected accumulation of blood lactate in VO_{2max} tests in native highlanders compared with lowlanders, and 2) lower than expected accumulation of blood lactate in VO_{2max} tests in hypoxia-acclimated lowlanders compared with patterns found in unacclimated or acute hypoxia responses.[13]

One explanation points to the reduced output of the glucose-mobilizing hormone epinephrine at higher altitudes. Glucose and glycogen are the only macronutrient sources for anaerobic energy and lactate formation. Reduced glucose mobilization blunts the capacity for lactate formation (McArdle et al. 2001, 612). The lactate shuttle might offer insight into this paradox, as it has been documented that Kenyan runners possess a high percentage of oxidative (Type I) muscles.

Lactate Threshold and Training

Lactate threshold is defined as the point at which lactate production exceeds removal, and lactate starts to accumulate in the blood. If the lactate threshold is reached at low exercise intensity, then the muscle oxidative energy systems (e.g., muscles, heart, and other tissues) are not good at extracting lactate from the blood. If these systems were performing at a high level, they would use oxygen to break lactate down to carbon dioxide and water, preventing lactate from entering the blood.[14] Raising the lactate threshold (with training) increases the oxygen and number of mitochondria inside muscle cells, and the concentration of enzymes needed to oxidize pyruvate at high rates. High-intensity aerobic training results in physiological changes similar to those resulting from living at medium altitude. These changes include cardiovascular, pulmonary, and metabolic changes.

Cardiovascular System Changes

1. Increased blood volume, muscle blood supply, and oxygen delivery to muscles and tissues.
2. Increased vascularization of capillaries surrounding the quadriceps. These muscle fibers contain more mitochondria and are thinner, for improved oxygen diffusion.

Pulmonary System Changes

1. Pulmonary ventilation increases. When cells require increased oxygen or need to dump carbon dioxide (toxic in high concentrations), the medulla processes inputs from central and peripheral receptors to produce an appropriate ventilatory response (Brooks 2000, 259). Arterial receptors are most important for controlling the ventilatory response to exercise (Brooks 2000, 260).
2. Pulmonary blood volume increases.
3. Diffusion capacity for oxygen increases.

Metabolic Changes

1. Arterial lactate concentration reduces during exercise by increasing the clearance rate. Training with large amounts of lactic acid in the system stimulates the production of enzymes that in turn increase the use of lactic acid as a fuel.
2. Muscular adaptations increase the rate of lactate removal. Major skeletal muscle adaptations include increases in the mitochondrial density and respiratory capacity of muscle fibers. Mitochondrial enzyme activity increases, improving performance and increasing the use of lipids as a substrate source (Hoppeler & Fluck 2003, 97).
3. Better circulation speeds the transport of lactic acid to tissues that can remove it from the blood.
4. Lower sympathetic nervous system activity causes reduced epinephrine release during exercise. Epinephrine is a stimulating factor for glycogenolysis, which reduces glucose and glycogen metabolism. Arterial blood lactate levels are highly correlated with epinephrine levels; the blood lactate inflection point in graded exercise coincides with the epinephrine inflection point.[15] The metabolic adaptation of muscles to en-

durance exercise is a slower utilization of muscle glycogen and blood glucose, corresponding to less substrate (glucose) available for lactate production.

The Crossover Concept

Brooks and Mercier propose the Crossover Concept as a means to understand the effects of exercise intensity and endurance training on the balance of carbohydrate and lipid metabolism. According to this concept, endurance training results in muscular biochemical adaptations that enhance lipid oxidation and decrease the sympathetic nervous system responses, promoting lipid oxidation during low-moderate intensity exercise.[16] In contrast, higher exercise intensity increases contraction-induced muscle glycogenolysis (increased epinephrine and use of glycogen), alters the pattern of fiber type recruitment, and increases sympathetic nervous system activity. Carbohydrates are the preferred energy source for high intensity exercise. Aerobic training results in a greater dependence on lipids. It follows, therefore, that exercise intensity (percent of VO_{2max}) is the determinant in the balancing of substrates. "Lipids play a predominant role in sustaining efforts requiring half or less aerobic capacity; however, greater relative efforts switch (crosses over) to blood glucose and muscle glycogen as substrates. To support the increased energy substrate flux necessary for muscle contraction in hard exercise, contraction induced and endocrine factors, along with other factors interact to determine fine setting of glucose, glycogen, lactate, free fatty acid and amino acid utilization patterns during exercise."[17] Moderate exercise intensity results in almost no increase in catecholamine (epinephrine and norepinephrine) levels. Beyond fifty to seventy percent VO_{2max}, however, the levels rise disproportionately. This contradicts the lactic acid/oxygen debt theory, as lactate accumulation results largely from the level of effort and associated hormonal release, not oxygen deprivation.[18] The inflection point in blood lactic acid level, mistakenly called the anaerobic threshold (the point at which muscle becomes oxygen-deficient), is an archaic concept. Several factors are responsible for lactate inflection point contractions, including hormone recruitment of fast/glycolytic muscle fibers, and the redistribution of blood flow from lactate-removing to lactate-producing glycolytic tissues (Brooks 2000, 219). The pattern of substrate utilization depends on the interaction between exercise intensity-induced responses (that increase carbohydrate utilization) and endurance training-induced responses (that promote lipid oxidation). The crossover

Table 4.1   Role of Lactate

Lactate clearance Lactate as fuel source used by oxidative muscles — Type I fibers, heart, and breathing muscles Lactate shuttle — (cell-cell) and intracellular Lactate is used without increasing insulin levels Lactate threshold — increased use of lipids as a substrate fuel source with training	George Brooks, Hochachka

point is the power output at which energy from carbohydrate-derived fuels predominates over energy from lipids.[19] The model is based on the control of enzyme activities both by enzyme and substrate concentrations. Because distance running causes a decrease in oxygen delivery, similarities exist between adaptations in metabolic pathways for endurance training and altitude acclimatization. The adaptations for both hypoxia tolerance and endurance performance may well have been applied simultaneously to East African runners.[20]

PART III

CULTURAL FACTORS:
HOW THEY DO THINGS

5

SOCIOLOGICAL FORCES

In whatever you do, to be considered a man in the village you must
be strong.

Hillary Lelei, pro runner and farmer in Nandi

Behaviorism: Creating the Individual

Behaviorism traces its origins to Russian psychologist Ivan Pavlov, who proposed that behavior could be shaped by learning situations. Common patterns
of social behavior exist—some unique to a culture, and some acquired
through enculturation (Wilson 1980, 159). This section examines Kenyan runners from the sociological perspective—how children and adolescents are
trained for social performance, the transmission of culture, their route to the
U.S., support systems, institutions, globalization, social channeling, and socialization.

Socialization

Socialization refers to the social experiences that alter an individual's development. In Kenya, socialization processes are more defined than in the U.S.
More emphasis is placed on conforming to gender and age norms (see Table 5.1).

Primary Socialization

Kenyan children learn both physical resilience and responsibility. In the
farm economy, the school year is divided into trimesters revolving around
crops, and agriculture is taught in secondary and high school. Boys milk the
cows and care for the animals before and after school, and girls collect fire-

Table 5.1   Traditional Life Stages in Kenya

Female	Male
Infant	Infant
Uncircumcised girl	Uncircumcised boy
Circumcised girl	Circumcised boy warrior
Married woman	Male elder
Female elder	

(Levine 1994, 81)

wood and water, take care of children, wash clothes, clean the house, and help prepare meals. Children are exposed to competitive athletics in primary school, especially football (soccer) and running.

In the communal lifestyle of Kalenjin society, children are disciplined and assisted by many adults within the clan. Visitors show up without notice. The host may provide shelter and food for extended periods of time. Within the family, the first-born child has more responsibility, looking after siblings and assisting his/her mother.

Clan members turn to elders for leadership. Men of status are selected to be elders because of their leadership skills and wealth (measured in animals, land, children, and wives. Typical responsibilities include managing the building of roads or houses, and choosing a replacement to raise children if a head of household dies.

Secondary Socialization

Theories have linked the traditional Kenyan initiation rite of passage to being a successful runner. The initiation takes place between thirteen and seventeen years of age, depending on the ethnic group. Those who do not participate run the risk of being labeled an outcast. An age-grade system prepares men aged twenty to forty for cattle raiding, and to defend cattle and property against attacks from other tribes. Each age-grade has three age sets, with members being initiated roughly every seven years to perpetuate war groups. A traditional initiation consists of several stages:

1. Preparation. Each boy lives in a temporary home in the forest for two weeks to prepare mentally for a new stage in life. An elder and a mentor play supervisory roles. In the past the mentor was compensated with a cow, but more recently he is paid the equivalent of twenty U.S. dollars. The boy sings songs and performs exercises to test strength, such as pulling a small tree from the ground. A modest structure is built for living arrangements following the initiation.

2. Circumcision. The elders witness the boy tolerating pain.

3. Recuperation. The boy recuperates in the temporary forest home for one week. The boy's mother leaves food at a location where it can be picked up (women are prohibited from coming in contact with the boy throughout the initiation).

4. Seclusion. The members of the initiation live in the forest for approximately six months. Members hunt, wear animal skins, eat from wooden bowls, and drink blood. Ethnic variations may include body mutilation such as scarring from a burning rolled leaf, or hunting wild animals.

5. Passing a Test. To transition from boy to manhood, the boy must pass a test of endurance and toughness. For an ethnic group living near a river, the test might be to cross the deep water where the current is the strongest.

6. Graduation Ceremony. Following a symbolic bathe in the river, a graduation ceremony takes place with clan members and others in the age-set. Knowledge is conveyed through proverbs, riddles, and political songs. Beer, food, and gifts or money are offered.

7. Warrior Status. After several months, men take an oath of secrecy and return home as warriors ready to enter marriage and war (Azevedo 1993, 29). The warrior has new living quarters (a separate building on the family farm), and a new status in society.

This initiation rite of passage educates on traditions, and inspires boys to renounce cowardice, embrace strength, and defend those in their ethnic group. As several Kenyan runners have said, "You have to do things, and not behave like a child."

Both private schools (based on the British system) and public schools are available for those able to afford them. Some students have developed a passion for running by the time they reach primary school. Their potential is recognized in competitions. With the opportunity to train with world class runners, their identity development begins as they imitate role models.

Gender Socialization

Kenyan gender roles are distinct and functional in all phases of life. Men and women are socialized to develop certain personality traits (e.g., discipline, respect, and specialization) in order to fulfill their societal roles. Sex education and the importance of marriage and children are taught. According to UNC Cultural Anthropology Professor and Kenyan specialist Dr. Robert Daniels, homosexuality and abstaining from marriage are not allowed. Rather, it is the first to marry and have children who achieves more status.

Traditional female initiation is structured around marriage. The steps include introduction, a pre-wedding ceremony or engagement, and then a civil (requires formal paperwork in court), traditional (when marrying within an ethnic group), or modern (Christian traditions and teachings from the bible) ceremony. In the past, men commonly took several wives. If members of two ethnic groups marry, children follow the customs of the husband's clan.

In a patrilineal society and farm economy, it is impractical for families to send daughters to school. Instead, the money is invested in a dowry, to be given to her future husband's family.

Globalization

Kenyans pursuing running as a career have several options. Some join college teams in Kenya, however these demand entrance requirements and provide few benefits. Some earn American college track scholarships. Most, however, prepare for professional status after high school. Kenya's training camps and cross country meets attract sponsors and agents from the U.S. and Europe. Successful athletes and external sponsors also set up training camps—Fila, for example, sponsors a junior camp that provides housing, clothing, and food to prospective professionals.

Social Channeling

According to the Functionalist view in social sciences, people are socialized for certain functions and social needs, and talented people are rewarded and channeled into roles of advanced training (Kornblum 1994, 374). According to Lubomir Kavalek, a chess grandmaster who coaches top international players, people dominate certain specialties because of a nurturing environment. Chess students (especially women who can be easily discouraged) tend to stick with the game if their families and social institutions are supportive. Runners

Table 5.2   Athletics Kenya Affiliate Bodies[1]

Athletics Armed Forces
Athletics Central
Athletics Coast
Athletics Eastern
Athletics KECOSO (post office)
Athletics Nairobi
Athletics North Eastern
Athletics Nyanza (Province in West)
Athletics Police
Athletics Prisons
Athletics Rift Valley
Athletics Western Province
Athletics Universities

are employed in government branches as prison guards, postal workers, police, presidential bodyguards, and the Armed Forces. They are able to train
and compete while receiving a salary. Paul Tergat and Paul Koech, for example, developed in the Air Force training camps. While they compete mostly in
Europe and the U.S., they are expected to return to Kenya to represent their
division in national competitions.

The Kenyan government supports its runners through the Federation
Athletics Kenya (see Table 5.2). The National Cross Country Camps at the
Kagiri Teacher's College in Embu prepare the squad for the World Cross
Country Championships. The government also provides national teams with
a month-long training camp at the Moi Sports Centre in Nairobi prior to
the World Championships, the Olympics, and other international competitions.

The Road to the U.S.

Kenya, a land of exotic Maasai, AIDS, malaria, and post-colonial politics,
is the training ground for an unprecedented number of world class distance
runners. Increasing numbers of Ethiopian, Russian, and Kenyan runners are
finding their way to road races in the U.S. Some will experience a life different to their own. Events in Canada, Puerto Rico, Europe, Brazil, Bermuda,
and Mexico vie to attract these international runners, hoping for new world

records. Airline tickets, meals, lodging, appearance fees, time bonuses, and apparel are among the perks used to lure the best athletes.

The Kenyan cross country races (November to February), arguably the most competitive races in the world, showcase new faces and provide a training ground for established talent. Agents, shoe company scouts, and race directors might invite aspiring professional athletes to races. The process for acquiring visas expressly for making money on the roads then begins.

Many Americans are unsure why Kenyans show up in mass numbers to road races. They see the runners as homogenous rather than individuals with their own stories. In March, the start of the road racing season, groups arrive in Georgia, Philadelphia, New Mexico, Ontario, North Carolina, New Jersey, Chicago, and Colorado. A second group arrives in the late summer for fall marathons. Runners typically stay three to six months, depending on their visas and race schedules. Then they return to Kenya to rest, work their crops, and train. The cycle is repeated the following year.

Runners with limited upward mobility are often forced to depend on others. Some train and compete at home with informal groups, and are in great shape upon arrival, posting fast times in 5 and 10Ks. Kibet Cherop, a Kalenjin, trained in Kenya with an informal group. His family was unable to afford private schools, and he did not attend college. After high school, he apprenticed with his neighbor, Reuben Chesang (1992 Commonwealth Games 1500m Gold Medalist) for several years. He never got a driver's license even though he won a car. His life in the U.S., therefore, consists of training, eating, sleeping, and being shuttled to the airport or a race on weekends.

In Kenya, Chesang works as a postal worker, a job that provides the government perks. When traveling to the U.S. in 2001, he had his passport stolen in Nairobi and sold back to him for five hundred dollars by a pick-pocket. In 2002, he attended the Athletics Kenya banquet honoring past medal winners, and was presented with a check from the new administration.

Similarly, Vincent Temu comes from a poor area in Kisii, and worked as a janitor at the National Stadium in Nairobi. He made it to the U.S. in his thirties with the assistance of neighbors. Joseph Nderitu (who trained with John Ngugi's camp in Kenya) received a Canadian visa, and trains with Tim Forrester's group in Hamilton, Ontario.

World half-marathon and marathon record holder Paul Tergat, who trains in Eldoret, takes in runners. Hillary Lelei, for one, went on to be successful enough to buy a car, a home, and three rental properties in Kenya. Lelei then allowed Augustus Kuvutu, a Kamba, to live in one of his homes while he trained. Kuvutu explains how he has several role models from his ethnic group; no one, however, is helping younger runners. Few runners today, therefore, come from Kamba unless they find others to train with, usually in Nandi.

Durham, NC is home to a diverse group of runners who ran on track scholarships at U.S. colleges. Elly Rono, Ben Kapsoiya (3:53 miler who was Rono's roommate at the University of Southern Indiana), and Amos Kipyegen (3:54 miler who ran for Tulane), have retired from competition and have taken different paths—Kapsoiya is a counselor, and Kipyegen is a second-year MBA student. Another U.S. college graduate Mbarak Hussein lives part of the year in New Mexico, and has a family in Kenya. Rono says "In Kenya sometimes people will just show up at your house and stay and expect you to support them while they train. I did it with my older brother when I was younger. It seemed normal to me then, but now it doesn't make sense. Now, I have to explain to runners that arrive in the U.S. for the first time, this is not the way it works here."

Paul Mwangi, based in Ossining, NY, is in a unique situation—he has a green card allowing him an extended stay. Nicknamed the 'Spaghetti Kenyan' by Toby Tanser, he has trained and raced long enough in the U.S. to become Westernized. I met Eliud Barngetuny and Daniel Kirwa Too through Mwangi and housemate Milka Jipchirchir. Barngetuny ran 8:06 in the 3000m steeplechase while based in Europe, faster than any American has run. In 1993, he was ranked third in the world. After racing in Europe for a number of years, he occasionally stays in New York or North Carolina to visit friends and experience road racing in the U.S.

Others choose to be full-time professional runners, training at altitude in sponsored camps in Kenya and flying to specific races in the U.S. Depending on their management, they may be based in Colorado or Europe. Daniel Komen, for example, was handpicked by Moses Kiptanui and the KAAA to represent Kenya. Ironically, he didn't make most teams, but was successful in breaking world records. He found his way to U.S. road racing, the Crazy Eights 8K, while visiting his sister in Michigan.

For every Kenyan runner in the U.S., hundreds of others aspire to be in their shoes. Everyone speaks of siblings and friends at home that are finishing high school and trying to become runners. Those without visas are trying to find a way to compete for prize money and develop their passion and identity as professional runners. Many are training with no guarantees. They are just contacting friends, fellow runners, and agents, hoping to find a support system in the U.S.

Table 5.3   **Sociological Forces, Factors, and Theories**

Social Class	Lack of opportunities.
Social Channeling	Institutional support from government and society.
Primary Socialization	Physical toughening, the ascetic lifestyle, and responsibility are taught early.
Secondary Socialization, Initiation Gender, and Psychological Socialization	Manners and Moore: Circumcision and initiation provide emotional strength under pressure, and tolerance of pain. Peer pressure to conform, shame, respect, and acquire traits as a result of gender and secondary socialization. Encouraged to develop certain personality traits for societal roles, strong gender schemas developed.

Support Systems in the U.S.: Who Works for Whom?

The right support group and management is crucial for success. Many athletes have great relationships with their managers, while others have not been so lucky. Some runners complain that they are working for their managers. Like other athletes, runners sometimes change management or work independently.

For foreign athletes, learning the American system takes time. Athletes, therefore, usually put their trust in a manager/agent to handle federations, embassies, travel, visas, customs, coaching, living arrangements, and sponsorships. Faced with high expenses (a percentage to the manager, a round-trip airline ticket from Kenya, and living expenses), runners are motivated to win.

6

Running in a 40 mph Headwind

Why are there so many joggers in the U.S.? Why do they train on the tarmac?
Why are those old people running? Why are those out of shape people running
with food on their backs? Why are they running with those heavy shoes? Why do
they have dogs in their houses? Why do they buy fast food everyday? Why do they
drink low fat milk?

Questions asked by Kenyan runners about American runners

Their Own (in the U.S.)

To be a professional runner in the U.S., Kenyans must adapt to new altitudes, climates, training regimes, diets, modes of transportation, traditions,
and cultures. American running products such as logs, heart rate monitors,
and energy bars are objects of curiosity to most Kenyan runners.

Simon Cherogony, farmer and former winner of the Mystic Places and
Steamtown Marathons, tires easier in the U.S. "I miss the smell of the flowers
from the peanut, tea, and coffee plants, and red soil," he says. "It doesn't feel
the same."

Indeed, anyone moving from Kenya's moderate equatorial climate to America's colder humid conditions must make behavioral and biological adjustments. My Kenyan friends have frequently worn track suits on humid eighty-
degree training runs.

"On our training runs in the mountain air in Kenya, we wear track suits,"
Cherogony explained.

Several days after he won the 2004 Big Sur Marathon, I went on an easy
run with Ibrahim Limo. A neighbor walking his dog asked Limo why he was
wearing long sleeves on such a humid North Carolina day.

"After an easy jog my insides will be warmed up, and then I will remove them," Limo responded. Then he asked the neighbor, "Why do Americans live together with dogs inside the house? In Kenya, the animals stay outside."

Why is Diet Important?

There is no single Kenyan diet—the diets of aspiring and successful world class runners vary based on geography, ethnic group, and socio-economic conditions. The pastoral Maasai, dominant in tribal competitions, subsist on beef, cow's blood, and milk.

Altitude initiates adjustments from the sympathetic nervous system that in turn increases the basal metabolism rate. Without increased caloric intake, body mass reduces. At altitude, the body dehydrates. Runners at altitude, therefore, must eat and drink more.

Paul Tergat tells his apprentices to eat a lot when training. "You cannot train well without lots of food," says Hillary Lelei. "He eats two large plates at lunch. Paul loves potatoes very much."In a traditional Kenyan household, women and children prepare the meals. When I hosted Kenyan women runners, I was not allowed in my own kitchen. Kenyan men in the U.S., however, become great cooks and prefer traditional staples to eating out. These staples include Kenyan tea, *ugali* (white cornmeal), *unga* (red millet flour for *uji*, similar to oatmeal), and milk. A glass of milk is customarily taken with *ugali*. Occasionally, warm milk or buttermilk is substituted at night. Runners arriving in the U.S. often comment that the milk and meat taste different (because of processing). Easygoing by nature, the only time I saw them become panicked or angry was when they were without milk. Each trip to the grocery store usually includes buying three gallons. "I think we need to buy a cow," I told marathoner Elly Rono."We have nowhere to keep it," he responded seriously. "In Kenya the kids and women would take care of that. It is easier to go buy it."

I am always amazed when I read about Kenyan runners' low fat diets. One cup of whole milk has a fat content 8.15 grams (saturated 5.07 grams and unsaturated 2.65 grams). They consume at least twenty to thirty grams of fat daily from milk. This does not include the fat consumed from cooking oil, beef, and chicken.Typically, a runner's day starts with several cups of Kenyan *chai*. More is taken after the morning training, in the afternoon, after the second training, and possibly after dinner. Made of half whole milk and half water, tea masala, sugar, and loose quality Kenyan tea, *chai* is boiled in a large pot and poured through a sieve. There are many individual variations. Rono, for example, uses more tea and milk, and cooks it slowly. Many visitors claim that his is the best tea they have ever had. For breakfast, runners eat *uji*, a porridge made from millet or *chapatti*. Milka Jepchirchir, a sub-fifteen 5000m runner, prepares *chapati*, a mixture of flour, eggs (optional), water, and salt, that is rolled like a pancake and fried (see figure 6.1). During hard training or after a race, *mandazi*, a donut-like deep-fried mixture of flour, baking powder, and sugar, is sometimes eaten for extra energy. During training, however, breakfast is usually several slices of bread.

Lunch usually consists of *githeri* (potatoes, corn, and beans), and rice or spaghetti. After a large lunch, runners usually nap.Kenyan runners eat dinner late, and go to bed soon after. Beef or chicken stew is eaten daily with cabbage, collard greens, or kale. The stew is made from imported Royco *mchuzi* spice mix, tomatoes, green or hot peppers, cilantro, onions, and water. *Ugali* is always part of dinner. White cornmeal is boiled, stirred with a *mwigo* (a large wooden utensil), and placed on a plate to cool until it resembles cornbread. Some runners grow and grind their own maize in Kenya and bring it with them to the U.S. For most runners returning home after a race, their first words are, "I have not had *ugali* or *chai* for three days. I need beef and *ugali*."

Training: From Casual to Organized

Those familiar with the Kalenjin anticipated the transition from pastoral lifestyle and tribal competitions to organized training with intense curiosity. According to John Manners, "At least a couple at every little school could step barefoot onto rough grass tracks at the start of the season and without training running at 6000 feet, turn in middle distance times that would have gotten them into the finals of most U.S. state meets. Training was remarkably casual in those days. We used to wonder what Kenyans would do if they ever started systematic, rigorous training. Now we're beginning to find out."[1] According to Tanser, organized training programs in Kenya have produced champions at an unparalleled rate. Kenyan champions make sacrifices, training in a Spartan lifestyle at camps away from family, night life, and television. Rising at five a.m. and asleep by nine p.m., they train sometimes three times daily at high intensity. Aspiring runners in Kenya carry a stick to ward off wild dogs, and train in second-hand shoes rather. The bulk of speed work includes tempo and Fartlek runs. Because tracks are not always accessible, some run diagonals in an open field. In a typical diagonal training session, runners run an X-shape inside a track, believing that this opens up the legs and is less likely to cause injury than intense speed work on a hard track. After leaving a problematic manager while training for the 2002 Pittsburgh Marathon, Margaret Kagiri stayed with me in Olde Town Alexandria, VA, for several months. Within two hours she had found trails in a wooded area that provided a great canopy for humid summer days.

Kibet Cherop: On the Roads
(*Haraka, Haraka haina Baraka*)

March 2000

Having placed thirty-fourth in a Kenyan cross country race, Kibet Cherop arrived in the U.S. in shape for the 2001 Shamrock 8K in Virginia Beach.

"I'm in the best shape of my life," he said. "Everybody in Kenya is running, running crazy."

A pack of Kenyans took it out fast. After three miles, Cherop and John Itati, Lisa Buster's newest sensation, dropped the field and sprinted to a 22:38 photo finish. Despite windy and cold conditions, they ran a current world best for 2000. They repeated the results in 2001.

April 2000

At the Sallie Mae 10K, Cherop and Joseph Nderitu, a Kikuyu living in Canada, ran with a large pack for four miles. Nderitu broke first. Cherop, with a four-minute road mile speed, sat on Nderitu and then noiselessly sprinted past him in the last few meters for the win. He savored the victory like a sated panther.

"Nderitu and several other Kikuyus were speaking in their dialect, so I knew something was going to happen," Cherop said after the race. "I just waited and kicked him at the end."

Ironically, it was at this event that Cherop met Andrew Masai, a top master's runner who had been on several Kenyan national teams when Cherop was a child. "I have heard of you," Cherop greeted him. "It is great to finally meet you."

October 2000

While staying with me in the DC area, Cherop competed in several low key races where the former local Reebok Enclave and Konstantin Selenivich's Red Square Sports train. At the Georgetown 10K, he ran the first half with the local elites, then broke away from the field with a 4:35 mile and won a five hundred dollar shopping spree at the Georgetown Mall. Andre Williams, the top local runner, dropped out at mile five on the instructions of Coach Matt Centrowitz, if he was going to lose.

After several hours of shopping the following day, Cherop was not tempted by anything. "I need to buy a chain saw," he said. Before leaving for Kenya, he filled four shopping bags at the Radio Shack with electronic gifts for his clan. Later that month at the Goblin Gallop 5K in Fairfax, VA, Kenyan runners placed first, second, and third. An editorial in the *Washington Times* suggested that they were not welcome; the provincial reporter implied that the race was for locals. When the runners asked why they shouldn't run, I explained that some people were frustrated and wanted their friends to win the prizes.

I alerted Selenivich, manager for Russian runners based out of Rockville, MD, to enter his female runners each year to pick up easy money. Urbane master's runner Jim Hage wrote an article in the *Washington Running Report*, stating how Americans need to run faster and road races are open to all unless otherwise stated.

November 2001

Reuben Chesang won the Richmond Marathon in 2:17:49. In the Ntelos 8K, Cherop came from behind to finish third (23:05), out kicking Andre Williams (23:06) in a rematch. In his American debut, Vincent Temu finished fifth (23:36).

June 2002

Cherop, Rono, and two retired milers mixed it up with top college teams at the Raleigh Relays 4x1500m (see Figure 6.1). Ben Kapsoiya and Amos Kipyegen ran respectable legs to lead the way. Rono, recruited because a fourth was needed, ran a slow third leg, leaving anchor Cherop with a sizable gap. Cherop pulled even with a Providence runner on the final turn, looked at him, and shifted to a faster gear for the win.

August 2002

In Durham, NC, Cherop and I took one of our many trips to an African grocery store to buy phone cards and food. The rush hour had begun—horns were blasting, and the highway was a parking lot.

"*Haraka, haraka haina baraka*," Cherop said with emotion.

Figure 6.1   4 x 1500m winners Ben Kapsoiya, Kibet Cherop, Amos Kipyegen, and
Elly Rono.

"What does that mean?" I asked.

"Hurry, hurry has no blessing. Just relax. Play this new tape from Zaire I
brought from Kenya. I know how you like their music like we Kenyans do."

June 2003

Cherop spent the racing season in Mexico. When he stopped in Durham
on the way back to Kenya, he said he'd won a car, but still couldn't drive.
Chesang, who had years earlier taken Cherop in as an apprentice, was also
racing in Mexico, and did. Chesang drove the car until he could sell it and
send the money to Kenya. Cherop asked me to take him shopping before he
departed. He took the allowable weight limit for international flights, with the
majority of gifts for Chesang's children.

Reuben Chesang and Simon Cherogony:
Thinking like a *Mzungu*

February 1999

The Pomoco Hampton Half-Marathon was too close to call. Reuben Chesang entered the finish chute first, but Andrew Letherby was given the win. After the event, Chesang, his teammates, and I had dinner at the mile seven marker, in the house in which I grew up. My father taught Chesang how to use a telescope, and talked about the NASA space program as they watched aircraft carriers in the harbor. That temporarily took Chesang's mind off the race, but unanswered questions lingered. Both runners ran 1:03:36, a course record; however, there remained a two thousand dollar difference in compensation.

October 1999

I hosted Cherogony and Rono the week of the Brew to Brew 8K in Baltimore and the Van Metre 8K in Northern Virginia. Neither offered much prize money, enough only to help pay rent and groceries. I invited a top local runner, Eron Ferrira, to train with them. The Kenyan duo alternated wins that weekend.

July 2000

Chesang, Rono, and Cherogony competed in a morning 8K in the Philadelphia suburbs, and the evening Rockville Rotary 8K in Gaithersburg, MD. Chesang broke from a large pack in the fifth mile of the Twiliter to beat the competitive field.

November 2000

When Cherogony arrived in DC to compete in the Veteran's Day 10K, I picked him up at the bus station. He hadn't been feeling well lately, he said.

John Tuttle won the 10K. Cherogony knew he should have won easily. On the way home, he complained of chest pains, and one side of his body began to feel numb. He refused, however, to see a doctor. Several days later, when his heart started beating fast, he went to the emergency room and was diagnosed with tetanus. According to the physician, he was hours from death.

July 2002

Simon Karori, formerly with the Kenyan military and KIM Management, spent his last year competing unsponsored as a master's runner. The 1992 fifth-ranked Road Racer of the Year was a role model for younger runners based in Durham, NC. He stressed the importance of being able to focus on professional running while simultaneously relaxing and having fun while training. The runners spent many hours watching African dance videos, relaxing their minds and bodies without losing their focus.

September 2002

Thinking like a *mzungu* (European or white person) became used more frequently as Cheregony acquired more American friends. He is a Kalenjin, sub-tribe Sabaot, who has partially resisted Westernization. He asked me several times to take him to meet someone, typically one to two hours late and without directions.

October 2002

Mary Mutua, a friend in Chapel Hill, NC, informed the Durham runners she had just received a shipment of food from Kenya.

"How do I get to your apartment?" I asked her.

"I do not know how to explain it to you," she said. "Ask Simon."

I asked Cheregony.

"We just go," he said. "I will show you. In Kenya you cannot use maps or directions."

November 2002

On our way to the Philadelphia Marathon and 8K, Jacob Kirwa, Cheregony, and I stopped in DC to have dinner with a traditional Tugen family. The wife just had a second child, and was relaxing for several months (the tradition in their sub-tribe). A friend had come from Kenya to prepare meals, perform daily chores, and care for the children. When we arrived, the wife was sleeping, a pot of tea was waiting for us, and dinner was prepared.

As I got up to refill my tea, I was told by the Kenyan visitor, "Don't go in the kitchen. Everything will be taken care of for you."

Consequentially, cups of tea kept appearing. It became late and we were invited to spend the night. After so much strong tea, I spent the night working on my laptop. At four a.m., the wife awoke and was curious about my computer. She had heard about them, she said, but had never seen one. At the time, the Kenyan presidential primaries were taking place. We read the Kenyan newspapers until six a.m., when the runners awoke for their training run.

The next day, Cherogony dropped out of the marathon and Kirwa ran poorly in the 8K. To this day, I have been accused of performing witchcraft late at night, resulting in their bad luck.

Elly Rono: Don't Call the Police, We're Just Running for Our Supper

When Reggae star Bob Marley died of brain cancer, his obituary included an interesting passage—while jogging in a rural area of Maine, a local filed a police report stating she had seen a monster.

When unshaven, Rono's imposing 6' 3", 150-pound frame bears a striking resemblance to Jimmy Cliff. He was a familiar sight cruising at a five-minute mile pace on the roads of Durham, NC.

"I have seen you running on Erwin road on my way to work," is a common greeting by locals.

He usually answers, "You must get up early because I have been running sometimes as early as four-thirty a.m. to avoid the summer heat and humidity."

The transformed marathoner has received a warmer reception. The second running boom of the 1990s has increased awareness among Americans of international elite runners. Rono has proudly worn a Durham-City of Medicine shirt to some races.

After two years of college and one year of teaching in Kenya, Rono received a track scholarship for two years at the University of Southern Indiana. He recalls being asked in his orientation if he had ever used an indoor restroom. While majoring in business and math, he was a Division II National Champion in cross country and track, running 28:42 for 10,000m. Rono moved to Durham after graduating in 1998.

April 2000

The George Washington Parkway 15K in Alexandria, VA, was a turning point in Rono's career. A college rival, Mark Coogan, easily dropped a good field with a 4:30 seventh mile, and Rono finished out of the money. He realized that he needed to train more seriously.

2001

Although a decent miler, 5K, 10K, and cross country runner in college, Rono worked odd jobs and had only moderate success on the roads. Before being able to support himself on road race winnings, he delivered pizzas and worked the midnight shift at a *USA Today* plant. After working on his weaknesses and building confidence, he decided to try the marathon. He competed in four in 2001, winning three with a 2:12 best.

The 2001 California International Marathon, where he placed second (2:23), was among the most memorable. Rono had to lean his upper body at a forty-five degree angle at times because of a forty mph headwind and occasional hail stones. Rather than complaining, however, he drew strength from the experience. After that, whenever his roommates complained, Rono said they were running in a forty mph headwind, meaning that they were losing focus by worrying about small things.

2002

Rono called 2002 the "Year of freezing out Chad Newton." Newton was a respectable sub-elite runner living and working on a North Carolina farm. In regional competitions in Ashville and Raleigh, Rono used Newton as training fodder. Newton and Rono became friends, and Rono and his training partners felt bad about not allowing Newton to participate in any awards ceremonies.

In 2002, Rono added five marathon wins to his resume—Grandma's (2:10:57), Providence (2:14), Richmond (2:16), CIM (2:11), and Mercedes (2:20). His training regime changed in two ways. Two daily one-hour runs remained the staple of his training. Every Sunday, he ran longer (2.25-2.5 hours), the last few miles on the Duke University track at a 4:50 pace. Eventually, he added another eight miles on Sunday night. Also, until 2002, most of his speed work was tempo runs. He gained a new level of confidence when he began weekly workouts of 10 x 1000m at 2:47, or 7 x a mile at 4:38.

July 2002

At the Crazy Eights 8K, Rono held back while many of his countrymen took it out fast. He recalls running beside a 5' 3" woman whose legs were mov-

Figure 6.2   Rono explaining to DeHaven he did not want to go for it due to the heat and humidity at the Parkerburg Half-Marathon. DeHaven is not buying it.

ing faster than anything he had ever seen. His goal became to beat her. His instincts were right since she set a world record. It was later discovered she was assisted with pacing by her husband. Later in the year it was revealed she had been assisted by something else, EPO, and consequentially banned from competition for two years.

Rono posted the cover of *Track and Field News* with Khannouchi, Gebreselasse, and Tergat in London on the living room wall as a constant reminder to keep focused. How does Rono race so frequently? He credits his ability to stay in world class shape year round to many hours spent on the treadmill through the winter. He says if he missed a few weeks of training, it would take too long to get back into shape.

2003

While the Duke University track was undergoing renovation in the spring and summer, Rono used the University of North Carolina track, running solo quarters to prepare for the 2003 New York Marathon. He also increased his long runs to six per month (2 x 1:45, 3 x 2:00, 1 x 2:20), competed in fewer races, and reduced his ten milers from 51:00 to 49:00. Two months before the race, he moved to Blowing Rock, NC, for focused altitude training at Zapfitness.

November 2003

Rono placed fourth in the New York Marathon (2:11), and two weeks later set a course record at the Richmond Marathon (2:15). Shrewdly and humbly, he invested his winnings in the Kenyan infrastructure. He has shunned material things, and drives an SUV with over three hundred thousand miles. He began searching for the secret to running a sub 2:10, waiting for his American citizenship paperwork to be approved, and hoping to make an Olympic team.

Friends, Rivals, or Friendly Rivalry?

The rivalry between Rono and Rod DeHaven, the only American 2000 Olympic marathoner, has been a windfall for race directors and journalists. Rono and DeHaven have competed many times, alternating wins at the Naples Half-Marathon and squaring off at the 2003 California International Marathon. "

Rod looked confident and tucked in behind me," Rono said after the race. "Joseph Kariuki, the former 25K world record holder, and I decided we needed to go sub-five at mile sixteen. We wanted to see if he was bluffing."

Rono easily dropped Kariuki and DeHaven for another win.

"I am going to drop to thirty-mile weeks and see you in Naples," DeHaven told Rono after the race.

Rono continued logging 140-mile weeks, and easily beat DeHaven in the Naples Half-Marathon. Several weeks later, Rono ran 2:12 for third in the Inaugural Miami Marathon. DeHaven and Rono met again at the 2003 Parkersburg Half-Marathon. The hilly race was filled with fresh Kenyans like Augustus Kuvutu and John Gwako. The multiple surges on the humid day were not what Rono needed to test his fitness. "

How many marathons are you running this year?" DeHaven jokingly taunted Rono after the race.

"I am just focusing on New York," Rono replied. "Today, I was not going to kill myself for five hundred dollars. Those guys were going for it. I just made it a training run."

"Maybe, you are the smartest one," DeHaven responded.

Hillary Lelei: How to Get Somewhere in Blowing Rock, NC

Hillary Lelei is familiar with the Kenyan running infrastructure. He worked on Moses Tanui's farm, lived and trained with Paul Tergat, and often speaks of his neighbors in his Nandi village (all winners of several major American road races). In the 1990s, he trained with the Fila junior camp. From 2000-02, he competed in London, and was a pacer for several major marathons. In 2003, his first U.S. racing season, he found American ways to be a significant adjustment.

"In Britain they do it like this," he often said. "In Kenya we do it like this. Why do you do it like this?" And when he left the U.S., he said, "I learned many things. When I come back again, I will know."

August 2003

At the Charleston 15 Miler, Lelei met up with former training partner Augustus Kuvutu. Kuvutu's manager, Tim Forrester, had four athletes working as a team, surging occasionally to tire Lelei out. But Lelei stuck to his game plan, surging with long strides on several downhill slopes—an attack formerly used by Bill Rodgers. Only Kuvutu responded, and Lelei got his first win on American soil.

The day before the race, Lelei avoided the other Kenyan runners, ate alone in his room, and was asleep by nine p.m. He later explained, "I know those guys and I used to train with them. Tergat told me to watch out for other runners and other agents. The day before the race, do not talk to the other runners and relax in your room. Talk to them after the race."

The same weekend, we drove to Virginia Beach for the Rock n' Roll Half-Marathon. Lelei's training partner in Kenya, Martin Lel, ran a 4:19 eleventh mile, breaking up a pack and finishing thirty seconds ahead of Paul Koech for the win.

September 2003

I took a group to Zapfitness to meet with Rono and train. Located near Boone, NC, Zapfitness is strategically placed off the beaten path. My directions included landmarks such as mailboxes, bulldozers, and dirt roads.

"We can find it, we are from Africa," Lelei exclaimed.

He is not a big fan of maps.

October 2003

I called several elite athlete coordinators, and decided to work with Steve Evans, from the Detroit Marathon. Evans wrote me the following congratulatory email:

From: Steve Evans sevans1956@comcast.net

Date: Sunday, October 05, 2003 4:09 PM

To: randy_mayes@msn.com

Subject: Hillary WON

Randy:

We tried to call you around 2:30. Hillary won with a 2:19+. He was behind until mile 24, when he pulled even with John Kariuki. They might have tried to work together, but John's Achilles was spent and Hillary won going away. Mike Dudley made a run at the end and finished 2nd to qualify for the Olympic trials. Another runner from Arlington, VA had been trying for several years to qualify and made it 12 seconds. Boy he was happy.

Hillary was a joy to have although a bit elusive as we could not find him a few times, including the VIP dinner. I told him he is as fast off the roads as he is on the roads. I also told him if he won, that he should bring his wife next year.

Again, Congratulations

My reply to Mr. Evans:

From: RANDALL MAYES

To: Steve Evans

Sent: Sunday, October 05, 2003 5:29 PM

Subject: Re: Hillary WON

His elusiveness is something that was taught to him by Paul Tergat. After the race he should be different. He is trying to avoid the distractions and other Kenyans before the race. Do not judge him by American ways of thinking. If he was thinking like us he would not be Hillary from Kenya. This is what my book is about. Thanks for your help.

October 2003

Lelei called Tergat after the Berlin Marathon.

It is crazy," Tergat said. "Reporters are everywhere. Let me call you back in a few minutes."

Lelei said, "Sometimes Tergat immediately asks to be taken to the airport in an ambulance so he can relax."

Tergat called back an hour later, expanding on the excitement and the history he had made that day. A number of major American newspapers failed to mention his accomplishment—an unbelievable 2:04 marathon. For elite runners, that psychological barrier was broken.

Their Own Worst Enemies

"How many Kenyans will be there?" is a common question asked before a race.

Kenyans compete mainly with other Kenyans. Established races with major sponsors such as the Cherry Blossom Ten Mile in DC and the Rock n' Roll Half-Marathon in Virginia Beach recruit straight from Kenya for forty-six minute and 1:01 times respectively.

A number of European management companies have training groups for top professional runners in Kenya, Europe, and Colorado. KIM Management has Tom Nyariki, Paul Koech, William Kiptum, Simon Rono, and Daniel Komen. The road racers train in Colorado, the track team in London and California.

Rono and I met with Daniel Komen at the Crazy 8's 8K race director's house in Kingsport, TN. Komen owns an internet café in Eldoret and a home in London where a number of runners live. He took out a laminated card with a list of KIM Management contacts. "These are the people who take care of us," he said. He called a number to find out the results from a track meet in Europe earlier that day. When he hung up, he said, "An Ethiopian won the 3000m."

In the late 1990s, Joseph Kimani set numerous records with a succession of sub-28:00 10Ks. In an interview at the Sallie Mae 10K, he disclosed that KIM Management encouraged him to move up to the marathon where more money could be made. He resisted the move, but succumbed to the pressure. Over time, the increased mileage injured his back; he never regained his invincible status.

Dr. Gabrielle Rosa and son Federico work with top runners such as Paul Tergat, Joshua Chelanga, Martin Lel, John Korir, and Robert Cheruiyot. Tergat agreed to help me with my story at the 2002 Rock n' Roll Half-Marathon. At mile eleven, he was running in the middle of a pack of ten men who had dominated major American road races earlier in the year. As the others began to lose form, Tergat's remained flawless. In the final two miles, he bolted from the pack and crossed the finish line first.

After the race, the television announcer called him John Tergat and commended him for his fifteen thousand dollar win. "You must be excited with

Table 6.1   "Their Own" Factors and Theories

Diet, physical training, mental training, recovery, and focus are all crucial to their peak performance.	Runner
Distractions hinder performance. The less distractions, the better they perform.	Manager

all that money," he said, not realizing that in Europe Tergat earned appearance fees fifteen times the amount.

Tergat smiled. "It's not bad."

I accompanied him to his hotel. His sister and terminally ill brother, Francis Kipkuna, were both there from New Jersey, along with a masseuse who went to work rejuvenating Tergat's legs. A full evening of festivities was scheduled for him before his return flight to Kenya the following day. Somehow, amidst the activity, he managed to sit down with me to explain his perspective on Kenyan running.

"It is simply how you see and do things. Do you know how we live?"

Gianni DeMadonna is another Italian manager and former colleague of Dr. Rosa. He works with Daniel Too, Reuben Cheriuyot, and Eliud Barngetuny, who occasionally race in the U.S. Jos Hermans has sent a number of runners to American road races, including Josephat Machuka and Felix Limo.

Several enclaves of Kenyan runners are based in the U.S. Some live in Albuquerque, NM, because it offers altitude and a favorable climate for training. Lisa Buster's group in Norristown, PA, comprised mainly of Kikuyu runners (including Catherine Nderba, Joseph Kariuki, Peter Githuka, John Kagwe, Gilbert Okari, Linus Maiyo, and John Itati) has won many major races. In Chicago, the *Kukimbia* club includes John and James Kariuki, and Joseph Kahugu among its members.

Living in the U.S. is a learning experience for Kenyan runners. Some prefer to live as they did in Kenya, isolated from distractions and focused on training and racing. Others are more curious and are only partially focused on their craft, at times forgetting why they came to the U.S. These runners tend to return home with less winnings.

7

KENYAN CULTURES

We are more modernized and were Christianized first, so we eat processed food. They (Kalenjins) mill their own corn maize, we buy it. The Kambas live in a more advanced society and are better off.

Mary Loko Mutua, a nurse from Kamba

Shortcomings in the Bush: Second and Third Order Cybernetics and Ethnocentrisms

"In athletics it is culture not biology, attitude not altitude, nurture not nature, which are the crucial variables which explain individual athletic success in the rationalized and regulated world of achievement sport (Bale & Sang 1996, 158)." Bale and Sang's book, *Kenyan Running*, has been described as a debunking of biological determinism. In the etic approach of ethnography, anthropologists invents categories through which to analyze a culture—an approach that reflects their own point of view. Upon becoming sociologically and ethnographically informed, anthropologists aim to use the emic approach by studying a culture without imposing their own cultural viewpoint on the analysis.

The lifestyles and cultures of Kenyan runners are mysterious, ironic, and different. Compared with the Maasai and the Kikuyu, little ethnographic research has been done on the Kalenjin. Tanser's *Train Hard, Win Easy* has increased awareness of the Kenyan running sub-culture.

When Amy Shipley visited a Kikuyu running enclave in Norristown, PA, she saw reigning New York City Marathon champion John Kagwe training in a woolen hat and gloves in sixty degree weather. She documented the cluttered apartment and communal lifestyle of the group that averaged forty-seven thousand dollars for six months' work, and wisely warned, "The American vantage point, clearly, should be set aside when considering these Kenyan athletes (Shipley 1998, A1)."

The running news website, www.letsrun.com, founded by professional runner Weldon Johnson and his brother Robert, a Cornell track coach, is an invaluable source of information for running enthusiasts. Posts on their chatboard suggest that Kenyan runners remain enigmatic. The contrasting ways of doing things perpetuate their enigmatic lifestyle.

Numerous lineages and ethnic groups make Kenya heterogeneous. Ethnic identities are reflected in naming systems and the concept of clan, and differences are expressed in the varying passions and beliefs. Their training is also mysterious to Westerners. Those living in rural areas far from the nearest track use diagonals and tempo runs rather than intervals for speed work. Some runners move to urban areas such as Iten, Nairobi, or Eldoret that have several tracks.

Kenyans' contrasting values and knowledge systems provide different ways of seeing things. Kenyans believe in making training fun, a different mindset from organized training—they have tea, relax, and train when they are ready rather than arriving at 4:00 p.m. to train. Because Kenyans typically do not run for recreation, they question why Americans jog when they are older and overweight to get in shape. When Kenyan runners retire after a short, but intense, career, they are accused of not lasting long in the professional ranks.

Kenyans are Great Runners Except for the Ones that Aren't

Do the Kenyan societal structure and its ethnic variations correlate to running success? Are these differences favorable for world class running? Kenyans are a heterogeneous group. Over forty ethnic groups inhabit specific geographic regions, and vary in ancestry, modernization, beliefs, and passions. Each speaks a different dialect (in addition to English and Swahili). Generalizations, therefore, are risky.

Lineage

The Kenyan running ethnic groups, Kalenjin, Kikuyu, Kamba, and Kisii, have patrilineal lineage. Men inherit land and cattle and are forbidden to marry women of the same clan. When intermarriage among ethnic groups occurs, the woman moves to the husband's village and joins his clan. Polygamy has been practiced for several centuries, but to a lesser extent today.

The Kenyan naming system typically includes a Christian first name, a family name, and an event occurring at birth. The runner may go by the middle or last name, so siblings may or may not use the same last name.

Kenyan lineages include three ancestries—Nilotes, Bantus, and Cushites. Among these, the Nilotes and Bantus have tribes with great runners. The major ethnic affiliations classified by geography and ancestry are as follows, with world class running tribes in bold.

1. Western Bantu—Luyia, **Gusii or Kisii**, Kuria
2. Central Bantu—**Kamba, Kikuyu**, Embu, Meru, Mbere, Tharaka
3. Coastal (Eastern) Bantu—Swahili, Mijikenda, Segeju, Pokomo, Taita, Taveta
4. Plains (Eastern) Nilotic—Maasai , Samburu, Turkana, Teso, Njemps, Elmolo
5. Highland Nilotic (**Kalenjin**)—Nandi, Marakwet, Tugen, Kipsigis, Keiyo, Sabaot, Pokot
6. Lake-River Nilotic—Luo
7. Southern Cushitic—Boni
8. Eastern Cushitic—Somali, Rendille, Orma, Boran, Gabbra[1]

Traditional vs. Modern

Modernization, Westernization, and privatization have magnified ethnic variations. The traditional-modern ratio varies depending on the ethnic group—some preserve their cultural traditions, while others embrace change. Of the top five modernized ethnic groups, four are considered the running tribes, producing most of the world class runners—Kamba, Kikuyu, Kisii, and Kalenjin. While the Luo are the most modernized, they have developed passions other than running. The Pokot, a Kalenjin sub-tribe, have resisted Westernization and produce the least number of elite runners in the tribe.

With the transition to the cash economy, education and jobs are not accessible to all. American road races, offering thousands in prize money (equivalent to much more in the Kenyan economy), are therefore appealing. With land inherited and food provided for in the agricultural economy, money is needed for schooling, cars, and modern homes.

Some traditional ethnic groups remain in a farm economy. The Pokots and Marakwets (and to a lesser extent, the Turkana) still practice cattle raiding. Several groups, including the Maasais and Turkana, have resisted the British school system and formal education. According to anthropology professor Peter Rigby, the Maasai's resistance to Westernization and their reluctance to enter the market system is ethnosuicide. He notes, however, that they are receptive to veterinary services for their livestock. "Their resistance is due to the importance of time as a utility in a truly capitalist system. Such a concept is quite incompatible with the Maasai perception of time and career progressions created in their age system (Rigby 1992, 31)." They remain pastoral; many do not send their children to schools. According to Hillary Lelei, they are notorious for refusing to stand in a queue in banks. A group of Maasai visiting Washington, DC made the Kenyan news when they stopped cars as they crossed the streets.

Geography

Great runners are not distributed equally throughout Kenya. The Kalenjin and the Kikuyu live at 2000-2500m altitude and produce many world class runners. The Kisii and Kamba live at lower elevations but also produce world class runners. The coastal ethnic groups have not produced world class runners. The correlation between geography, climate, and running is discussed in chapter two.

Beliefs

Ethnic groups that resist assimilation hold on to different beliefs and values. The Plains (Eastern) Nilotes have taboos against agriculture, hunting, and fishing. The Kikuyu once had taboos against eating fish and game. The coastal Cushites and Bantus have an Arabic-Moslem influence. Some traditional tribes such as the Samburu have adopted cultivation, and the Turkana, fishing. In the pastoral cattle-based economy, there is minimal need for cash. Cattle provide milk, blood, meat, sacrifices to ancestors or spirits, leather, dowries, and dung for fuel and building homes. To avoid overgrazing and to be close to water, some tribes are nomadic.

Table 7.1   **Ethnographic Factors and Theories**

Ancestry or lineage	Nilotes and Bantus are producing world class runners
Geography	Rift Valley and Kikuyu homeland at medium altitude
Modernization, transition from traditional to modern society	Farm to cash economy, economic motivation, less traditional, more Westernized
Beliefs	Links with cattle and lifestyle
Passions	Soccer, politics, business, running, craftsmen

Passions

In Manners' *The Running Tribe*, he discusses how the Kalenjin are a tribe with an affinity for running. They not only ran as a means of survival historically, but enjoy running today. Other ethnic groups are known for other specialties. The Gusii, or Kisii, are noted for their soapstone carvings, the Kamba for their wood carvings. The Kikuyu, the largest and wealthiest group, own the majority of businesses and are involved in politics and religion. According to Rebecca Kiplagat, a Cultural Affairs Officer at the Kenyan Embassy in Washington, DC, "The Kikuyu are more outgoing than Kisii, and the Kisii are more outgoing than the Kalenjin."

The Luyia have produced several sprinters. The Luo, many of whom are agricultural scientists and doctors, have a passion for soccer and fishing. Soccer is more popular than running in Kenya, although the Kenyan National Team is not exceptional. It also receives more news coverage and government funding. A possible explanation for the lower international ranking in soccer is possibly linked to the phenomenal success in endurance events. The majority of Kenyan ethnic groups do not have the West African muscular build that is essential for success in sprinting and soccer. The Luos are more representative of the West African build.

PART IV

PSYCHOLOGICAL FACTORS: HOW THEY SEE THINGS

8

Belief and Knowledge Systems

The formality and structure are not natural, and the Kenyans will return to their own traditions.

John Bale and Joe Sang

We can find it (Zapfitness), we're from Africa.

Hillary Lelei

What is African Philosophy?

The notion of African philosophy has been ambiguous since it was first used in the 1910s (Mudimbe 1991, 32). Writings from the crossover disciplines of philosophy, ethnography, and literature are divided into four schools of thinking. The rift centers on the definition of African philosophy, and whether it is different from other philosophies.

Self-definition in the post-colonial era has been problematic, as Africans have had to combine tribal and colonial beliefs (Wiredu 1995, 9). Traditional African ways of thinking have become fused with Western, Christian, and Moslem thought. Wiredu suggests a need for retradition—the conceptual decolonization of African minds. This would differentiate foreign conceptual schemes in language, religion, and politics (Mudimbe 1988, 169).

Ethnophilosophy

Students of African thought, or ethnophilosophers, contend that African thinking is unique—there exists an African and European experience (Imbo

1998, 22). Accordingly, differences are expressed in belief and knowledge systems.

Belief Systems: It Depends on How You See Things, Religion vs. Spirituality

"To believe you can win is like any other kind of faith. You can think about it, talk about it, write about it. But it doesn't matter, belief is a simple thing. The Kenyans believe they will win as simply as the sun shines. And even if you match their training, to beat them, you would have to match their faith. In my mind I am a Kenyan (Bale & Sang 1996, 105)."

What is the basis for this Nike advertisement slogan? Physical talent alone does not guarantee victory. Confidence, passion, and motivation are also necessary.

According to Paul Tergat, Kalenjin runners are dominant because, "It depends on how you see and do things. All Kalenjins are not the same. I am very competitive. I set a goal and ask myself each day what I need to do to get there. Because of the way we are raised, we do things differently. Our beliefs and spirituality are different. My spirituality is not organized religion, but drums, kids, nature, and music."

The African belief system affects many aspects of their daily life. "If we (The Armed Forces Team) train, we know we can win," says Tergat. "If someone is running faster than I am, then I must train harder to beat them." Before setting a 26:27 10,000m world record, he said, "You have to believe everything is possible." When Naoko Takahashi broke the women's marathon sub-2:20 psychological barrier, Catherine Ndereba and Paula Radcliffe soon ran faster times. Similarly, Roger Bannister's sub-four-minute mile was soon repeated.

According to Alphonse Mutima, a Duke University and University of North Carolina Swahili professor who was selected at a young age to spread seeds for villagers whose crops were not producing, the traditional Kenyan belief system is difficult for Westerners to understand. Because he was innocent and respected adults, it was believed that the spirits would honor him. Pregnant women believed that he could guess the gender of their baby. For many Kenyan runners, this belief system comprises their psychological mindset—a stark contrast to Western psychology.

Mary Loko Mutua, a Kamba, says that in some tribes children rarely misbehave because they believe that if their parents curse them they will not have a good life. A blessing from the elders is very important and influences the collective behavior.

Second and Third Order Cybernetics and Belief Systems

Western and traditional African concepts of religion have different mean-ings. According to Kwasi Wiredu, it is unclear whether the word 'religion,' or the concept of organized religion, is applicable to African life and thought (Wiredu 1996, 45). The African perspective is sometimes overlooked or seen from different viewpoints. "When the British arrived in Kenya they did not realize the significance of certain buildings, gatherings, and large trees. These were sacred places (Holdstock 2000, 166)."

Many Kenyans influenced by missionaries remain Christians, some prac-tice tribal religion, and some belong to African branches of the Christian church. These African Independent Churches reflect more upon the tradi-tional beliefs. Their spirituality is less about priests and churches, and more about nature, animals, music, drums, dancing, and children. Physical close-ness to nature is important in all aspects of life (Holdstock 2000, 181).

Knowledge Systems: Selection Based on Intuition; Experience vs. Reason

To think of Africa as the right hemisphere and the West as the left offers an interesting psychological way to examine the two areas (Holdstock 2000, 203). The scientific, analytical, or Western way of looking at the world is structured rather than spontaneous or based on personal experience.

Len Holdstock, a psychologist who has taught in Europe, Africa, and the U.S., notes, "Like the South Americans, Africans play soccer with a sponta-neous joyfulness that contrasts starkly with the organized skills of European teams (Holdstock 2000, 194)." According to cultural sociologist Niels Larsen, "The rhythm between hard and systematic training and the playful means a great deal to the continuous motivation. The true artists' talent is to combine potential and hard training with the playful and pre-conscious, where one doesn't deliberate rationally, but allows the bodily rhythm and pulse to ex-pand and live entirely in the present (Larsen 1998, 5)."

Clement Oniang'o, Dean of Social Sciences at the University of Nairobi, ar-gues that essential differences exist in traditional African and Western thought. "The African culture does not assume that reality can be perceived through reason alone. There are other modes of knowing such as imagination, intu-itive experience, and personal feelings. This is why the deepest expression of the African culture has been through art, myths, and music rather than through the European mode logical analysis (Oniang'o 1995, 1)."

Oniang'o elaborates on the relationship between Western and traditional African knowledge.

> The epistemological foundation of the African thought offers the uni-
> tary cultural view about reality and nature. This foundation proposes
> the thesis that the African concept of reality could offer the possibil-
> ity by which humanity could eliminate the errors of the European
> epistemology in conflict: rationalism (analytical) vs. empiricism (ob-
> servation and experimentation). The European cultural attempt to
> grasp reality has created two incompatible and contradictory theories
> of knowledge. On the one hand the rationalists thought the world
> was a pure idea independent of sense experience; while on the other
> hand the empiricists thought the world was that of natural reality in-
> dependent of reflection. Without any reference to other cultural
> modes of thought, it was naively supposed that these duelist theories
> applied to all cultures in the world. Let us examine two possible views
> of reality:

> a. Knowing is a process which may involve immediate and direct ex-
> perience; we shall call this the personal experience mode, or the
> African mode;

> b. Knowing may also involve an impersonal and mediate or indirect
> experience. We shall call this the scientific experience mode, or the
> European mode.

> The limitations of the scientific mode are the elements of personal
> experience. The scientific mode demands self-detachment. This mode
> is irrelevant to the African experience (Oniang'o 1995, 2).

Philosophers differentiate what is learned through the senses or experience as phenomenal as opposed to cognitive thought or intuition (Chalmers 1996, 11). "Personal experience refers to people acquiring knowledge and skills from observing life and in engaging in behavior without having been instructed in such matters (Thomas 2001, 57)."

Second and Third Order Cybernetics and African Knowledge Systems

Ethnophilosophers believe that humans are essentially different, and African knowledge systems are unique. Universalists, on the other hand, be-

lieve that African knowledge systems are not unique, but instead are the result of historical differences that have caused ethnic variations.

Sagacity or Sage Philosophy

Leading Sage Philosopher Odera Oruka criticizes ethnophilosophy for sharing beliefs throughout an ethnic group, arguing that philosophy ought to con-
sist only of the thoughts of the wisest individuals.

African philosophy is passed down orally by elders through proverbs, folk-
tales, rituals, beliefs, and myths (Imbo 1998, 38). Kwasi Wiredu warns us not
to compare African with Western philosophy (Wright 1979, 141). Elders,
which Wiredu refers to as aged peasants, are individuals and do not include
the group's diverse beliefs. Philosophers agree that no clear distinction between folk and philosophical sages exists.

Hermeneutics

Is sport an indicator or expression of culture? Can sport symbolize the social system? Literature, philosophy, and ethnography interpret rituals and examine how people live in order to understand other cultures. An ethnographer interprets symbolic behavior as a critic does novels or movies,
encouraging discussion and other interpretations (Patton 2002, 498).

Cricket

English colonies India, Pakistan, and the Trobriand Islands were cultur-
ally influenced by cricket. "If cricket did not exist in India, something like
it would have certainly have been invented for the conduct of public exper-
iments with the means of modernity (Appadurai 1996, 112)." The sport includes spectators, male domination, and social class division (Appadurai
1996, 110). Further, cricket offers an outlet for aggressive behavior; racial
and cultural tensions are acted out symbolically, thereby reducing actual
conflict.

According to Grant Farred, members of public and private cricket clubs in
Trinidad represent the political and social strata. "The sport was transformed
into a vehicle for Caribbean resistance. The resistance is such an integral part
of the game it fundamentally remakes Trinidadian society. It is more than a

metaphor for Caribbean politics, and it is more than a weekend game, it is a medium of expression of latent political hostilities (Farred 1996, 171)."

Baseball

In the U.S., baseball evolved from cricket, and football from rugby and soccer—both acts of independence against the English (Van Bottenburg 2001, 72).

Dominican baseball is both a symbol of American hegemony and a path of opportunity. As sport anthropologist Alan Klein explains, "Americans are beaten at their own game and symbol of superiority. It is a symbolic victory for baseball in the Dominican Republic, but a trade off between resisting American culture while maintaining pride, self identity, traditions, and modernity (Klein 1991, 111)."

The Dominican Republic has become dependent on the U.S. and its high salaries, losing talent and resources while absorbing American culture. There exists a complex relationship between modernity and nationalism.

Kenyan Running

Bale and Sang offer similar interpretations of Kenyan running. "It maybe symbolic, beating the British at their own game. It is a decolonization of the mind (Bale & Sang 1996, 190)." Kenyans' psychological motivation to train twenty miles daily comes from their history. "Each title won by a Kenyan is a triumph for their compatriots at home. They now dominate their former oppressors. One interpretation might be that the Kenyans have successfully manipulated and controlled the means of socially controlling them (Bale & Sang 1996, 182)."

Kenyan running reflects a different rationality. "To make running more their own, Kenyans had to loosen the English elements. In fact it was running with *e'lan*, something that had become suppressed in the rational world of modern runners (Bale & Sang 1996, 178)." *Élan* is a vigorous spirit or enthusiasm revealed by poise, verve (spirit animating artistic composition), or imagination.

Universalists

Cybernetics, Ethnocentrisms, and the Way They See Things

In direct opposition to ethnophilosophy, Universalists dismiss essentialism in post-modern literature and contemporary ethnographic writings. Wiredu denies that African philosophy is related to language and culture, and argues that a unique African philosophy does not exist. Rather, African thought parallels the development of philosophy in Europe.

Valentin Mudimbe proposes that Africa is a Western invention, based on a series of writings he refers to as a colonial library. Attempting to make sense of it all, he describes the missionary, African, and ethnographic views of African thought (Mudimbe 1988, 44). Philosophy professor Dismas Masolo says, "The power of Mudimbe's work is the illustration of the ways in which Western anthropological and missionary interpretations of African life and thought have induced distortions, not only for Westerners, but also for Africans who try to understand themselves by means of Western epistemological models (Masolo 1994, 182)."

According to Mudimbe, the missionary and ethnographic viewpoints resulted in an invented space—an African historical philosophy in which place, time, and consciousness are the determinants. Mudimbe describes this as a problem with self definition, because multiple worldviews results in collective unconsciousness. Education has changed mindsets. At the national level, colonialism and the church have created a double consciousness (Western and traditional). In the process of conversion, Christianity used religion to colonize minds (Mudimbe 1991, 4). The Church aimed to convert pagans to Christianity, and civilize primitives. British education was used to make the unscientific scientific. Today, the Kenyan government and people are searching for ways to combine traditional and modern culture with a Kenyan identity.

Table 8.1   Belief and Knowledge Systems, Factors, and Theories

Ethnophilosphy: Essentialism, playful, present, spiritual, informal, spirituality vs. religion, belief vs. science, left vs. right brained, analytical vs. intuition and personal experience, analytical vs. spontaneous, passion vs. structure.	Oniang'o, Bale and Sang
Sage philosophy: Belief and knowledge systems passed down.	Oruka
Universalists: Deny essentialism, rather a juncture in time and place.	Wiredu, Mudimbe
Hermeneutics:	
Decolonization of the mind, structure vs. passion, nationalism.	Bale & Sang
Their (Kenyan) own, modernity, globalization, acting out aggression and tensions.	Holdstock
Class politics, social structure. Identity, independence.	Appadurai, Klein, Farred, Van Bottenburg

9

INSIDE THE MIND OF THE
HIGHLY EVOLVED RUNNER

You line up for the London Marathon, clad in skimpy clothing and running shoes: the unadorned man of King Lear, reduced to your essentials. All you have to do is get yourself from here to there with whatever capacities you can mobilize—not just legs and lungs, but your head as well. Especially your head: the best physique is no better than the brain that drives it.[1]

Norman Myers, Oxford University Professor and Duke University Visiting Professor

Second and Third Order Cybernetics and Western Psychology

There is more to the East African success than physiology. Regardless of physical attributes, the psychologically tougher athlete usually prevails. According to coaches and running experts, competitive distance running is at least fifty percent mental. How, then, has a third world country that does not use Western psychology, sports psychology, and structured mental techniques become so dominant?

Similar to early ethnography, Western psychology is based on Eurocentric values and customs. "The reason why Western psychology has not taken off on the African continent possibly relates to the fact that the ideologies and the methodologies of contemporary psychology do not fit into the inclusive value system of the African people (Holdstock 2000, 201)."

"The underlying cultural values in Western psychology are Eurocentric, male, and middle class," explains South African psychologist Anthony Naidoo. Therefore Western psychology is ethnocentric in theory and practice (Naidoo 1996, 2)." Where Naidoo identifies the problem, Holdstock offers a solution. "The Achilles heel of psychology is being a Western and European discipline, it neglects the indigenous psychology of areas like sub-Sahara Africa (Holdstock 2000, 74)."In Western sport psychology, the ability to relax and focus is called 'flow,' or 'the zone.' Chinese martial artists call it *chi*, and the Japanese, *ki*. The average runner calls it having a good day. Many strive to reach peak performance physically, mentally, and spiritually; few, however, achieve such a state. For thousands of years, the attainment of *chi* has been a tradition in the Orient, and been a lifestyle for monks in the Shaolin Temple and Monastery. Phil Jackson, former coach of the Los Angeles Lakers, used Zen to supplement a void in Western sport psychology—a technique that had similarities to Kenyan indigenous psychology. In martial arts, achieving *ki* or *chi* provides focused energy enough to break objects, perform feats of strength, or maximize performance. In such a state, pain and fatigue is overcome. Wasting mental energy on worries, distractions, and negative thinking causes performance to suffer.[2] Bruce Lee taught lessons learned from Zen, including removing barriers to optimal performance. Shaolin Monks develop skills through repetition, concentration, and imagery. Repetition, a form of visualization, proactively trains and disciplines the mind. The monks practice distraction, mood, and stress control, and think about spirituality, patience, and humility.

Western Sport Psychology

The Americans that ruled the track and roads in the 1970s did not use structured mental techniques in preparation for racing.

Jack Bacheler, one of the few Americans to have beaten Steve Prefontaine, said "I did absolutely nothing."

"I relied mainly on instinct," said Frank Shorter.

According to Bill Rodgers, "You must empty yourself physically and psychologically as the race progresses. Successful marathoners must lose their cool, and allow their irrational, animal consciousness to take over (Rodgers 1980, 111)."

Gerry Lindgren's approach is to "Run with your heart, not your mind."

In the 1990s, the mental preparations used by American runners included social support groups (e.g., friends, family, or team members), positive thinking, faith, goal-setting, and visualization.

Competitive runners obtain confidence while training hard towards a goal. Both Western sports psychology and Zen use visualization, which uses repetition. For others, visualization is used to make cognitive changes. According to sport psychologist Dr. Wayne Hurr, the most common problems among runners are anxiety, lack of confidence, and negative thinking. Solutions vary, but usually require relaxation and positive thinking. If the coach or athlete is unable to resolve the situation, sport psychologists can help bring about cognitive changes.

Sport psychologist Dr. Jim Loehr breaks down the achievement of maximum performance into steps. First, relaxation clears the mind of clutter and lowers the heart rate. Second, the next step is planned in the preparation phase. Finally, the body and mind achieve an internal state of rhythm and readiness in the ritual phase. The more evolved the athlete, the more elaborate the ritual becomes.[3]

Traits

Elite athletes have unique psychological and personality profiles. At the entry level of a sport, the range of personalities is diverse (Cox 1990, 41). Certain personalities, traits, and temperaments provide a mental edge in middle and long distance running, allowing certain individuals to overcome the demands of the sport and advance to higher levels. Research indicates that successful female athletes have personalities similar to successful male athletes, but different from female non-athletes who tend to be more submissive, dependent, emotional, and passive (Williams 1980).

The psychological profile of an elite runner is not based solely on personality—studies correlating personality with performance have been unreliable at predicting success. More reliable has been the correlation of temperament and individual traits or socialization of cultural and collective personality traits to success (Cox 1990, 37).

The Interactional Model

Most Western sport psychologists have adopted the Interactional Model, which incorporates physical ability with how personality influences performance through interaction between the person and the situation (Cox 1990, 10).

The Yerkes-Dodson Law, also referred to as the Inverted-U Hypothesis, suggests that each athlete has an optimal level of arousal. With increased arousal, body chemistry changes—adrenaline surges, and attention becomes more focused. At low levels of arousal, individuals attend to both task-relevant and task-irrelevant cues. At moderate levels of arousal, individuals attend only to task-relevant cues. At high levels of arousal, individuals may fail to attend to task-relevant cues. Optimal performance is the point at which further increases in arousal lead to decreased performance.

The Information Processing Theory

The Information Processing Theory states that brain cells become active with arousal. With high levels of arousal, there is a trade off between information processing and performance (Cox 1990, 107). With too much information, the mind becomes cluttered and the ability to focus and relax is compromised. Peak performance requires a mental state in which fears, insecurities, and inhibitions can dissipate, and minimal calculating or thinking is occurring (Anshel 1994, 42–43).

Data is infinite, and much is useless. Information is useful data, but finite. For professional runners, information can be separated into training and racing files (see Table 9.1). Training and relaxation are equally important for peak performance. Boxers are known to train at an isolated training camp in order to focus on achieving peak performance.

Table 9.1   Files in Brain

Training File	Racing File	Useless Data File
Physical training and confidence. Mental Training. Spare time: recovery.	Running your own race, breaking the race into components and utilizing your strengths.	Clutter: the media, gossip. Extra arousal: problems, can't let go, can't focus, over thinking.

Top U.S. runners have diverse racing tactics—Steve Prefontaine was a front runner, Bill Rodgers surged down hills, Frank Shorter surged mid-race, Rich Kenah and Bryan Woodward kicked at the finish, and Steve Spence practiced detailed visualization.

- **Steve Holman.** In 1995, Holman placed well enough in European track meets to rank fourth in the world for the 1500m. National championships, however, eluded him. While his training was going well, his state of increased arousal prevented him from relaxing, and prompted negative thinking. By relaxing and thinking positively, he was able to control the situation; he won an Outdoor National Championship before retiring. Jokingly, he called his triumph a long overdue 'demonkeyfication' (Mayes 2000, 44).

- **Rich Kenah.** Kenah mastered the skill of separating training and racing mental files. In 1997, his most successful year, he was able to tune out external pressures and focus on racing tactics and goals. He won the 800m bronze medal at the World Indoor and Outdoor Championships.

- **Steve Spence.** In 1991, Spence won the marathon bronze medal at the World Championships and was ranked the top road racer in the world. His race plan and visualization included a hot weather strategy, a devised race pace, and knowledge of the course and competition.
- **Dan Browne.** Commenting on making the 2004 Olympic Marathon Team, Browne said, "That was the critical point in the race for me, no doubt. My body was getting crampy. I knew I had two good competitors ahead. I ran this race for a purpose to make the team. I ran this race to honor my West Point classmates who have died over in Iraq. With three miles to go, I thought of them, and knew I wouldn't quit."[4]
- **Keith Brantly.** In addition to visualization, Brantly would plant doubt in other runner's minds. Before a race, for example, he would tell Kenyan competitors that they did not look well, and ask if they felt okay.

What is the Kenyan Equivalent to Western Sport Psychology?

The Kenyan mindset might be better understood by comparing cultural values from the anthropological perspective and individual traits from the psychological perspective. Indigenous psychology is based on native norms and values. The African worldview includes the following components: social class, gender, ethnicity, historical psychological oppression, self-consciousness, and cultural values (e.g., being communal, spiritual, and interdependent) (Ajani ya Azibo 2003, 133).

Performance can be considered a function of the interaction of intrapersonal and interpersonal factors such as belief in oneself, motivation, and achievement orientation.[5] Professional runners have certain collective personality traits and mental skills derived from their history, culture, environment, and temperament.

Traits

1. *Focus.* World class runners must be able to resist acquiring useless information and over thinking. Multitasking is discouraged—Kenyan runners put away their work and listen to music or talk during meals, and get off the treadmill while watching track meets on television. Tuning out unnecessary distractions (e.g., the media, marketing people, and gossip) may make professional runners seem aloof, but is a necessary skill for success. Paul Tergat

is known for his focused training. This focus was tested at the 2000 World Cross Country Championships in Vilamoura. His individual five-time winning streak on the long course ended because of low team moral and sleepless nights over federation politics. Amazingly, the team managed to continue its winning streak with Tergat placing third individually, the top Kenyan.

2. *Playfulness and the ability to relax.* My first experience watching Kenyan runners at Hains Point in Washington, DC, left a lasting impression. Their smooth, graceful cadence can be described as similar to ballet. As I interviewed them before competitions, they seemed relaxed and playful. Alphonse Mutima says "running can be liberating." It is similar to golf. To some it is serious, maybe too serious depending on how it fits into your life. Brother Colm O'Connell, coach of St. Patrick's High School in the Rift Valley of Kenya, observed, "Kenyans are conditioned from birth to deal with the boredom that can accompany long hours of training. They don't have any problem sitting around doing nothing."[6]

3. *Intuition.* Using the terms right brain and left brain dominance to describe ways of thinking may be too simplistic (see Table 9.2). Thinker vs. feeler, however, is a self description. While providing commentary at the 2003 American Outdoor Championships, Steve Holman said, "Kenyans just run, Americans have a technical approach." Inger Miller said, "As an athlete, I'm a thinker more than a feeler. It takes a lot for me to get my mind and body in sync. Rather than just going out and doing it, I tend to think about what I have to do (Bloom 2000, 56)."

Being spontaneous, learning by doing, and navigating by places are all right brained (creative)/feeling mode. During training and performance, the right brain performs imagery and coordinates skills into one flowing performance. The left brain (analytical) tells the right that the pace is too fast, the distance too long, and the race too hard.

4. *Belief.* Top Kenyan runners earn a good living—they receive six-figure appearance fees and win a substantial amount of prize money on the European Grand Prix circuit, at international marathons, and at American road races. In Kenya, large homes with expensive cars are scattered among traditional homes. Aspiring runners can train with champions at training camps; this opportunity to escape the ascetic tradition their role models were raised in is often motivational.

"Kenyans believe they are capable of what their tribesmen have been capable of (Tanser 1997, 96)." When Emily Samoei needs inner strength to finish strong, she tells herself, "Others have done it, I can do it."

Table 9.2   General Cultural Comparison of African and Western Value Systems

	Traditional African	Western
Ethos	Group harmony: part of clan and nature	Survival of the fittest, control nature
Psychology	Spiritual, interdependent, communal	Materialistic, independent, organized religion, structured
Knowledge system	Socialization-traditional Education/socialization-modern	Education
Reasoning	Right hemisphere, feel	Left hemisphere, think
Time	Event to event	Schedule

5. *Ability to let go.* When Kenyan runners call home, they hope not to learn that someone is sick, the cows were stolen, the farm equipment needs repairs, or the crops and animals are suffering in a drought. In Swahili, *hakuna matata* means 'don't worry' or 'let it go'—a concept similar to a Zen saying used in martial arts, "a tree that bends will not break during a storm." Like self-talk and affirmations used in Western sport psychology, letting go allows runners to deal with problems.

When Simon Cherogony's father and daughter were sick at home in Kenya, he was having trouble focusing on training. Elly Rono told him that there was nothing he could do, so he shouldn't worry about it. He needed to focus on running. He told Cherogony to win the marathon for his family.

When an elite Mexican runner was interviewed before a major U.S. marathon, he was asked why his region, Kenyans, and Ethiopians were dominating the field. He responded, "What we have in common is a tough life. When we are successful, it makes a better life for our whole village. The Americans have a different mindset and motivation. I know an American runner who could not run well because his cell phone was not working."

Kenyans learn to be easy on themselves. Paul Tergat teaches his apprentices that only one person can win—if they have a bad day, they'll make it next time. His mindset dismisses self-imposed pressures that interfere with arousal state and relaxation needed for peak performance.

6. *Ascetic, patience.* According to Brother Colm O'Connell, "Kenyans are conditioned from birth to be distance runners. Their lifestyle compels them to develop stamina, endure tedium, and tolerate pain."[7] *Polepole*, which means 'drop by drop' in Swahili, conveys the concept that a task turns out better if one takes the time to do it correctly. After years of training, a shy runner develops confidence, and will gradually improve both physically and mentally. "The Kalenjin are different than other tribes, they are willing to sacrifice and defer gratification (Bale & Sang 1996, 150)."

Paul Koech says that with an ascetic lifestyle, the transition to hard training is natural. At the 2003 Rock & Roll Half Marathon, he decided that the only way he could do well in the Chicago Marathon was to return to Kenya to train.

James Menon, America's fastest 10,000m runner in 1998, explains why Americans chase Kenyans: "They train harder. They have a different way of approaching training. The other challenge is understanding that improvement cannot be hurried (Menon 1999, 51)."

7. *Passion.* Brother Colm O'Connell says, "You have to give the European a motive to train…but with the Kenyans they will train just because they love to run." Kip Keino, a Kalenjin, said, "Running is in our blood."

8. *Spiritual, communal.* Kenyans are socialized to think about nature, their clans, and spirituality. Whether sharing shoes at the Raleigh Relays or a hotel room, these schemas are present in all aspects of their lives. Community takes priority over the family, as the family takes priority over the individual. "You hear them speaking of uncles as fathers, cousins as brothers or sisters. The mentality is community."[8]

According to Dr. Robert Daniels, who studied the initiation at Fort Bragg, NC, soldiers internalize courage and confidence on the individual level, and groupthink as an ethos. Similarly, in Kalenjin initiation, boys are taught not to accept or initiate attacks, and to keep social cohesion in the group.

9. *Willfulness.* Defined as persistence and power of control over one's actions, willfulness may be what separates the great from the greatest. All runners possess varying degrees of will. At the top of the hierarchy is Paul Tergat, who said, "I have the will and determination to achieve my goals."

Military strategists say that a battle is won before stepping foot on the battlefield. Some Kenyan runners also follow this principle, revealing the link be-

Table 9.3   Indigenous Psychology Factors and Theories

Psychological traits essential to achieving peak performance and inner strength	Focus, playfulness, intuition, belief, ability to let go, ascetic, passion, and willfulness
Schemas	*kuvumvilia* *tayari* In our blood *polepole*

tween training and successful racing. Training is not just physical, but mental and spiritual.

- **Hillary Lelei.** We train at five a.m. to become accustomed to discipline and pain. Several concepts taught in our culture reflect our mindset and preparations for running—*kuvumulia* means perseverance or to endure, and *tayari* means to be ready physically, mentally, and spiritually.
- **Kipchoge Keino.** "Far from any alleged genetic influences, it is achieving a balance of hard work and mental attitude that counts," said Keino, the Kenyan distance runner and winner of four Olympic medals. "In the training regimen of the best athletes, seventy-five percent is physical training and twenty-five percent is mental. Then, in the race itself it's the mental process—thinking ahead and planning your moves—that comes to the fore, and proves most valuable."[9]
- **Daniel Komen.** "For me, if my training is good, then I will have a good racing season."

It appears as though Kenyans, for the most part, rely on inner strength. In the U.S., a large commercial market exists for self-discipline and self-esteem. Are Americans searching for inner strength? Is something essential missing in the psychological socialization process? Americans seek what they are missing in yoga, religion, therapy, and Tae Kwon Do. Psychologists note that females in Galloway training groups draw strength from others, typically people they do not know. Ariana Huffington suggests that the American value system may be responsible. Obsessed with muscles and plastic surgery, Americans are focused on their looks when they should instead pamper their inner consciousness (Huffington 1994, 79).

10

PSYCHOLOGICAL ANTHROPOLOGY

It depends on how you see and do things.

Paul Tergat

Cognitive Sciences and Anthropology

Over the years, ethnographers and psychologists have searched for methods to best understand the cognitive processes of how knowledge is learned and processed (Strauss & Quinn 1997, 57). Early cognitive anthropology was based partially on Karl Mannheim's study of concepts, categories, and systems of ordering. In the early 1900s, anthropologist and ethnographer Franz Boas performed studies on tribal categories of sense and perception that became the foundation for cognitive anthropology (Demeterio III 2001). Through the 1940s and 50s, studies based on psychoanalytic theories focused on cross-cultural variations in personality. Today, controversies exist regarding the usefulness of linguistic concepts and the relationship between culture and cognition.

Psychological anthropology developed further during the 1960s and 70s, when mental processes were used for insights and languages were studied to understand cognitive processes. Called personality and culture studies in the 1970s, a new field emerged within psychological anthropology, called cognitive anthropology. In *A Cognitive Theory of Cultural Meaning*, Strauss and Quinn argue that internalized cultural knowledge typically consists of adaptive understandings, similar to Bourdieu's habitus and Levi-Strauss' structuralism (Strauss & Quinn 1997, 45).

Schemas and Connectionism

Today, cognitive schema is considered one of the most powerful concepts in cognitive anthropology; it has become the primary means of studying psychological aspects of cultures. "Schemas are the learned patterns of connections among units of different parts which will be activated in any given situation (Strauss & Quinn, 83)." Strauss and Quinn call schemas 'cultural models.' "Meanings generated by schemas, in connectionist models, are mental states but are shaped by the learner's specific life experiences and are sensitive to activity in a particular context. While often similar from person to person, context to context, and one period of time to another, they can vary and change (Strauss & Quinn, 50)." To understand language or cognition, it is important to understand that intelligence results from processing symbolic expressions (Pinker & Mehler 1989, 74).

Information processing is mediated by learned or innate mental structures that organize related pieces of knowledge. Connectionism, or neural network modeling, is a way to model cognition (Strauss & Quinn, 11). To best explain cultural meanings, psychology (how the mind works) merges with cultural anthropology (the dynamics of interpersonal and extrapersonal factors in the socialization process) (Strauss & Quinn, 8). Working under the assumption that the concept of 'self' in the individual and culture is not innate or fixed, the task facing psychologists and anthropologists is to understand identities, gender, and ethnic and national identity in a dynamic psychological model (Strauss & Quinn, 9). Given social variation and differences in individual experiences, cognitive networks develop differently; an object or event will evoke separate interpretations.

Several factors determine whether culture is internalized. Certain properties of culture, called centripetal tendencies, act as forces that serve to continue the existence of the culture (Strauss & Quinn, 85). These centripetal tendencies include:

1. Durability of individuals;
2. Emotional and motivational, and individuals will act on them;
3. Historical durability (over generations);
4. Thematic-useful in a variety of contexts; and
5. Shared by the social group.

Strauss and Quinn use speech clues to learn about shared cognition and determine what motivates people to say the things they do. Several factors indicate schemas: patterns of speech, repetition of key words and phrases, use of metaphors, and commonalities in reasoning. Connected or disconnected discourses reveal if the schemas are used in multiple contexts.

Kenyan Runner Schemas

Little research is available on the relationship between culture, thought processes, and Kenyan running success. I have had many conversations with world class runners about their mental skills and the impact of their culture on performance. They showed patterns of thinking both collectively and individually. The following conversations reveal their perspective on their running success. Unless otherwise noted, the runners are Kalenjin.

Why are you great runners?

Amos Kipyegen: "I do not know, there has to be something in the genes, also upbringing."

Andrew Masai: "Many tribes are talented, some are just now developing."

Kibet Cherop: "Our culture and we develop because of few options."

Paul Tergat: "Passion, individual motivation, African spirituality, and we train very hard. Each culture has its own discipline they excel in. Americans are good in many things."

Daniel Komen: "All drink lots of fresh milk with calcium making strong bones. Also, where you are from and how you are raised."

Peter Rono: "Several things—how you live and grow up, how you do things. Tradition, food, environment, how you are brought up."

Elly Rono: "I don't know. Other tribes try to run, but they just are not as good. We (Kalenjins) are the best."

Paul Mwangi (Kikuyu): "Where you come from, most are from the same region, certain areas are good for training due to altitude and weather."

Eliud Barngetuny: "The culture is supportive and many people are talented."

John Korir: "If you have talent and want to train, there are places to train with many good runners. Then it is up to you to sacrifice and train hard."

What made you start running?

Daniel Komen: "I was good in high school."

Paul Mwangi (Kikuyu): "I saw Margaret Kagiri training and was inspired by her."

Kibet Cherop: "Run to school, back home for lunch, transportation."

Paul Tergat: "I qualified for the Air Force by passing tests, then joined and developed as a runner."

Elly Rono: "I was good in high school, taught in Kenya, and then received a scholarship in the U.S."

Is your cultural upbringing helpful for being a professional runner?

Paul Tergat: "It depends on how you see and do things."

Daniel Komen: "[I was] raised in a harsh environment and saw the success of others."

Elly Rono: "Tradition in Kalenjin area, lifestyle, and economic situation."

Kibet Cherop: "Others will help you become a runner and many people to train with."

Reuben Cheruiyot: "The Rift Valley is good for training with many great runners."

Ben Kapsoiya: "Peer pressure and kinship pressure to behave. If you are considered a family failure, it reflects on your sub-tribe, village, and clan."

Julius Kimtai: "I am from a very poor family. Most great runners are from poor backgrounds and want to make life better for their families."

Paul Koech: "When you are raised with a very hard life, hard training is natural."

Hillary Lelei: "In whatever you do to be considered a man in the village you must be strong."

Is there a correlation between initiation and running?

Ben Kapsoiya: "A shorter adolescent period, discipline, and after initiation you cannot act like child. You learn discipline and behavior which are useful not just as an athlete, but in all aspects of life. Shame and respect are taught in socialization when becoming part of a group called an age-set."

Paul Tergat: "No correlation, it is our way of preparing for adulthood and marriage."

Elly Rono: "None."

Daniel Komen: "None."

Paul Mwangi (Kikuyu): "None."

Kibet Cherop: "None."

Figure 10.1   Paul Tergat

Paul Koech: "When you become a runner, your group will tell you what to do and what not to do. The initiation is not important, it is inside you [the individual]."

Does initiation make you mentally and emotionally tough?

Ben Kapsoiya: "Willpower over alcohol and other temptations. You can see what it has done to others. Lessons are taught which can be used in all aspects of life."

Paul Tergat: "No, it our way of becoming adults. It depends on the person—their desire."

Elly Rono: "No."

Daniel Komen: "No."

What do you do to mentally prepare for a race?

Daniel Kihara (Kikuyu): "Religious beliefs and inspirational music for inner strength."

Paul Mwangi (Kikuyu): "Money and food on the table are good motivators."

Kibet Cherop: "I know others good runners will be there. I will try to beat them."

Peter Rono: "Nothing, just train."

Simon Rono: "I gear up by relaxing. If my training is not good, I will not race."

Reuben Cheruiyot (shaking his head): "Nothing."

Elly Rono: "It is a constant learning experience. Training for the 3,000m to 10,000m was pretty much the same. Learning the marathon game is different. If you take time off, it takes a long time to get back in shape. So, I do not take time off from training. So I have confidence from getting better and wiser each year."

Daniel Komen: "Set a goal and train very hard. That is all."

Paul Tergat (led to 26:27 10,000m world record): "Set goals, hard work, believe everything is possible."

Simon Karori (Kisii): "Stay focused on your job. We are not joggers."

Do you have anxieties or lack of confidence going into a race?

Elly Rono: "If a small race, the answer is no. If it is a world class race it can affect you."

Daniel Komen: "I know other good runners will be there. If your training is good or if your training is not good, it will make a difference."

Paul Tergat: "You have to believe you can win. You have to believe it is possible."

Kibet Cherop: "If they beat me they are in better shape, it is okay, I will train harder. I have to compete and see who wins. Next time I will be in shape. I have to try to beat them."

Paul Mwangi (Kikuyu): "If you know someone is running well like a race horse (referring to Cherop), you hope they do not show up. It is not the end of the world. Next time, train harder. I'm not bad, he is strong today. Only one person can win."

As a professional runner, how do you stay focused?

Paul Tergat: "Drive, another goal—the marathon. The challenge in the marathon is you cannot predict what is going to happen after 35 Km. I am highly competitive and have the will to achieve. I want to be competitive on all surfaces and many distances (10,000m, marathon, and cross country). When I wake up in the morning I ask myself what I need to do."

Elly Rono: "I am going to train very hard, so I can beat those guys. I set higher goals and do not worry about unimportant things."

Simon Karori (Kisii): "It is a serious business, a profession, not a hobby. I need to pay for schooling for children in Kenya. We do not pay taxes for public school. Private school is more expensive. If we do not pay our children do not go to school."

Who (or what) are you running for?

David Kipngetich: "Being the best in your school has high status and opportunities for the future."

Paul Tergat: "To be the best on many surfaces and events. I love competition."

Paul Mwangi (Kikuyu): "Money."

Elly Rono: "Times, money, and to win."

Kibet Cherop: "The motivation is money and to better myself. I have few job skills or choices for survival."

Daniel Komen: "Set goals for world records. Moses Kiptanui and the KAAA motivated me."

Reuben Chesang: "Commonwealth 1,500m gold medal and money."

Margaret Kagiri (Kikuyu): "Money for shamba (farm)."

Ben Kapsoiya: "College scholarship."

Amos Kipyegen: "College scholarship and brother (Nixon Kiprotich) won an Olympic silver medal."

Simon Karori (Kisii): "Money for family and businesses."

The multiple schemas binding the running subculture make it distinct. Individuality also plays a role in motivation. Each runner's goals are unique, and depend on focus, passion, drive, confidence, and the will to achieve.

Table 10.1   Cognitive Anthropology Factors and Theories

Schemas: Broader Meanings

1. Where you are from. Environment, weather, infrastructure, role models, the Rift Valley, altitude, having many training partners.

2. How you see things.

   a. Spirituality: Drums, nature, children, belief, indigenous psychology, communal, ability to excel with training groups.

   b. Belief: Strong belief that you can win or excel in competition. Confidence correlated with training.

3. How you do things. Culture, food, walking and running daily, upbringing, clan, ascetic lifestyle, few options, clan and peer pressure to act responsibly and represent the group.

4. Social channeling limited choices. Football (soccer) or running identity is developed in primary school.

5. Individual desire. Drive, goals, confidence, focus, motivation, competitive, traits that come from within, will, passion. Run for many reasons.

6. Training. Physical and mental components of the job. Ability to stay focused, let go, relax, and minimize mental distractions. Hard physical training.

7. Racing file. If they do not win there is always another race. Only one can win.

PART V

ANALYSIS: CYBERNETICS AND REVERSE ENGINEERING

11

THE CYBERNETICS
OF KENYAN RUNNING

Cognitive power remains useful even though humans are subjective, emotional, and slower than computers. Limitations in computing also exist. They currently have inferior abilities to use common sense and multiple perspectives.1

Nicholas Negroponte, Chairman of the MIT Media Lab

The Kenyan Ethnosystem

The nature vs. nurture dialogue remains at the forefront of the discussion over Kenyan running success. While some argue for one or another, Margaret Mead's husband Gregory Bateson uses ecology as a metaphor to process information on interrelationships between many disciplines. Ethnicity is a broad concept; it encompasses genetics, culture, genotype, and phenotype. To capture the interrelationships between biological, cultural, psychological, and historical components of Kenyan running success, I have used the concept of an ethnosystem. While enculturation and socialization describe processes, ethnosystem incorporates the linkages between and the dynamics of these components.

Assuming that ethnicity is a product of nature and nurture, the genetic code will not accurately portray a complete blueprint. The ethnic code is a combination of necessary variables—biological, cultural, and psychological—that work in a symbiotic relationship (see Table 11.1).

Kenyan runners must have certain qualities in order to succeed—some essential, others contributing. No single factor has been correlated to success. Rather, it is a combination of components that seems to result in peak performance. I have separated the factories and theories discussed in the previous chapters into essential, contributing, and possible (or having no merit).

Table 11.1   The Ethnic Code

A	Ascetic lifestyle. Ability to train hard. Adaptations.
C	Channeling. Cognitive socialization.
G	Globalization. Gene Expression.
T	Training. Transition to modernity. Traits.

I have divided the essential factors into several different models that are summarized in Tables 11.2 – 11.6.

Environmental-Biological Model

Adaptations and Gene Expression

Physical adaptations to a pastoral lifestyle, warm climate, and medium altitude include the following:

1. A high percentage of slow twitch oxidative Type IIa muscle fibers;
2. Biomechanics, running economy, ectomorphic frames;
3. Bioenergetics—a complex linkage with muscle type, enzymes, substrate for fuel source, and environmental factors;
4. Lactate shuttle; and
5. Ability to sustain a high percentage of VO_{2max} and fatigue resistance.

Ability to Train Hard

In 1996, Sam Walton went to the IBM school to learn the most efficient method to manage distribution and logistics in his small business. To shorten lead times, he linked computers to stores and suppliers (Walton & Huey 1992, 207). In 1992, he invested seven hundred million dollars to update to a bar coding satellite system that would receive information quicker (Walton & Huey 1992, 213). Today, Wal-Mart's communications and distribution systems provide a real competitive advantage, allowing the company to sell items at lower prices with greater profits than competitors. This is the competitive edge business analysts refer to that Wal-Mart has over its rivals.

Nature has written an analogous software program in the human body. Kenyan adaptations to altitude, heat, and a pastoral lifestyle correlate to success in running. However, if running success was correlated simply with liv-

Table 11.2   Environmental and Biological Model

Gene expression resulting in an ability to train at a high intensity may have resulted from: 1. Natural selection—adaptations to climate, altitude, and pastoralism. 2. Other methods of producing alleles such as genetic drift, mutations, and epigenetics. 3. Sociobiological factors including temperament, hormones (testosterone), indigenous psychology, and ascetic lifestyle.

ing at altitude, for example, then athletes from other regions at altitude would likely experience similar success. Neighboring counties Tanzania and Uganda, however, produce a small number of world class runners, while Ethiopia produces many. Biological components are necessary but work in conjunction with other necessary factors.

Cultural Model

Channeling

The government, schools, and families can significantly affect the development of a runner in both a negative and positive manner. People from the middle and upper classes, for example, may not be channeled into running as a profession. In the U.S., football and basketball have more status than running as early as junior high school. They also have higher professional status, with accordingly higher salaries.

Ascetic Lifestyle

For the young and old alike, activity is a way of life in Kenya. For centuries, Kenyans were pastoral, tending to cattle and moving to water. For many today, walking remains the primary means of transportation whether going to the market, school, or to visit friends. Many run to school, run home for lunch, run back to school, and run home again at the end of the day—for some, a 10K run at altitude. Even if vehicles are available, roads do not always exist (Tanser 1997, 96). It is common for the elderly to walk up to 10K daily. In some cases, individuals walk fifty to sixty miles daily (Bale & Sang 1996, 52).

Table 11.3   Cultural and Psychological Model

Inner strength and traits such as belief, passion, ability to let go, motivation, will, feeler vs. thinker, spiritual, and communal may have resulted from:

1. Social Darwinism—channeling, financial motivation.
2. Primary Socialization—ascetic lifestyle, diet.
3. Secondary Socialization—initiation, peer pressure.
4. Gender and Cognitive Socialization—indigenous psychology.

This active lifestyle not only results in tough joints, ligaments, tendons, and muscles, but provides a ten-year base by the time children reach high school. Becoming a professional runner, therefore, is not a dramatic transition.

Former Surgeon General David Satcher and the National Institute of Health have estimated that between fifty and sixty percent of Americans are overweight, and roughly half of these are obese. If someone is unable to walk long distances or chooses not to lead an active lifestyle, it is unlikely that they will ever run long distances. Because Kenyans walk daily from childhood to old age, it is not surprising that they can run faster.

Kenyan runners live an ascetic lifestyle with a mindset of *polepole* (developing slowly) and self-discipline. According to former *Running Times* journalist Tom Kennedy, the ascetic tradition is not a determining factor or answer to Kenyan dominance. "Acclimating ones self to the discomfort of running fast is best done through hard training, not meager living. If culture and environment alone could explain the Kenyan success, other countries with similar circumstances such as Tanzania would be producing hordes of world class runners. Kenyan runners who settle outside their national boundaries continue to perform superbly (Kennedy 1998, 60)."

Psychological Model

Traits and Cognitive Socialization

Kenyan runners' indigenous psychology is formed from historical, cultural, and environmental factors. Select mental traits are required for runners to succeed—belief, motivation, and the ability to focus. Schemas and traits are formed in cognitive socialization. Clan and peer pressure are major socialization factors.

External Factors Model

Transition to Modernity

The transition to modernity often incorporates the dynamics of social class, economic motivation, and globalization. Professional runners endure their demanding life for a variety of reasons—some are economically motivated, while others strive to attain a higher social class. Elly Rono recalls how, in high school, a well-off friend was beating current 800m world record holder Wilson Kipketer. Because of his financial situation, however, he lacked the motivation to develop his talent.

The British introduced a number of sports to Kenya that are all linked to socio-economic classes. Milcah Chepkemei, a Nandi nursing student living in Minnesota, says, "Some people in Kenya consider running as a lower class sport and have interests in other sports recreationally."

As Jon Entine explained in a May 2000 NPR *Talk of the Nation* debate with Grant Farred, "Oh, I'm not saying that social and cultural factors don't play a role. I'm saying that reducing success to a social phenomenon really doesn't do justice to what the individual does in becoming a successful athlete. If you take, for instance, all of the Olympic sporting events, ninety percent or so of the athletes come from rather middle class or even above circumstances. And, frankly, the argument that African Americans succeed because they're escaping the ghetto is quite racist. Look at someone like Donovan Bailey, who's the reigning gold medalist in the 100m and Donovan had to give up his job on the Toronto Stock Exchange and put his Porsche in hock to pursue his dream and that was to become a 100m runner and an elite one. So we don't know—the characteristics that lead to great success are very individual. Sometimes it's economic deprivation and sometimes it's not."[2]

Globalization

Race directors, shoe sponsors, and managers provide opportunities that conflict with national interests. The costs for individual means to modernity may include a loss of self identity and national pride.

Table 11.4   Historical and External Forces Model

The external forces of colonization, globalization, modernization, and Westernization may be responsible for historical factors:

1. Indigenous psychology, dual consciousness.
2. Decolonization of the mind.
3. Social control.
4. National Pride.
5. Social Darwinism.
6. Transition to modernity.
7. Accusations of performance enhancement.

Contributing Factors and Theories

Contributing factors to running success provide an edge, but are not essential. These factors are biological, cultural, and psychological (see Table 11.5).

Table 11.5   Contributing Factors and Theories

Biological	Cultural	Psychological
1. Temperament 2. Testosterone levels	3. Diet 4. Tradition and role models 5. Gender socialization 6. Representing clan, shame, respect, peer pressure	7. Groupthink 8. Additional traits a. Feeler vs. thinker b. Spiritual and communal

Possible Factors and Theories

The following theories are currently being debated. They will either fade, or prove to be factors to success.

Speed Gene

There is no evidence available proving the existence of a speed gene. In Spencer Wells' *Journey of Man*, human origins are traced to common ancestors in East Africa whose survival depended on their ability to raid cattle and flee from enemies or wild animals. Doesn't it make sense, therefore, that all of mankind has some form of a speed gene?

Initiation and Circumcision

Modernization and exposure to the West have modified socialization, specifically initiation. For several reasons, the four major Kenyan running ethnic groups no longer practice traditional initiation—it is impractical for boys to be away from school for six months, and the warrior mentality is useless in a cash economy. Initiation ceremonies today, therefore, last approximately one month. Increasing numbers of runners are being circumcised in hospitals. As with traditional initiation producing warriors and cattle raiders, running camps weed out those not possessing the appropriate physical and mental traits. In the traditional society the most suited would become warriors, not the whole age-set according to Elly Rono. All warriors were not training to be runners. Some were defending from outside tribes.

Emotional Strength

Milcah Chepkemau, a Kenyan student living in the U.S., says that boys are not the same when they come back from initiation. Through the psychological socialization process, young men internalize shame, respect, confidence, and courage, all traits required for their societal roles. Both distance runners and warriors need emotional strength and a high pain tolerance. Kalenjins are able to summon a supreme effort when it matters most.[3] Females are also extremely successful runners, even though they received no warrior training.

Pain Threshold

According to Manners, circumcision without anesthetic might result in a high pain tolerance, which could be the magical ingredient to Kenyan running success. Such a theory seems logical—circumcision without anesthetic makes training for and racing long distances seem relatively painless. It is difficult, however, to show a causal relationship between circumcision and an increased pain threshold necessary for running performance. The top Kenyan runners do not believe that initiation is responsible for running success. Initiation is their society's way of becoming responsible and representing their clan and ethnic group.

Socialization differs for everyone. No two individuals participate in quite the same way because of different dispositions, situations, and agents of socialization (e.g. teachers and parents). According to cultural anthropologist Fred Plog, socialization describes part, but not all, of the relationship between the individual and the culture (Plog & Bates 1976, 125).

National Pride

Kip Keino's idea that "talent opens doors to college scholarships and team medals" (Kennedy 1996, 31) is not the prevailing schema among Kenyan runners. Most have chosen not to attend college or run on national teams, instead aiming at financial rewards.

Performance Enhancement

Other ethnic groups and American sprinters have been under fire for testing positive to illegal performance enhancement drugs. While reports have come out on Americans and altitude tents, Finnish blood doping, and Russian and Chinese military research on the pharmacological effects of natural herbs and synthetic equivalents, it is widely believed that Kenyans rely on training. Shame and peer pressure discourage most from using illegal performance enhancers.

Temptation exists, however, to correlate Kenyan running times with illegal substance use. Former Chairman of the U.S. Anti-Doping Agency Frank Shorter noted that the increasing number of 2:06-2:08 times being recorded by Kenyan marathoners doesn't correspond to their 10,000m times. The Kenyans' lactate clearance advantage accounts for the difference.

In 1993, John Ngugi was accused of taking performance enhancing drugs. While he never tested positive, his image was tarnished. "He was approached outside of a training camp, however the tester did not present Ngugi with proper papers," explains his manager, John Bicourt. "The tester eventually agreed to postpone the test for seven days, which eventually proved negative. However, the refusal had already been reported in the Press and the International Association of Athletics Federation (IAAF) was forced to take action."[4]

According to John Manners, "There isn't a whiff of evidence of Kenyan drug use beyond baseless rumors from frustrated Western athletes and their supporters." Since 1996, several Kenyan runners have tested positive for banned substances. In 1999, Delilah Asiago was suspended for a positive ephedrine test at the Sao Silvestre 15K. Also in 1999, Laban Kagika tested pos-

Table 11.6   Possible Factors and Theories or No Merits

Biological	Cultural	Psychological
1. Speed gene, cattle raiding	2. Initiation, circumcision 3. National pride 4. Performance enhancement 5. Social control	6. Decolonization of the mind

itive for ephedrine and methylephedrine at an international meet, and later admitted to taking the banned substances.

Simon Kemboi, a 400m runner, tested positive at the 2000 Sydney Olympics for the anabolic steroid nandrolone. Pamela Chepchumba tested positive for EPO at the 2002 World Cross Country Championships. Ambrose Bitok, sixth in the 5,000m in Austria in 2003, tested positive for norandrosterone.

European managers and the naivety of some athletes have also fueled speculations. Athletics Kenya chief Isaiah Kiplagat, commenting on Chepchumba's positive tests, said, "If we find that somebody somewhere was a party to this, then I must assure you that drastic action will be taken. It doesn't matter who it is. It is well known that drugs are becoming a very serious issue that even the European Parliament has now passed a law that athletes or any sportsman, irrespective, found having used prohibitive drugs, will not only be banned, but will be punished by way of imprisonment."[5] Many accusations made by frustrated runners have been without evidence. In August 2002, the IAAF introduced compulsory athlete licenses as a means of control, and began revoking licenses to discipline those making unsubstantiated accusations.

Decolonization of the Mind

Mental and spiritual movements are taking place in Kenya — retradition, liberation psychology, and reversion of African consciousness. Interestingly, the Kalenjin feel no hostility toward the British people — rather, they like the Western culture. As a Kalenjin runner explained to me, "The British came with the Bible and we had the land. Soon, we had the Bible and they had the land."

12

CULTURAL EVOLUTION AND BEHAVIORAL EXPRESSION

Running is in our blood.

Kipchoge Keino

Tabula Rasa vs. Human Sociobiology and Evolutionary Psychology

It is unknown to what extent behavior is innate as opposed to learned. Linking social behavior with genetics implies a Darwinian evolution (Layton 1997, 159). Sociobiologists support the notion of behavior having a genetic component. In 1964, William Hamilton's theories on fitness and animal altruism launched the field of sociobiology. With the 1970s publication of Harvard biology Professor Emeritus Edward O. Wilson's book *Sociobiology: The New Synthesis*, sociobiology became a formal discipline.

It is important to differentiate sociobiology from human sociobiology. Wilson's ideas were based on zoological studies. When his theories underwent scientific scrutiny, questions arose concerning their applicability to humans. Much sociobiological literature discusses pre- and post-Wilson politics. A sociobiological basis for human behavior remains controversial. Its critics include religious fundamentalists and some social scientists, cultural anthropologists, and psychologists, who advocate that socialization and conditioning determines behavior.

Psychologist J. Philippe Rushton debunks the view that humans are all identical at birth, stating that races differ in appearance, size, biochemistry, and brain size. He goes on to question whether there is any reason why humans should not vary in behavior.[1] Evolutionary psychology has offered many theories to explain human behavior. While evidence of gender and ethnic differences exists, institutional barriers keep the findings from mainstream thought. Rushton proposes that aggression and criminal behavior are genetically programmed. MRI scans revealing brain size differences between ethnic groups (combined with varying testosterone levels) correlate with patterns of crime, parenting, and success in school and sports.[2] Brain imaging studies provide visual proof that innate gender differences exist.[3] It has been further proposed that gender differences in reasoning skills are linked to hormone expression, the size and shape of the *corpus callosum*, and increased communication in females between the right and left hemispheres of the brain.

Sociobiology offers a way to explain patterns of cooperation (reciprocal altruism) and competition. Community interaction, problem-solving, and competition seem to be key behaviors in nature. In *The Selfish Gene*, Richard Dawkins argues that humans are born selfish and must learn generosity and altruism. This theory promotes survival, competition, and even exploitation, resulting in colonialism and other social inequities. Creationists advocate social responsibility and compassion to compensate for such actions.

"Wilson argues that the future of science resides in reductionism. Sociology should ultimately be reduced to its underlying sociobiological mechanisms. In turn, sociobiology needs to be reduced to biology, which will eventually be completely explicable by chemistry. Ultimately, all knowledge can be explained by physics. To discuss the sociology of gender without grasping the sociobiology of why evolution instilled different reproductive goals in males and females is useless (although that doesn't stop feminist verbalizers). In turn, those contrasting sociobiological drives emanate from chemicals like testosterone and estrogen, which can be understood in terms of the physics of protons and electrons."[4]

A controversial book, *The Bell Curve*, links levels of intelligence with ethnic groups. Similar to the controversy surrounding the usefulness of SAT scores, it implies that culturally-biased questions place certain groups at a disadvantage. Howard Gardner's Multiple Intelligences Theory challenges the traditional view that the IQ test is an adequate measure of intelligence. He proposes that intelligence is better measured through skills including intrapersonal, interpersonal, logical, musical, linguistic, kinesthetic, artistic, and spatial intelligences. University of Sydney professor Clive Harper found that Australian aborigines earned low scores on Western IQ tests. Aboriginal children's visual processing scores, however, are twenty-five percent above average.[5] Harper suggests that for the Aborigines, being able to remember landscapes might be an adaptation because the skill is required for survival.

Humans are born with innate traits, or temperament. Some traits are common among groups, while others are individual. Certain behavior patterns, including cheerfulness verses moodiness, patience verses speediness, preference of routine verses new experiences, sensory verses analytical, and the ability to focus, can be seen by the age of three (Oldham & Morris 1991, 359).

Biologists and anthropologists agree that behavior between the sexes has a biological component. Research has shown that pheromones, through neurotransmitter and receptors sites, affect behavior.

The Junk in the Trunk Mystery

Some Kenyan runners relax by listening to African dancing tapes. In Central Africa, watching three generations of African women dancing with their buttocks is considered family entertainment.

"Kenyans they like their women with big butts and they mosey," said former Olympian Juli Henner.

In an interview with Jack Bacheler (Elly Rono accompanied me), Bacheler asked Rono if he was related to Henry Rono.

"I am not," Rono replied.

Bacheler spread his arms wide. "That guy was always with three hundred pound women."

On another occasion, a Kenyan runner friend asked me, "Do you read the front or back page?"

"What are you talking about?" I responded.

"Do you see that lady? She is the kind of woman you need in Kenya."

This was spoken after never seeing the woman's face, but sighting her globular muscle containers from afar.

"Why would one need so much junk in the trunk?" I asked.

"She is a powerful, strong woman," he replied. "She can do a lot of work and have lots of babies."

According to Duke University Swahili instructor Alphonse Mutima, "In our culture big bodies signify babies, warmth, and tenderness, and strong and productive women." In *Evolution of Endurance*, John Langdon explains that when climbing was a daily activity, power was derived from the hamstrings. At some point, the ischium bone of the pelvis shortened for terrestrial movement, and power shifted to the gluteus maximus.[6] Pulitzer Prize winning author Natalie Angier describes the female breasts as mobile pantries and visual lures. Similarly, she sees female buttocks as globular containers for a large muscle. "Estrogen and fat deposits display fecundity, the ability to bear children," she explains (Angier 1999, 149).

Evolutionary psychology proposes that men are hard-wired to notice waist-to-hip ratios, and are most attracted to women with waists seventy percent of hip size, the ratio most conducive to producing healthy offspring (Bellafante 2003, 9). If this theory is true, then it is the Western media (along with other factors) that has made small hips more desirable. Current fashion trends have focused attention on a new area of the female body—the stomach. A flat belly is a modern fertility symbol. Low riding pants and short tops are analogous to Egyptian belly dancing and naval jewelry (Bellafante 2003, 9).

Social Darwinism

A successful cultural adaptation can be acquired from anyone, not just from one's parents.

Steven J. Gould

Herbert Spencer's theory of Social Darwinism proposes that the environment conveys information to an organism, dictating behavioral changes required for survival. These changes are handed down to the next generation in socialization practices. In modern society, for example, money and education will increase the likelihood that children become successful. It was Spencer, not Darwin, who coined the concept 'Survival of the fittest.'

The theory of natural selection, on the other hand, proposes that the environment selects only those organisms displaying certain characteristics needed to survive.

Humans don't have to evolve through natural selection. Cultural evolution is much faster in responding to environmental conditions. In the 1880s, Jean Baptiste Lamarck proposed the inheritance of acquired characteristics. A successful cultural adaptation can be acquired from anyone, not just from one's parents—a concept Steven Gould called diffusion.

Essentialism vs. Historical Factors

Three major forces of social change have resulted in Kenyan cultural adaptations:

1. *Colonization.* Exposure to the British and missionaries impacted the Kenyan culture and psyche. Organized running was introduced. Since

independence, a post-colonial movement promoting cultural identity has occurred.

2. *War.* With independence, ethnic fighting was replaced by cooperation and a unified direction for the country. Similarly, some historians speculate that the launch of the Russian satellite Sputnik was the single most important event responsible for the quality of life in the U.S. today.

3. *Modernization.* The post-colonial period in Kenya is a complex coexistence of tradition and modernization. There is a simultaneous attempt to maintain traditional culture and identity while moving from a farm to cash economy. For professional runners, modernization means opportunity. Because traditions and social customs are changing in some ethnic groups, there is more freedom to waiver from traditional socialization. For modern runners, several traditions remain essential to making it through the weeding-out process—training without modern conveniences, living close to nature, and retaining one's beliefs. These are being replaced, however, by the cash economy, value on education, and formality.

Internalizing Conflicting Schemas

When a conflict arises between an individual and societal demands, the conflicting discourses can be internalized in several ways. Strauss and Quinn propose the compartmentalization of separate and unconscious schemas that can be activated in different contexts. One schema can be repressed while another is more accessible, both can be equally accessible, one can be chosen, or they can be mixed (Strauss & Quinn, 213).

On an individual basis, a re-socialization process can internalize and adjust mental schemas to resolve a conflict. Cultural practices vary in durability when schemas meet with new world conditions (Strauss & Quinn, 86). Strauss and Quinn classify four schemas for the existence of a culture. Referred to as centrifugal tendencies (Strauss & Quinn, 85), these include:

1. Changeable in persons and generations, where schemas do not filter out new information;

2. Unmotivating and emotional and do not act on them;

3. Contextually limited; and

4. Shared by relatively few people.

Ethnosystem

The modern Kenyan ethnosystem is changing rapidly. Exposure to external forces has altered ethnic groups, depending on the durability of individuals within each. This durability is analogous to the plasticity of genes during gene expression where certain proteins are repressed or activated. A combination of historical factors, culture, environmental factors, and cognitive socialization affect psychological makeup and, eventually, behavior.

Modernization has diminished the traditional, ascetic Kalenjin culture. Today, a number of traditions are being dropped or reconsidered. In some ethnic groups, for example, it is customary for male elders to eat bull testicles. Simon Cherogony, a Sabaot, says that many in his generation are not carrying on this tradition.

Hillary Lelei grew up in a rural area, but invested his European race winnings in a home in Eldoret, an urban area. While visiting, Lelei's mother said she didn't like the stove and electrical lighting—she preferred cooking with firewood and using paraffin or kerosene lamps. Lelei, in turn, sees differences in the village children, potentially the next generation of runners. Some, he says, want to ride the bus to school rather than run, and want to use machines on the farm rather than working manually.

Globalization and external support systems have created social forces at odds with Kenyan traditions, government institutions, and the Sports Ministry and Federation. In several ethnic groups today, social channeling is directed towards running. As different opportunities arise, however, the forces of social Darwinism may result in less channeling towards running. When athletes such as Wilson Kipketer gained citizenships in other countries, they had to overcome peer and societal pressure. More recently, as acquiring foreign citizenships has become more commonplace, the Kenyan government struggles to find a solution.

Gender Roles

Male roles have shifted with new passions and opportunities. Female roles, however, have been more rigidly defined, their transition to modernity more complex. In the patrilineal farm economy, there is little incentive to invest in a daughter; traditional females are ideally domesticated and clan-oriented. According to Cultural Anthropologist Robert Daniels, the society has resisted changes in female roles because women are considered valuable assets. In the cash economy, where women have traditionally been considered liabilities, the desire for modernization has increased the number of females pursuing nursing and other medical professions.

For modern Kikuyu and Kalenjin, less traditional roles for females have been accepted, but with resistance. As the economy changed from traditional to cash, some men had to move to cities to work. Consequently, women became responsible for work both in and out of the home. For some aspiring female runners, therefore, finding the time to train was impossible.[7] According to Kibet Cherop, in the traditional system women had to join the Armed Forces or work in the prison system to be able to train and compete. Esther Kiplagat recalls how it wasn't easy being a runner—boys made fun of her, and her family and village did not support her training because they thought she should be working on the farm.[8] Even with such cultural barriers, Kenyan women have managed to be competitive at the world class level. One can argue, however, that they have not reached their potential.

With modernization, women (including two of Kenya's most successful female runners) holding non-traditional occupations have served as new role models for the next generation. Catherine Ndereba's (a Kikuyu and former marathon world record holder) choice to have a career and a child has the full support of her husband Anthony Maina. Centered on her professional running career, his lifestyle is a radical role reversal from the traditional culture.[9] Lornah Kiplagat's (Kalenjin) running camp to empower women will provide a forum in which a whole new generation of professional women runners can develop.

Knowledge Systems: Socialization to Education

In traditional initiation, becoming a man meant becoming a warrior. Today, both the concept of manhood and the initiation process have changed. As most men are no longer preparing to live a pastoral lifestyle as a warrior, certain rites of passage have become a mere part of their heritage (e.g. living for months in the forest). Modern initiation continues to prepare members to defend their ethnic group, however as leaders, not warriors. Hospital circumcision is becoming more common.

Western education is becoming increasingly valued. Traditional initiation, requiring much time away from school, is therefore no longer practical. Many occupations in the new cash economy demand education and computer literacy. For those lacking such skills, professional running offers an option.

The Maasai's resistance to Westernization reveals the importance of ethnic affiliation in professional running. Paul Tergat's mother was raised a Maasai, his father a Tugen. Had the ethnicities been reversed, Paul Tergat would have been socialized as a Maasai and would likely never have become a professional runner.

Why does the Maasai culture remain traditional? What holds their culture together? Hiram Kabui, a U.S.-educated Kikuyu anthropologist, offers insights into their traditional culture that help explain its survival. The Maasai are less susceptible to government and media influences. The Kenyan government has asked the Maasai to send their children to school for fear that they would fall behind as the country modernizes. In Kenya, however, the primary agent of socialization is the family—not the government. Today, many Maasai children are taught the traditional way of life rather than attending school.

Modernized ethnic groups have been influenced by the mass media and other cultures. On a recent visit to Kenya, Kabui noticed that the *matatus* (taxi-vans) had names on them—Michael Jordan and Mississippi.

Traditional Kenyans value a sense of belonging to and receiving blessing from their clan, ethnic group, or religion. The age-sets hold a special bond. Peer pressure within the age-set acts as a disincentive to improper behavior—children do not want to reflect badly on each other, as they will need their friends in the future. The clan-owned land (that each male will inherit) serves as further incentive to conform.

Belief Systems: Spirituality to Organized Religion to Spirituality

Kenyans have long practiced spirituality. With the British occupation, however, many converted to organized religion. African churches today are retaining Christian doctrines, but are becoming African Independent Churches to differentiate themselves.

In some ethnic groups, the reversion of consciousness or returning to the previous practices coexists with modernization. For example, several options are available for couples choosing a wedding ceremony—a traditional wedding for those within the same ethnic group who practice tribal beliefs, a civil wedding in which legal papers are signed, or a Christian wedding with a religious ceremony.

Essentialism vs. Individualism

Kenyans appear homogeneous. Each, however, has his own story, identity, varied paths to the U.S., and motivations. Bruce Lee would likely prefer to say that the Tao (or way) of Kenyan running over Kenyan running reflects their individual paths. This confirms Tergat's belief that Kenyan running success is individual. As discussed in chapter 10, it is clear that motivations comprise several categories:

1. Social status and fame.
2. Competition, world records, national records, national teams, and the Olympics.
3. Passion. Will they become joggers or run for fun when they become older? Most say they will.
4. Economic motivation, to better self and clan, and college scholarships.

Individuals make the change from tradition to modernity. Motivations vary, as do circumstances. Some runners are products of the farm economy. Some run to school, some don't. Ethnic group altitudes vary, as do lineages. Some have traditional initiations, while some are circumcised in the hospital. Some aim to make a national team, while others run to make money. Those fortunate enough to receive college educations and/or running visas typically do not forget their families—Amos Kipyegen and Ben Kapsoiya, for example, used running to help their clans. Male runners often train away from home in camps, and then compete in Europe or the U.S. Rather than buying luxury items, most send their winnings home to fund school tuition, family members (often several families if the runner's father practiced polygamy) unable to find work, and the operation of the modern farms. Some start businesses and invest in the modern Kenyan infrastructure. Independence is gradually replacing the communal lifestyle. Interdependence is being replaced by the runner's independence and the clan's dependence on the runner. It has become less acceptable for clan members to show up expecting the runner to provide shelter for extended periods of time (as Elly Rono did).

How will Resocialization Play Out?

Today, several Kenyan ethnic groups possess the traits needed to be superior. Whatever the motivations and circumstances, it is crucial that professional Kenyan runners be able to balance their double consciousness between tradition and modernity. Certain characteristics must remain unchanged in order for them to dominate world class running. When they travel to the U.S. to race or attend college, they become partly westernized, trading off culture, identity, and values. Elly Rono emphasizes to his training partners that they should minimize distractions and keep focused on their training and goals.

Rono understands both the Kenyan and American worldviews, and sees the good and the bad in each. He sees the need for an orientation for Kenyan runners first arriving in the U.S., to familiarize them with necessities such as food, transportation, banking, indoor restrooms, and weather.

After college, Rono lived in a low-income housing development in Durham, NC. Neighbors wanted to borrow money, trollops wanted to earn money, car tires were stolen or punctured, drunk men chased women in their underwear through the courtyard, someone was murdered, garbage was scattered on the grounds, dumpsters overflowed with cheap broken furniture, and kids played in contaminated water. After three years, Rono said, "These people are backwards." In August 2002, Rono moved his hundreds of trophies, ribbons, plaques, and running shoes to an upscale tobacco warehouse that was renovated to resemble the Village in New York City. His neighbors were successful, many Duke students driving Range Rovers. When entertaining, he occasionally cooked Italian dishes, and even offered his visitors wine. These living conditions contrasted those from his upbringing. His focus and will to compete, however, were never stronger.

Paul Tergat has the third fastest 10,000m time in history. He is the world record holder in half-marathon and marathon. In addition, he owns five world cross country titles. In his first serious race, when he was in the Kenyan Armed Forces, he watched experienced runners finish far ahead of him. By studying their training and diet, he developed his talent and eventually beat them. "I have the drive and will to be the best," he says. "I stay motivated by setting new goals in running on different surfaces."[10] Will is defined as the power of control over one's own actions or emotions. It is used to express determination, insistence, persistence, or willfulness.

What Country or Ethnic Group Will Dominate Next?

Today, it is no longer a given that Kenyan runners will win major marathons, road races, cross country meets, or track events. What is a given is that they will be represented by their sheer number of world class runners. "I can beat these guys (the Kenyans)," Ethiopian Worku Bikila said before the 1999 Nortel Networks Cherry Blossom 10 Mile Run in Washington, DC.

Figure 12.1   Kikuyu's #3 James Kariuki (John Ngugi's brother), #5 Joseph Kimani, and #4 William Kiptum (Kalenjin)

Table 12.1   1999 Nortel Networks Cherry Blossom 10 Mile Run Results[11]

1. Worku Bikila	Ethiopia	46:59
2. Lazarus Nyakeraka	Kenya	47:01
3. James Kariuki	Kenya	47:03
4. William Kiptum	Kenya	47:07
5. Joseph Kimani	Kenya	47:31
6. Josphat Machuka	Kenya	47:33
7. Julius Randich	Kenya	47:37
8. Leonid Shvetsov	Russia	49:10
9. Reuben Chesang	Kenya	49:22
10. Daniel Kihara	Kenya	49:23
11. Kibet Cherop	Kenya	49:26
12. Ben Kimondieu	Kenya	49:37
13. Jacob Kirwa	Kenya	50:05
14. Simon Cherogony	Kenya	50:17

Table 12.2   Cultural Evolution and Behavioral Expression Factors and Theories

Sociobiology	Temperament
	Testosterone
	Howard Gardner's Multiple Intelligences Theory
Social Darwinism	*Traditional Lifestyle*: Schemas not compatible with professional running (e.g. the Maasai)
	Double consciousness: Transition to modernity, changing factors, changing gender and generational roles, ethnic variations
	Modernity: Choose other sports associated with middle and upper classes, children provided with more options

13

THIRD ORDER CYBERNETICS

The will to find and tell the truth is the goal of scholarship.[1]
Valentin Mudimbe

Evolving Historical Western Schemas

What a person sees depends upon his or her background.
Stuart Umpleby

Perspectives regarding Kenyan running success vary between Kenyan runners, ethnographers, sociologists, sociobiologists, social Darwinists, psychologists, biologists, historians, and philosophers. I have presented several sides of the story. But who is telling the truth? And what is the reader's role in the conversation in relation to the observed system? Third Order Cybernetics investigates this interrelationship. To form their own perspective, the reader must evaluate multiple perspectives and their respective merits. The various perspectives presented include ethnocentrisms, schemas, ideologies, and dogmas. Some help bring clarity and understanding, while others create barriers to the truth.

Ethnocentrisms and New Social Science

Early cultural anthropology was seen from the Western perspective. "When the British went to Kenya and proselytized organized religion, they did not understand the significance of the gathering places under trees, drums, nature, and African spirituality (Holdstock 2000, 166)." African philosophy is problematic even to African philosophers.

What if history had been different and Kenya had invaded Great Britain? When Richard Williams, father of top women tennis players Serena and Venus, invaded Wimbledon in the 1990s, he commented on the event's stiffness.

There was no singing, music, dancing, spirit, or rhythm, he said. What they needed was some Rap music up in here.

The result of the historically one-sided perspective of African culture is the proliferation of post-modern genres that crossover in philosophy, literature, and ethnography.

Olympics vs. Road Racing

In the 1960s, 6'6" Jack Bacheler was a basketball player at Miami University in Ohio. When his basketball coach (who also coached track) encouraged him to run track to stay in shape, Bacheler discovered that he was a natural runner. After college he went on to do his graduate studies at the University of Florida, and competed as an elite runner. When Frank Shorter sought him out as a training partner in the early 1970s, the Florida Track Club (modeled after the successful New Zealand and British cross country clubs) became an enclave of professional runners.

At the time, Gainesville locals thought it peculiar to see grown men with long hair running daily on the streets. It was only when people learned that the men were potential Olympians did they begin to respect them. Several runners called this era the non-supportive 1970s. Bacheler made two Olympic teams, then married and become an entomology professor at North Carolina State. Bacheler said he ended his professional running career when he decided it was time to get married and find a full time job.

Meanwhile, Steve Prefontaine (or PRE, as he was called) was training to make the 1972 Olympic team while attending the University of Oregon. He lived in a mobile home and qualified for food stamps. He made the team, and placed fourth at Munich in the 5000m. In his short post-collegiate career, he had a number of confrontations with the Amateur Athletic Union (AAU) when the organization kept the appearance money he had earned at international track meets. While PRE had financial offers to run professionally, he turned down the money and remained focused on the 1976 Olympic final.

Shorter continued to run professionally, earned gold and silver medals in the marathon, and pursued his and PRE's goal of elevating running to professional status in the U.S. As society began to place a higher priority on fitness, the first running boom began. Grown men running around city streets were no longer considered strange. The opposing Olympics vs. earning a living as a professional runner schemas remain today, but to a lesser extent.

While preparing for the New York City Marathon in 2003, Elly Rono spent two months with elite American runners at Zapfitness. For mental recovery while training to make national teams, elite American miler Dan Wilson played ice hockey video games and drank beer. Rono relaxed by taking tea, entertaining visitors, and checking his online stock portfolio. Despite their cultural differences, each had a successful year—Dan Wilson was ranked eighth for U.S. milers, and Rono placed fourth in the New York City Marathon.

Gender Roles

In the twentieth century, women were thought to be too fragile to run marathons. Women's track and field was finally introduced at the 1928 Olympics; three women, however, collapsed during the 800m race. Consequently, women's events longer than 200m were discontinued until 1960, and the women's marathon was only introduced at the 1984 Los Angeles Olympics.

Several women proved that women could not only compete, but achieve stellar performances. Joan Benoit Samuelson won a gold medal in the 1984 marathon even though she'd had knee surgery seventeen days earlier, and Paula Radcliffe ran an incredible 2:15:25 at the 2003 London Marathon.

New Science

Evolution vs. Creationism. In 1860, Bishop Samuel Wilberforce defended Christianity against Darwin's evolution by natural selection in a formal debate at Oxford University. Because the theory was not written in the scripture, he declared the idea that he was related to monkeys preposterous (Wells 2002, 4).

In 1925, John Scopes was tried and found guilty of teaching evolution to his biology class. The Butler Law prohibited such teachings in Tennessee. Prosecutor William Jennings Bryan opposed the theory of evolution because of the implication of social Darwinism (2) (because social Darwinism implied the evolution of culture, the church did not hold it in high regard). While the conviction was overturned on appeal, any mention of the theory was removed from school biology texts until the 1960s.

Adaptationists vs. Evolutionists. Darwin's Natural Selection Theory proposed that new gene pools evolved from the organism's interaction with the environment. Neo-Darwinists, or Adaptationists, combine his concept with Mendelian genetics (proposes the storage and transfer of heredity information). Like every scientific theory, the theory of evolution is being continually refined and critiqued. Harvard professors and Evolutionists Steven J. Gould and Richard Lewontin claimed that Adaptationists are blind to non-adaptive explanations such as the possibility of genetic variations (e.g., genetic drift and mutations). Some philosophers of biology further criticize the Adaptationist's position, claiming that heritable traits acquired by an organism in response to the environment are random variations, and the survival of the fittest is a circular argument because the fittest are the ones to survive.

Nature vs. Nurture. Popular opinion assumes that genes play specific roles. Several prominent scientists, however, have expressed reservations. According to Bengt Saltin, humans are approximately seventy percent genetically programmed; a complex relationship exists among genes, culture, and performance. Identifying genes will not resolve the nature vs. nurture issue, as genetics coexist with the environment in an endless loop.[3] Current research has shown a complex integration of nature and nurture—in some cases, the integration is polygenic because multiple genes are involved in a physiological phenotype (Hochachka & Somero 2002, 206).

The Human Genome Project has offered a better explanation of the relationship between genes and the environment. Dr. Craig Venter, a founder of Celera Genomics, worked with the National Institute of Health in developing the human genome sequence. "…Our understanding of the human genome has changed in the most fundamental ways," he stated in a press release. "The finding that we have far fewer genes than expected suggests that environmental influences play a greater role in our development than was previously thought. The small number of genes—thirty thousand instead of one hundred and forty thousand—supports the notion that we are not hard-wired."[4]

He further revealed a new understanding of the genetic and environmental factors causing diversity among individuals. "We now know that the notion that one gene leads to one protein and perhaps one disease is false. One gene leads to many different products and those products—proteins—can change dramatically after they are produced. We know that regions of the genome that are not genes may be the key to the complexity we see in humans. We now know that the environment acting on these biological steps may be the key in making us what we are. Likewise the remarkably small numbers of genetic variations that occur in genes again suggest a significant role for environmental influences in developing each of our uniqueness."[5]

Barriers to Knowledge

By an error repeated throughout the ages, truth, becoming a law or a faith, places obstacles in the way of knowledge. Method, which is in its very substance ignorance, encloses truth within a vicious circle. We should break the circle, not by seeking knowledge, but by discovering the cause of ignorance.

Bruce Lee

Politics: Scientific and Institutional Dogma

Neo-Darwinism, which insists on the slow accrual of mutations, is in a complete funk.[6]

Lynn Margulis

In his book *Darwin's Radio*, Greg Bear warns of the scientific communities' politics and institutional dogmas, and the repercussions of religious fundamentalists. He claims that these dogmas have impeded the war on AIDS by subordinating science to politics. When words once considered esoteric are introduced (e.g., mad cow disease is caused by a prion), Bear's concept hits closer to home. Prions, transposons (jumping genes), and transgenic protein alterations are shifting from science fiction to mainstream journalism. Our understanding of the Central Dogma, introduced by Francis Crick, is being constantly revised as we learn more about the human genome.

New scientific ideas take time to be accepted. Because of the Human Genome Project, transposons and epigenetics, which violate the central dogma, can no longer be ignored. New sciences, however, remain partially underground; people aren't supposed to talk about them. According to Greg Bear, "The unfortunate aspect of the rancorous debate on evolution in the last seventy or more years has been the fossilization of hypotheses. One side says God and God only, the other says, random mutations and natural selection and nothing more. Both are likely wrong. A third variety of intelligent design has long been awaiting our attention."[7]

In 1892, biologist August Weissman proposed that hereditary information moves from genes to body cells, but not vice versa—a concept called the Weissman Barrier. Since it germ cells are separate from somatic cells, it was believed that it prevents the transmission of acquired traits. Recent experimentation has proven epigenetic inheritance in fruit flies, flatworms, hydra, pepper moths, *E. coli* bacteria, plants, and transgenic mice. Epigenetic inheritance is not the result of changes in DNA sequence, but through post-translational modifications. Ultimately, the same DNA (gene) does not always lead to the same mRNA. The discovery of alternate splicing discredited the theory that one gene produces one protein.

Political Correctness and Taboos

The process of learning requires an open mind, a dialogue, a debate and a search
for the truth, and unless you approach education on that basis you are not going
to be educated.

William F. Buckley, Jr.

The discussion of race, ethnicity, and evolution elicit diverse responses—
the religious right attacks Darwin's theory of what animals evolved from, and
the left and center attack Darwin's theory of what humans evolved to.[8] UCLA
physiologist Jared Diamond says that even today, those who study racial origins risk being branded a racist.[9]

By definition, Darwinism requires hereditary inequalities. Walter E.
Williams, economics professor at George Mason University, believes that ethnic discussions are not inherently racist. "If decent people don't discuss human
biodiversity, we concede the turf to black and white racists." Jon Entine coun-
tered the same point in a May 2000 NPR debate with Grant Farred called Relationship between Race and Athletic Achievement. "The argument of the
book *Taboo*—or part of the argument of the book—reflects very mainstream
science, and that's human populations have evolved in different parts of the
world primarily, have different body types and this is not a black-white issue,
because East and West Africans are very, very different in body types as are
East Asians, the rest of Asia, whites and so forth. So each area, the more it was
insular, the more likely we're able to find certain diseases and certain body
types and that's reflected on the athletic field."[10]

Constructive Dialogue

Conformers are second hand artists.[11]

Bruce Lee

In the politically-correct U.S., people are only able to discuss controversies
such as race and athletic performance in several arenas—anonymous chat
boards, therefore, have sprung up as a forum for debate. Several essayists, too,
are researching and discussing these sensitive topics (e.g., Steven Sailer and
Jon Entine). Their controversial articles help break down taboos by forcing
readers to take positions and support their beliefs.

Liberal academic institutions with interdisciplinary studies and tenured
professors are major players in the civilized debate on controversial topics.
Tenured professor Valentin Mudimbe, for example, has spent his distinguished

career writing about the decolonization of the mind. According to his secretary, he doesn't worry about these things.

In many cases, it is those researchers who think outside the box who ultimately determine how most of us see and do things. When Dr. Robert Atkins presented his radical approach to nutrition, the medical establishment attacked him and his ideas. His approach, however, ended up changing people's understanding of nutrition. Despite the hurdles at the time, Bruce Lee refused to accept ideas and doctrines at face value, but on their merits. He reinterpreted and eventually revolutionized the field of martial arts. Finally, Sam Walton's initially unorthodox business philosophy is now considered a model. In his book, *Sam Walton: Made in America*, he discusses the merits of thinking outside the box. "Rule Ten Swim Upstream: Go the other way. Ignore the conventional wisdom. If everybody is doing it one way, there's a good chance you can find your niche by going in exactly the opposite direction. But be prepared for a lot of folks to wave you down and tell you you're headed the wrong way (Walton & Huey 1992, 249)."

What can we learn from such thinking? Dr. Susana Zabala de Utreras, a clinical psychologist, says approximately ninety-eight percent of her patients are undeveloped in the individualization process. "We are continually discovering who we are," she says. Psychologist Carl Jung spoke of the inner journey, and the undiscovered self and consciousness, and advised followers to be themselves.

Are Kenyans really different? Their genes are expressed differently because of environmental factors, they are socialized differently, and they experienced a colonization of the mind. Consequently, they have their own worldview. Professor Mudimbe suggests that they have a dual consciousness. They are not, however, mentally homeless. "It is I that am mentally homeless," he says. "I'm not sure if I'm African, European, or American."

ENDNOTES

Introduction

1. Ridley, M. 2003. What Makes You Who You Are. *Time* 161(22): 59–63.

2. Connell, D. J. 2002. Symbolic Interactionism to Luhmann. Paper presented at the Society for the Study of Symbolic Interaction Conference. <www.djconnell.ca/papers.html>.

3. Kleine, M. 1990. *Beyond Triangulation: Ethnography, Writing, and Rhetoric.* P. 2. <http://jac.gsu.edu/jac/10/Articles/9.htm>.

4. Lee, B. Jeet Kune Do—Toward Personal Liberation. pp. 8–14. <www.brucelee.com/jeet.htm>.

5. Ibid.

Chapter 1

1. Kennedy, T. 1996. Waiting for Machuka: The Pre-Olympic Drama of the World's Best Distance Runners. *Running Times* (November): 30–32.

2. Moore, K. 1990. Sons of the Wind Out of Africa. *Sports Illustrated* (February 26).

3. Ibid.

4. Manners, J. H. 1997. Kenya's Running Tribe. *The Sports Historian* (November) 17(2).

5. Okoth, O. 2002. Dane Experts Attempt to Unravel Kenya's Athletics. *The East African Standard* (November).

6. Manners, J. H. 1997. Kenya's Running Tribe. *The Sports Historian* (November) 17(2).

7. Ibid.

8. Ibid.

9. Bellamy, R. 1999. No Barriers for Kenyans. *The Register-Guard* (May).

10. *Running Times Magazine* 1992. Rankings provided by intern Lucas Meyer.

11. *Running Times Magazine* 1993. Rankings provided by intern Lucas Meyer.

12. Manners, J. H. 1997. Kenya's Running Tribe. *The Sports Historian* (November) 17(2).

13. *Running Times Magazine* 1993. Rankings provided by intern Lucas Meyer.

14. Ibid.

15. www.trackandfieldnews.com.

16. Sandrock, M. 2001. Running with the Kenyans. *Marathon & Beyond* (March/April).

17. Mitchell, K. 2000. Genetic Story Should Be Told. *The Observer*.

18. <www.trackandfieldnews.com>.

19. Ibid.

20. Ibid.

21. Ibid.

22. Kennedy, T. 1996. Waiting for Machuka: The Pre-Olympic Drama of the World's Best Distance Runners. *Running Times* (November): 30–32.

23. Sailer, S. 2000. *Kenyan Runners—what's their Secret?* UPI Newswire (September).

24. Kennedy, T. 1996. Waiting for Machuka: The Pre-Olympic Drama of the World's Best Distance Runners. *Running Times* (November): 30–32.

25. Okoth, O. 2003. Broke and Angry, Ngugi seeks Help. *The East African Standard* (December 8).

26. Kennedy, T. 1996. Waiting for Machuka: The Pre-Olympic Drama of the World's Best Distance Runners. *Running Times* (November): 30–32.

27. Macharia, D., and S. Kiragu. 2003. This is a Runner's Paradise. *The Nation* (September).

28. Reavis, T. 2004. Who's in First? (January). www.runnersworld.com/home/0,1300,1-0-0-6066,00.html.

29. Toohey, K., and A. J. Veal. 2000. *The Olympic Games: A Social Science Perspective.* CABI Publishing.

30. Grytting, W. 2003. American Newspeak, Buy American. *The New York Times* (March 16).

31. William, J. 2000. *Relationship between Race and Athletic Achievement.* NPR Talk of the Nation (May 8). <www.jonentine.com/reviews/NPR_TOTN_5_2000.htm>.

32. Salazar, A. 2003. Racing the Kenyans. <http://nikebiz.com/media/n_salazar.shtml>.

Chapter 2

1. Moore, K. 1990. Sons of the Wind Out of Africa. *Sports Illustrated* (February 26).

2. Entine, J. 2001. Why Race Matters in Sports. <www.jonentine.com/reviews/AOL_Why_Race_Matters.htm>.

3. Anderson, O. Dad, Mum and You: How Much do your Genes Really Influence Your Performance? *Peak Performance Newsletter.*

4. Grossier, R. 2002. Researchers and their Research. <www.vuhs.org/apbio/html-ryan/research.html>.

5. Graetzer, D. High Altitude and its Effects on Exercise Performance. <www.sumeria.net/oxy/altitude.html>.

6. <www.nsbri.org/HumanPhysSpace/introduction/intro-environment-atmosphere.html>.

7. Munce, T. Physiological Responses to Altitudinal Hypoxia, Part I. <www.personal.psu.edu/staff/t/a/tam275/performance.html>.

8. Munce, T. Effects of Altitude on Athletic Performance, Part II. <www.personal.psu.edu/staff/t/a/tam275/Lactate.html#LE>.

9. Campbell University faculty website. Fuel reserves for a typical 70-kg man. Available energy (kcal) is dependent on CHO intake. <http://www.campbell.edu/faculty/bergemann/exph04.htm>.

10. Brooks G. A. 1987. Amino Acid and Protein Metabolism during Exercise and Recovery. *Medicine and Science in Sports and Exercise* (October). <www.ncbi.nlm.nih.gov/entrez/query.fcgi?cmd=Retrieve&db=PubMed&list_uids=3316914&dopt=Abstract>.

11. Saltin L. H., N. Terrados, J. Bangsbo, T. Bak, C. Kim, J. Svedenhag, and C. Rolf. 1995. Aerobic Exercise Capacity at Sea Level and at Altitude in Kenyan Boys, Junior and Senior Runners Compared with Scandinavian Runners. *Scandinavian Journal of Medicine and Science in Sports* (August) 5(4).

12. Booth, F. W., M. V. Chakravarthy, and E. E. Spangenburg. 2002. Exercise and Gene Expression: Physiological Regulation of the Human Genome through Physical Activity. *Journal of Physiology* 543(2). <http://216.239.37.104/search?q=cache:00MgfVL7kbwJ:www.aktivitetogsundhed.dk/frankboothartikel.pdf+lactate+saltin+kenyan&hl=en&ie=UTF-8>.

13. Saltin B., C. Kim, N. Terrados, J. Svedenhag, C. Rolf. 1995. Morphology, Enzyme Activities and Buffer Capacity in Leg Muscles of Kenyan and Scandinavian Runners. *Scandinavian Journal of Medicine and Science in Sports* (August) 5(4). <www.ncbi.nlm.nih.gov/entrez/query.fcgi?cmd=Retrieve&db=PubMed&list_uids=7552767&dopt=Abstract>.

14. Weston, A. R., O. Karamizrak, A. Smith, T. D. Noakes, and K. H. Myburgh. 1999. African Runners Exhibit Greater Fatigue Resistance, Lower Lactate Accumulation, and Higher Oxidative Enzyme Activity. *Journal of Applied Physiology* (March) 86(3): 915–23. <http://jap.physiology.org/cgi/content/full/86/3/915>.

15. Karp, J. R. *Muscle Fiber Types and Training*. <http://www.coachr.org/fiber.htm>.

Chapter 3

1. Noakes, T. D. 1997. Challenging Beliefs: Ex Africa Semper Aliquid Novi. *Medicine and Science in Sports and Exercise* (May) 29(5).

2. Weston A. R., Z. Mbambo, and K. H. Myburgh. 2000. Running Economy of African and Caucasian Distance Runners. *Medicine and Science in Sports and Exercise* (June) 32(6): 1130–34.

3. Noakes, T. The Governor: How the Brain Protects Your Vital Organs by Inducing Exercise Fatigue. <www.pponline.co.uk/encyc/0873b.htm>.

4. Noakes, T. D. 2000. Physiological Models to Understand Exercise Fatigue and the Adaptations that Predict or Enhance Athletic Performance. *Scandinavian Journal of Medicine and Science in Sports* 10: 123–45.

5. Ibid.

6. Noakes, T. The Governor: How the Brain Protects Your Vital Organs by Inducing Exercise Fatigue. <www.pponline.co.uk/encyc/0873b.htm>.

7. Ibid.

8. Noakes, T. D. 2000. Physiological Models to Understand Exercise Fatigue and the

Adaptations that Predict or Enhance Athletic Performance. *Scandinavian Journal of Medicine and Science in Sports* 10: 123–45.

9. Ibid.

10. Pohl, O. 2002. Improving the Way Humans Walk the Walk. *The New York Times.* Science Section (March).

11. Noakes, T. D. 2000. Physiological Models to Understand Exercise Fatigue and the Adaptations that Predict or Enhance Athletic Performance. *Scandinavian Journal of Medicine and Science in Sports* 10: 123–45.

Chapter 4

1. Brooks, G. A. 1991. Current Concepts in Lactate Exchange. *Medicine and Science in Sports and Exercise* (August) 23(8).

2. Fahey, T. 2003. Ten Things You Should Know About Lactic Acid: Old Myths and New Realities. <www.cytosport.com/science/lacticacid.html>.

3. Ibid.

4. Brooks, G. A. 2000. Intra- and Extra-Cellular Lactate Shuttles. *Medicine and Science in Sports and Exercise* (April) 32(4). <www.ncbi.nlm.nih.gov/entrez/ query.fcgi?cmd= Retrieve&db=PubMed&list_uids=10776898&dopt=Abstract>.

5. Ibid.

6. Ibid.

7. Saltin L. H., N. Terrados, J. Bangsbo, T. Bak, C. Kim, J. Svedenhag, and C. Rolf. 1995. Aerobic Exercise Capacity at Sea Level and at Altitude in Kenyan Boys, Junior and Senior Runners Compared with Scandinavian Runners. *Scandinavian Journal of Medicine and Science in Sports* (August) 5(4).

8. Interview with Dr. George Brooks, Professor of Integrative Biology at the University of California at Berkeley.

9. Brooks, G. A. 1985. Anaerobic Threshold: Review of the Concepts and Directions for Future Research. *Medicine and Science in Sports and Exercise* 17. <www-rohan.sdsu.edu/ dept/coachsci/csa/vol46/brooks5.htm>.

10. Brooks, G. A. 1998. Mammalian Fuel Utilization during Sustained Exercise. *Comparative Biochemistry and Physiology* (May) 120. <www.ncbi.nlm.nih.gov/entrez/ query.fcgi?cmd=Retrieve&db=PubMed&list_uids=9787780&dopt=Abstract&itool=iconabstr>.

11. Interview with Dr. George Brooks, Professor of Integrative Biology at the University of California at Berkeley.

12. Fahey, T. 2003. Ten Things You Should Know About Lactic Acid: Old Myths and New Realities. <www.cytosport.com/science/lacticacid.html>.

13. Hochachka, P. W., C. L. Beatty, Y. Burelle, M. E. Trump, D. C. McKenzie, and G. O. Matheson. 2002. The Lactate Paradox in Human High-Altitude. *Physiological Performance News in Physiological Sciences* (June) 17 (31). <http://nips.physiology.org/cgi/content/full/17/3/122>.

14. Anderson, O. Report on Blood Lactate 1: Things your Mother Forgot to Tell you About Blood Lactate. *Peak Performance Newsletter.* <www.pponline.co.uk/encyc/0175.htm>.

15. Brooks, G. A. 1991. Current Concepts in Lactate Exchange. *Medicine and Science in Sports and Exercise* (August) 23(8). <www.ncbi.nlm.nih.gov/entrez/query.fcgi?cmd=Retrieve&db=PubMed&list_uids=1956262&dopt=Abstract&itool=iconabstr>.

16. Brooks G. A., and J. Mercier. 1994. Balance of Carbohydrate and Lipid Utilization During Exercise: The "Crossover" Concept. *Journal of Applied Physiology* (June) 76(6). <www.ncbi.nlm.nih.gov/entrez/query.fcgi?cmd=Retrieve&db=PubMed&list_uids=7928844&dopt=Abstract>.

17. Brooks, G. A. 1998. Mammalian Fuel Utilization during Sustained Exercise. *Comparative Biochemistry and Physiology* (May) 120. <www.ncbi.nlm.nih.gov/entrez/query.fcgi?cmd=Retrieve&db=PubMed&list_uids=9787780&dopt=Abstract>.

18. Brooks, G. A. 1991. Current Concepts in Lactate Exchange. *Medicine and Science in Sports and Exercise* (August) 23(8). <www-rohan.sdsu.edu/dept/coachsci/csa/vol46/brooks2.htm>.

19. Brooks G. A., and J. Mercier. 1994. Balance of Carbohydrate and Lipid Utilization During Exercise: The "Crossover" Concept. *Journal of Applied Physiology* (June) 76(6). <http://jap.physiology.org/cgi/content/abstract/76/6/2253>.

20. Hochachka, P. W., H. C. Gunga, and K. Kirsch. 1998. Our Ancestral Physiological Phenotype: An Adaptation for Hypoxia Tolerance and for Endurance Performance? Proceeding from the National Academy of Sciences (February) 95 (4). <www.pubmedcentral.gov/articlerender.fcgi?artid=19213>.

Chapter 5

1. <www.athleticskenya.org/aff_bodies.php>.

Chapter 6

1. <http://www.kenyarunners.com/pages/167372/index.htm>.

Chapter 7

1. Bliss, T. F., and L. Beth. 2002. People of Kenya. <http://www.blissites.com/kenya/people.html>.

Chapter 9

1. Meyers, N. 1994. Marathon Mind. *The Guardian* (April 12).

2. Manktelon, J. 2002. Focus and Flow. <http://members.tripod.com/~tesur/sp2.html>.

3. Meyers, R. 2002. Sports Psychologists: Rituals Help Win in Tennis and Business. *Abilene Reporter-News* (March 25).

4. Brown, H. 2004. Culpepper, Keflezighi, Browne Claim Olympic Marathon Spots. *Running USA Wire* (February 7).

5. Hamilton, B. 2000. East African Running Dominance: What is Behind It? *British Journal of Sports Medicine* 34: 391–94.

6. Doxsie, D. 2001. Running Defines a Nation. *Quad-City Times*. <http://apse.dallas-news.com/contest/2000/writing/40-100.enterprise.first1.asp>.

7. Ibid.

8. Moore, K. 1990. Sons of the Wind Out of Africa. *Sports Illustrated* (February 26).

9. Entine, J. 2001. Black Athletes: A Race Apart? <www.joneetine.com/reviews/chronicle_world.htm>.

Chapter 10

1. Demeterio III, F. P. A. 2001. Critical Aesthetics and the Social Significance of Jose Reyes' Film Toro. Diwatao 1(1). <www.geocities.com/philodept/diwatao/cognitive_anthropology.htm>.

2. Ibid.

Chapter 11

1. Lecture at Duke University in 2003.

2. Williams, J. 2000. *Relationship between Race and Athletic Achievement.* NPR Talk of the Nation (May 8). <www.jonentine.com/reviews/NPR_TOTN_5_2000.htm>.

3. Manners, J. H. 1997. Kenya's Running Tribe. *The Sports Historian* (November) 17(2). <www.kenyarunners.com/pages/167371/index.htm>.

4. Okoth, O. 2003. Broke and Angry, Ngugi seeks Help. *The East African Standard* (December 8).

5. <http://uk.sports.yahoo.com/030702/323/e3n9a.html>.

Chapter 12

1. Reed, F. 2003. *Race, Rushton, and Us.* <www.fredoneverything.net/Rushton.shtml>.

2. Ibid.

3. Doyran, M. A. 2000. *Human Nature: Born or Made* (March) <http://csf.colorado.edu/mail/matfem/current/msg00173.html>.

4. Sailer, S. 1999. *A Miracle Happens Here: Darwin's Enemies on the Right* (November). <www.isteve.com/Darwin-EnemiesonRight.htm>.

5. Entine, J. 2001. Why Race Matters in Sports. <www.jonentine.com/reviews/AOL_Why_Race_Matters.htm>.

6. Langdon, J. H., and S. P. Nawrocki. 1997. *The Evolution of Endurance—Toward a Synthesis of Skeletal and Soft Tissue Evolution.* <http://biology.uindy.edu/Biol345/ARTI-

CLES/evolutionofendurance.htm>.

7. Shontz, L. 2002. Fast Forward: The Pioneers Who Led the Way. *Pittsburgh Post-Gazette* (May 6). <www.post-gazette.com/sports/other/20020506kenya0506p2.asp>.

8. Ibid.

9. Shontz, L. 2002. Fast Forward: Crazy Catherine, On Top of the World. *Pittsburgh Post-Gazette* (May 7). <www.post-gazette.com/sports/other/20020507kenya0507p3.asp>.

10. Interview with Paul Tergat at the 2002 Rock and Roll Half-Marathon in Virginia Beach ,VA.

11. <www.cherryblossom.org>.

Chapter 13

1. Interview with Valentin Mudimbe.

2. Ongley, J. 2001. The Scopes Trial and Social Darwinism. <www.iit.edu/departments/humanities/impact/colloquium/ongley_2001f.html>.

3. Entine, J. 2000. Breaking the Taboo: Why Black Athletes Dominate Sports and Why We Are Afraid to Talk About It. *Public Affairs.* <www.jonentine.com/skeptic/entine.htm>.

4. <http://askwaltstollmd.com/archives/genome/65745.html>.

5. Ibid.

6. <www.christiankeys.ca/Creation73.html>.

7. <www.gregbear.com/A55885/Bear.nsf/ea0abde639de22eb882568b4002c920c/32efe95dade0174388256b3e001a06b4!OpenDocument>.

8. Sailer, S. 1999. The Coming War over Genes: Darwin's Enemies on the Left. (December). <www.isteve.com/Darwin-EnemiesonLeft.htm>.

9. Entine, J. 2001. Why Race Matters in Sports. <www.jonentine.com/reviews/AOL_Why_Race_Matters.htm>.

10. Williams, J. 2000. *Relationship between Race and Athletic Achievement.* NPR Talk of the Nation (May 8). <www.jonentine.com/reviews/NPR_TOTN_5_2000.htm>.

11. Lee, B. Jeet Kune Do—Toward Personal Liberation. <www.brucelee.com/jeet.htm>.

Appendix A

Glossary

Adaptionists. Advocates of natural selection.

Anaerobic threshold. The upper limit of exercise intensity that can be sustained aerobically. A point just prior to metabolic acidosis.

Catecholamines. Released during hypoxia and cause circulatory changes including increased blood pressure, heart rate, and cardiac output.

Cell-cell lactate shuttle. George Brooks' observation that lactate can be produced by one cell and used by another.

Cognitive anthropology. The study of thought in a cultural context.

Consciousness. Awareness of the external world.

Crossover Concept. How the body selects combinations of fatty acids, carbohydrates and amino acids for use for fuel during sustained exercise.

Emic. Attempting to understand a native culture without imposing one's own viewpoint.

Epigenetics. The way in which an organism develops because of the interaction of genes and environment through post translational modifications.

Enculturation. Socialization unique to a culture.

Essentialism. People are different and possess certain properties, as opposed to being products of historical circumstances.

Ethnic Code. Genetics and cultural factors that comprise a person.

Ethnocentrism. Viewing another culture from one's own perspective.

Ethnophilosophy. Philosophy unique to an ethnic group.

Ethnosystem. The dynamics of the biological and cultural factors that comprise a person.

Etic. A cultural analysis using categories that reflect the point of view of the anthropologist.

Evolutionary psychology. Sociobiology relating to humans.

Evolutionists. Consider both non-adaptive reasons (e.g., genetic drift and mutations) and natural selection as a way to understand human evolution.

Exon. Protein coding DNA.

First Order Cybernetics. The study of systems and the interaction of the variables in a system.

Gluconeogenesis. Process of making new glucose.

Glucose Paradox. Why lactic acid is converted to liver glycogen rather than blood glucose.

Glycogenolysis. The increased use of glycogen with high intensity exercise and increased epinephrine. Glycogen is reduced to glucose.

Glycolysis. The metabolic pathway of glucose breakdown.

Hakuna matata. No worries.

Haraka haraka haina baraka. Hurry hurry has no blessing.

Hermeneutics. The theory and methodology of interpretation.

Hypoxia. The condition resulting from decreased oxygen supply to body tissues. Can occur as a direct response to lower atmospheric pressures at altitude.

Hypoxemia. Deficient oxygenation of the blood.

Indigenous psychology. A mindset native to a particular region, people, and culture.

Individuation. Jung's term for the process of approaching personal wholeness by integrating the conscious and unconscious aspects of personality.

Intracellular Lactate Shuttle. Mitochondria take up and oxidize lactate directly within a cell.

Kukumvilia. Perseverance. An individual must be ready physically, mentally, and emotionally.

Lactate paradox. How lactate accumulation is reduced without a concomitant increase in tissue oxygenation (when hypoxemia should promote lactate accumulation).

Lactate shuttle. Lactate produced in one tissue can be used as fuel in another.

Lactate threshold. The point at which lactate production exceeds lactate removal and lactate starts to accumulate in the blood.

Lactate turnover. Balance between production and removal of lactate.

Lamarckism. A theory of evolution claiming that acquired characteristics are transmitted to offspring.

Meta-ethnography. A research methodology that can be used to integrate the findings of qualitative research. It can be considered a complete study in itself—it compares and analyzes texts, and creates new interpretations.

Mzungu. A white or European person.

Myoglobin. The form of hemoglobin found in muscle fibers.

Natural selection. The Adaptionists' view of evolution. This theory postulates that interaction with the environment causes new gene pools to form.

Parasympathetic nervous system. The part of the autonomic nervous system that slows the heart and dilates the blood vessels.

Phenomenal. Known through the senses or experience rather than through cognitive thought or intuition (noumenal).

Polepole. Slowly, when it is ready.

Psychological anthropology. The interrelationships among psychological, social and cultural phenomenon.

Reverse Engineering. The process of analyzing an existing system both to identify its components and their interrelationships, and to create representations of the system in another form or at a higher level of abstraction. For example, the process of inferring an adaptation's function from its design.

Schemas. Point of view affecting judgment and governing inner life.

Second Order Cybernetics. The study of observing systems and the interaction between observer and observed. In social sciences, collected data is considered subjective.

Self consciousness. Awareness of self.

Semiotics. The study of signs and symbols.

Socialization. Social experiences that alter an individual's development.

Sociobiology. The scientific study of the biological basis of forms of social behavior in all organisms.

Sub-maximal exercise. Less than one hundred percent intensity.

Sympathetic nervous system. The part of the autonomic nervous system speeding up the heart and contracting the blood vessels.

Third Order Cybernetics. Social and intellectual ideas and their relation to the individual.

Universalist. Philosophical approach to humanity believing humans are similar.

Ventilation. Movement of air into and out of the lungs.

VO₂ₘₐₓ TEST —ELLY RONO

Name: _Elly Rono_   Age: _3 2_   Date: _7/24/02_

Gender: _M_   Height (in): _75.25_   Weight (lbs): _156.60_

Stage		Minute (min)	Speed (mph)	Grade (%)	HR (beats/min)	RPE (6-20 Scale)	METS
1		1	1.7	10			
		2	1.7	10			
		3	1.7	10		__	4 - 5
2	start	4	2.5	12			
		5	2.5	12	101		
		6	2.5	12		7	6 - 7
3		7	3.4	14	121		
		8	3.4	14			
		9	3.4	14	129	11	9 - 10
4		10	4.2	16			
		11	4.2	16	135		
		12	4.2	16		12	12 - 13
5		13	5.0	18	146		
		14	5.0	18			
		15	5.0	18		14	14 - 15
6		16	5.5	20	157		
		17	5.5	20			
		18	5.5	20		17	17 - 18
		19	6.0	22	163		

Total Treadmill Time Completed: _18 min, 20 min_   HR_max_ = 163

Test Terminated Due To: _Fatigue_

Measured VO₂ Max (ml·kg⁻¹·min⁻¹): _69.38_

Predicted VO₂ Max (ml·kg⁻¹·min⁻¹): _67.1_

Predicted VO₂ max for Males: VO₂ max (ml·kg⁻¹·min⁻¹) = 14.76 – 1.379*Time (min) + 0.451*Time² – 0.012*Time³

Predicted VO₂ max for Females: VO₂ max (ml·kg⁻¹·min⁻¹) = 4.38*Time (min) – 3.9

Cardiorespiratory Fitness Classification (See Table 1): _Olympic_

DUKE UNIVERSITY MEDICAL CENTER
K-LAB—SPORTS PERFORMANCE PROGRAM

MAXIMUM TREADMILL TEST (BRUCE PROTOCOL)

The Bruce protocol is by far the most common maximal graded exercise test. The conventional Bruce protocol involves performing up to six 3 min stages (stages 1-6) with speeds, grades, and METS for each stage shown below. The conventional Bruce protocol is an uphill walking test for stages 1-3, and then becomes an uphill running test for stages 4-6. For subjects who have difficulty starting off with the 10% grade in stage 1 for conventional Bruce protocol shown below, a modified Bruce protocol can be used by adding two stages at the beginning of the conventional Bruce protocol. The first stage begins with the subject walking at 1.7 mi/hr at a 0% grade for 3 min, while in the second stage the subject walks at 1.7 mi/hr at a 5% grade for 3 min. Subsequently, the conventional Bruce protocol shown below is followed. When maximal exertion is achieved and subject is unable to continue, the time completed in minutes is recorded.

Using 200 symptomatic and asymptomatic male subjects (mean age of 48.1 ± 16.3 years), both active and sedentary, Foster et al. (1984) developed the following generalized regression equation ($R = 0.98$; SEE = 3.35 ml·kg^{-1}min^{-1}) for the conventional Bruce protocol (stages 1-6) to order to estimate VO_2 max for both active and sedentary (symptomatic and asymptomatic) males:

$$VO_2 \text{ max (ml·kg}^{-1}\cdot\text{min}^{-1}) = 14.76 - 1.379*Time \text{ (min)} + 0.451*Time^2 - 0.012*Time^3$$

Using 49 asymptomatic female subjects (age range between 20-42 years), both active and sedentary, Pollock et al. (1982) developed the following generalized regression equation ($R = 0.91$; SEE = 2.7 ml·kg^{-1}min^{-1}) for the conventional Bruce protocol (stages 1-6) to order to estimate VO_2 max for both active and sedentary females:

$$VO_2 \text{ max (ml·kg}^{-1}\cdot\text{min}^{-1}) = 4.38*Time \text{ (min)} - 3.9$$

c:\turbofit\rono.xls

VacuMed (TurboFit V4.047, Dec 10, 1999)
4483 McGrath Street #102
Ventura, CA 93003 - (805) 644.7461

Patient Information

Id		**Protocol**	
First Name	Simon *Elly*	**Temperature**	22.0 degree C
Last Name	Rono	**Baro**	756 mm Hg
Weight	156.6 Lbs	**Height**	75.3 inches
Date	07-24-2002	**Time**	13:16:25
Humidity	68	**Filter**	20 seconds (BBB)

TIME(min)	VO2(Kg)	VCO2(Kg)	RER	VE(btps)	SaO2	REE	METS	Watts	VE/VO2	VE/VCO2	TV(atps)	HR
00:23	30.32	8.17	0.27	31.69	0	13.043	8.66	0	12.07	44.78	1.14	97
00:41	22.08	14.21	0.64	39.58	0	10.430	6.31	0	20.69	32.16	1.15	104
01:01	21.13	15.82	0.75	41.46	0	10.230	6.04	0	22.64	30.24	1.14	102
01:20	27.54	19.11	0.69	48.11	0	13.165	7.87	0	20.18	29.08	1.30	101
01:41	26.77	20.10	0.75	50.53	0	12.967	7.65	0	21.82	29.05	1.50	100
02:00	26.50	20.05	0.76	48.73	0	12.855	7.57	0	21.24	28.08	1.37	104
02:20	27.61	21.66	0.78	53.29	0	13.482	7.89	0	22.29	28.42	1.38	103
02:42	26.22	21.47	0.82	51.17	0	12.904	7.49	0	22.51	27.50	1.52	111
03:01	26.90	22.56	0.84	54.05	0	13.296	7.69	0	23.21	27.67	1.48	119
03:20	25.64	21.82	0.85	52.79	0	12.710	7.33	0	23.77	27.94	1.52	130
03:40	33.60	27.04	0.80	59.31	0	16.480	9.60	0	20.35	25.30	2.09	122
04:00	34.62	28.69	0.83	64.25	0	17.074	9.89	0	21.44	25.87	1.94	123
04:20	31.28	26.74	0.85	59.73	0	15.519	8.94	0	22.06	25.80	2.07	118
04:40	32.10	27.17	0.85	59.90	0	15.896	9.17	0	21.57	25.48	1.74	113
05:01	31.31	26.05	0.83	57.70	0	15.452	8.94	0	21.25	25.54	1.90	118
05:21	34.54	28.33	0.82	61.51	0	17.001	9.87	0	20.57	25.08	1.94	118
05:40	33.31	28.27	0.85	62.52	0	16.503	9.52	0	21.67	25.53	1.90	117
06:00	36.69	31.45	0.86	69.63	0	18.212	10.48	0	21.89	25.53	2.00	125
06:22	34.65	30.19	0.87	66.49	0	17.254	9.90	0	22.18	25.45	2.22	136
06:40	45.87	38.49	0.84	81.14	0	22.676	13.11	0	20.42	24.34	2.28	140
07:00	42.23	36.62	0.87	78.54	0	21.012	12.07	0	21.47	24.76	2.23	141
07:20	49.09	40.72	0.83	83.01	0	24.215	14.03	0	19.53	23.55	2.33	142
07:40	47.97	41.88	0.87	90.02	0	23.898	13.71	0	21.69	24.84	2.44	144
08:00	48.90	43.59	0.89	93.08	0	24.464	13.97	0	21.97	24.65	2.38	143
08:21	47.14	43.16	0.92	94.02	0	23.711	13.47	0	23.04	25.16	2.37	142
08:40	45.12	41.22	0.91	88.63	0	22.684	12.89	0	22.68	24.82	2.48	146
09:00	52.70	47.03	0.89	99.46	0	26.370	15.06	0	21.84	24.47	2.39	146
09:21	47.93	46.07	0.96	103.24	0	24.357	13.70	0	24.85	25.85	2.58	156
09:40	50.79	46.06	0.91	97.71	0	25.497	14.51	0	22.22	24.51	2.49	154
10:01	54.25	48.43	0.89	101.04	0	27.147	15.50	0	21.50	24.08	2.56	154
10:21	56.93	52.59	0.92	109.77	0	28.689	16.27	0	22.27	24.11	2.88	157
10:40	58.31	55.02	0.94	114.24	0	29.515	16.66	0	22.59	23.94	2.67	154
11:00	56.41	54.77	0.97	117.10	0	28.728	16.12	0	23.96	24.68	2.66	152
11:21	57.88	55.52	0.96	116.54	0	29.399	16.54	0	23.24	24.23	2.58	163
11:40	55.26	52.61	0.95	109.29	0	28.021	15.79	0	22.83	23.98	2.54	162
12:00	61.29	58.35	0.95	121.01	0	31.079	17.51	0	22.77	23.92	2.70	160
12:20	57.97	58.02	1.00	125.23	0	29.717	16.56	0	24.95	24.93	2.75	157
12:40	59.78	59.01	0.99	123.83	0	30.549	17.08	0	23.89	24.20	2.79	157
13:01	63.25	63.82	1.01	130.29	0	32.479	18.07	0	23.82	23.61	2.79	88
13:20	63.39	65.41	1.03	134.69	0	32.716	18.11	0	24.53	23.77	2.82	9
13:40	62.82	66.01	1.05	137.48	0	32.556	17.95	0	25.28	24.06	2.71	9
14:00	63.91	67.64	1.06	140.20	0	33.176	18.26	0	25.32	23.93	2.77	
14:20	63.90	68.80	1.08	144.36	0	33.302	18.26	0	26.10	24.24	2.76	
14:40	64.92	70.41	1.08	150.80	0	33.892	18.55	0	26.78	24.70	2.78	
15:00	64.72	70.91	1.10	154.61	0	33.867	18.49	0	27.60	25.19	2.87	4
15:20	67.38	75.27	1.12	170.08	0	35.422	19.25	0	29.14	26.09	2.79	4
15:40	62.71	72.28	1.15	168.15	0	33.220	17.92	0	30.96	26.86	2.80	3
16:01	58.84	64.28	1.13	133.65	0	29.971	16.24	0	27.16	24.02	2.66	

c:\turbofit\rono.xls

VacuMed (TurboFit V4.047, Dec 10, 1999)
4483 McGrath Street #102
Ventura, CA 93003 - (805) 644.7461

Patient Information

Id		**Protocol**		
First Name	Simon	**Temperature**	22.0 degree C	
Last Name	Rono	**Baro**	756 mm Hg	
Weight	156.6 Lbs	**Height**	75.3 inches	
Date	07-24-2002	**Time**	13:16:25	
Humidity	68	**Filter**	20 seconds (BBB)	

TIME(min)	VO2(Kg)	VCO2(Kg)	RER	VE(btps)	SaO2	REE	METS	Watts	VE/VO2	VE/VCO2	TV(atps)	HR
16:20	46.46	54.06	1.16	105.28	0	24.670	13.28	0	26.17	22.49	2.47	155
16:40	35.64	44.99	1.26	93.71	0	19.318	10.18	0	30.38	24.06	2.22	131
17:00	27.13	39.86	1.47	92.22	0	15.340	7.75	0	39.26	26.73	2.15	119
17:21	17.35	27.68	1.60	68.77	0	10.059	4.96	0	45.64	28.61	1.80	114
17:40	18.06	27.35	1.51	69.03	0	10.312	5.17	0	44.10	29.15	1.74	110

Table 10. Cardiorespiratory VO_2 max ($ml \cdot kg^{-1} \cdot min^{-1}$) fitness norms and classifications. Reprinted with permission from (Astrand 1960; Nieman 1999).

Fitness Classification	Low	Fair	Average	Good	High	Athletic	Olympic
Male							
Age Group							
20-29	<38	39-43	44-51	52-56	57-62	63-69	>70
30-39	<34	35-39	40-47	48-51	52-57	58-64	>65
40-49	<30	31-35	36-43	44-47	48-53	54-60	>61
50-59	<25	26-31	32-39	40-43	44-48	44-49	>56
60-69	<21	22-26	27-35	36-39	40-44	45-49	>50
Women							
Age Group							
20-29	<28	29-34	35-43	44-48	49-53	54-59	>60
30-39	<27	28-33	34-41	42-47	48-52	53-58	>59
40-49	<25	26-31	32-40	41-45	46-50	51-56	>57
50-65	<21	22-28	29-36	37-41	42-45	46-49	>50

Appendix C

World Road Racing Rankings

1982   2/10 Kenyan   Kamba, Kikuyu
1. Alberto Salazar 2. Michael Musyoki (Kamba) 3. Jon Sinclair 4. Greg Meyer 5. Rodolfo Gomez 6. Rod Dixon 7. Nick Rose 8. Gabriel Kamau (Kikuyu) 9. Benji Durden 10. Dick Beardsley and Bill Rodgers (tie)

1983   2/10 Kenyan   2 Kamba
1. Michael Musyoki (Kamba) 2. Rod Dixon 3. Joseph Nzau (Kamba) 4. Alberto Salazar 5.Greg Meyer 6. Paul Cummings 7. Gidamis Shahanga 8. Geoff Smith 9.Pat Porter 10. Nick Rose

1984   4/10 Kenyan   2 Kamba, 1 Kalenjin, 1 Kikuyu
1. Carlos Lopes 2. Steve Jones 3. Michael Musyoki (Kamba) 4. John Treacy 5.Joseph Nzau (Kamba) 6. Rob de Castella 7. Charlie Spedding 8. Simeon Kigen (Kalenjin-Nandi) 9. Marcus Nenow 10. Gabriel Kamau (Kikuyu) & Nick Rose (tie)

1985   2/10 Kenyan   Kalenjin, Kamba
1. Carlos Lopes 2. Simeon Kigen (Kalenjin-Nandi) 3. Steve Jones 4. Michael Musyoki (Kamba) 5. Mark Curp 6. Bruce Bickford 7. Ken Martin 8. Rob de Castella 9. Paul Davies-Hale 10. Phil Coppess

1986   2/10 Kenyan   Kalenjin, Kamba
1. Arturo Barrios 2. Peter Koech (Kalenjin-Nandi) 3. Ed Eyestone 4. Keith Brantly 5. Michael Musyoki (Kamba) 6. Jon Sinclair 7. John Doherty 8. Rob de Castella 9. Bill Donakowski 10. Bruce Bickford

1987   1/10 Kenyan   Kalenjin
1. Arturo Barrios 2. Steve Binns 3. Rolando Vera 4. John Gregorek 5. Marcos Barreto 6. Ed Eyestone 7. Mark Curp 8. John Doherty 9. Keith Brantly 10. Ibrahim Hussein (Kalenjin-Nandi)

1988   2/10 Kenyan   2 Kalenjin
1. Arturo Barrios 2. John Doherty 3. John Treacy 4. Ed Eyestone 5.Peter Koech (Kalenjin-Nandi) 6. Mark Curp 7. Steve Spence 8. Steve Jones 9. Joseph Kipsang (Kalenjin-Nandi) 10. Jon Sinclair

1989   3/10 Kenyan   Kalenjin, Kamba, Kisii
1. Arturo Barrios 2. John Halvorsen 3. Ed Eyestone 4. Yobes Ondieki (Kisii) 5. Ibrahim Hussein (Kalenjin-Nandi) 6. Marc Nenow 7. Keith Brantly 8. Steve Spence 9.Andrew Lloyd 10. William Musyoki (Kamba)

1990   No Kenyans in top 10
1. Dionicio Ceron 2. Steve Moneghetti 3. John Halvorsen 4. Martin Pitayo (Mexico) 5. Ed Eyestone 6. Steve Spence 7. Jon Sinclair 8. Brian Sheriff 9. John Campbell 10. Mark Curp

1991   2/10 Kenyan   Kalenjin, Kamba
1. Steve Spence 2. Alejandro Cruz 3. Frank O'Mara 4. Steve Kogo (Kalenjin-Nandi) 5.Dionicio Ceron 6. John Halvorsen 7. Ed Eyestone 8. Mark Plaatjes 9.William Musyoki (Kamba) 10. Bill Reifsnyder
1. Liz McColgan 2. Lynn Jennings 3. Jill Hunter 4. Wanda Panfil 5.Francie Larrieu-Smith 6. Delilah Asiago (Kisii) 7. Judi St. Hilaire 8. Susan Sirma (Kalenjin) 9. Kim Jones 10. Shelly Steely

1992   9/10 Kenyan   5 Kalenjin, 3 Kisii, 1 Kamba
1. William Mutwol (Kalenjin-Marakwet) 2. Benson Masya (Kamba) 3. Dominic Kirui (Kalenjin-Kipsigis) 4. William Sigei (Kalenjin-Kipsigis) 5. Simon Karori (Kisii) 6. Sammy Lelei (Kalenjin-Nandi) 7. Lameck Aguta (Kisii) 8. Ondoro Osoro (Kisii) 9.Boay Akonay (Tanzania) 10. Godfrey Kiprotich (Kalenjin-Keiyo)
1. Lynn Jennings 2. Liz McColgan 3. Lisa Ondieki 4. Olga Markova 5. Uta Pippig 6. Judi St. Hilaire 7. Jill Hunter 8. Wilma Van Onna 9.Albina Galliamova 10. Lorraine Moller

1993   5/10 Kenyan   3 Kalenjin, 2 Kisii
1. Phillimon Hanneck 2. Lucketz Swartbooi 3. Arturo Barrios 4. Simon Chemoiyo (Kalenjin-Nandi) 5. Thomas Osano (Kisii) 6. Sammy Lelei (Kalenjin-Nandi) 7. Simon Karori (Kisii) 8. Mark Plaatjes 9. Dominic Kirui (Kalenjin-Kipsigis) 10. Valdenor Dos Santos
1. Lynn Jennings 2. Uta Pippig 3. Anne Marie Letko 4. Carmen de Oliveira 5. Lisa Ondieki 6. Judi St. Hilaire 7. Colleen De Reuck 8.Caroln Schuwalow 9. Gladys Odeyo 10. Olga Appell

1994   6/10 Kenyan   2 Kalenjin, 1 Kamba, 3 Kisii
1. William Sigei (Kalenjin-Kipsigis) 2. Benson Masya (Kamba) 3. Phillimon Hanneck 4. Josphat Machuka (Kisii) 5. Armando Quintanilla 6. Lazarus Nyakeraka (Kisii) 7. Jon Brown 8.Thomas Osano (Kisii) 9. Simon Chemoywo (Kalenjin-Nandi) 10. German Silva
1. Elana Meyer 2. Tegla Loroupe 3. Olga Appell 4. Lynn Jennings 5.Anne Marie Letko 6. Jane Omoro 7. Delilah Asiago 8. Laura Mykytok 9.Nadia Prasad 10. Carmen de Oliveira

1995   6/10 Kenyan   1 Kalenjin, 2 Kikuyu, 3 Kisii
1. Ismael Kirui (Kalenjin-Marakwet) 2. Josphat Machuka (Kisii) 3. Phillimon Hanneck 4. Joseph Kimani (Kikuyu) 5. Simon Morolong (S. Africa) 6. Thomas Osano (Kisii) 7. Joseph Kamau (Kikuyu) 8. Armando Quintanilla 9. Peter Whitehead 10. Simon Karori (Kisii)
Top 3 women Kenyan
1. Delilah Asiago 2. Rose Cheruiyot 3. Tegla Loroupe 4. Uta Pippig 5. Lynn Jennings 6. Joan Nesbit 7. Olga Appell 8. Collette Murphy 9. Kamila Gradus 10. Colleen De Reuck

1996   7/10 Kenyan   2 Kalenjin, 3 Kikuyu, 2 Kisii
1. Joseph Kimani (Kikuyu) 2. Joseph Kamau (Kikuyu) 3. Lazarus Nyakeraka (Kisii) 4. Peter Githuka (Kikuyu) 5. Simon Rono (Kalenjin-Nandi) 6. Phillimon Hanneck 7. Thomas Osano (Kisii) 8. Khalid Khannouchi 9. James Bungei (Kalenjin-Nandi) 10. Jon Brown
1. Catherine Ndereba 2. Hellen Kimaiyo 3. Colleen De Reuck 4. Tegla Loroupe 5. Anne Marie Lauck 6. Lynn Jennings 7. Elena Meyer 8.Valentina Yegorova 9. Libbie Johnson 10. Liz McColgan

1997   8/10 Kenyan   4 Kisii, 2 Kikuyu, 2 Kalenjin
1. Joseph Kimani (Kikuyu) 2. Khalid Khannouchi 3. Paul Koech (Kalenjin-Nandi) 4. Thomas Nyariki (Kisii) 5. Peter Githuka (Kikuyu) 6. Godfrey Kiprotich (Kalenjin-Keiyo) 7. Ondoro Osoro (Kisii) 8. Hexron Otwori (Kisii) 9. Lazarus Nyakeraka (Kisii) 10. Jon Brown
1. Colleen De Reuck 2. Sally Barsosio 3. Elana Meyer 4. Hellen Kimaiyo 5. Libbie Hickman 6. Delilah Asiago 7. Lornah Kiplagat 8. Joyce Chepchumba 9. Jane Omoro 10. Elena Viazova

1998   8/10 Kenyan   3 Kalenjin, 2 Kikuyu, 3 Kisii
1. Khalid Khannouchi 2. Simon Rono (Kalenjin-Nandi) 3. Hezron Otwori (Kisii) 4. Peter Githuka (Kikuyu) 5. Ondoro Osoro (Kisii) 6. John Korir

(Kalenjin-Kipsigis) 7. Joseph Kariuki (Kikuyu) 8. Gert Thys 9. Thomas Nyariki (Kisii) 10. Moses Tanui (Kalenjin-Nandi)

1999   8/10 Kenyan   4 Kalenjin, 2 Kikuyu, 2 Kisii
1. Khalid Khannouchi 2. Simon Bor (Kalenjin-Nandi) 3. John Korir (Kalenjin-Kipsigis) 4. Moses Tanui (Kalenjin-Nandi) 5.Joshua Chelanga (Kalenjin-Kipsigis) 6. Joseph Kimani (Kikuyu) 7. Lazarus Nyakeraka (Kisii) 8. David Makori (Kisii) 9. Peter Githuka (Kikuyu) 10. Armando Quintanilla

2000   6/10 Kenyan   4 Kalenjin, 1 Kikuyu, 1 Kisii
1. Reuben Cheruiyot (Kalenjin-Nandi) 2. Joseph Kimani (Kikuyu) 3. Khalid Khannouchi 4. Mark Yatich (Kalenjin-Nandi) 5. Faustin Baha 6. David Makori (Kisii) 7. Antonio Pinto 8. Hendrick Ramaala 9. John Korir (Kalenjin-Kipsigis) 10. David Chelule (Kalenjin-Nandi)
1. Tegla Loroupe 2. Catherine Ndereba 3. Naoko Takahashi 4. Lornah Kiplagat 5. Lidia Simon 6. Derartu Tulu 7. Elana Meyer 8. Joyce Chepchumba 9. Esther Wanjiru 10. Restituta Joseph

2001   5/10 Kenyan   5 Kalenjin
1. Paul Tergat (Kalenjin-Tugen) 2. John Korir (Kalenjin-Kipsigis) 3. Haile Gebrselassie 4. John Koskei (Kalenjin-Nandi) 5.Shadrack Hoff 6. Evans Rutto (Kalenjin-Marakwet) 7. John Yuda 8. Abdelkader El Mouaziz 9. Hendrick Ramaala 10. Peter Chebet (Kalenjin-Marakwet)
1. Susan Chepkemei 2. Lornah Kiplagat 3. Catherine Ndereba 4. Derartu Tulu 5. Lidia Simon 6. Misuki Noguchi 7. Elana Meyer 8. Edith Masai 9. Pamela Chepchumba 10. Fernanda Ribiero

2002   5/10 Kenyan   4 Kalenjin, 1 Kikuyu
1. Paul Kosgei (Kalenjin-Nandi) 2. Haile Gebrselassie 3. Chales Kamathi (Kikuyu) 4. James Koskei (Kalenjin-Nandi) 5. Paul Tergat (Kalenjin-Tugen) 6. Khalid Khannouchi 7. John Yuda 8. Tesfaye Jifar 9.Hendrick Ramaala 10. Jackson Koech (Kalenjin-Nandi)
4/10 women Kenyan
1. Paula Radcliffe 2. Lornah Kiplagat 3. Birhane Adere 4. Susan Chepkemei 5. Catherine Ndereba 6. Sonia O'Sullivan 7. Deena Drossin 8. Asmae Leghzaoui 9. Isabella Ochichi 10. Mizuki Noguchi

2003   6/10 Kenyan   5 Kalenjin, 1 Kisii
1. John Korir (Kalenjin) 2. Paul Kosgei (Kalenjin) 3. Kenenisa Bekele 4. Robert Cheruiyot (Kalenjin) 5. Dejene Berhanu 6. Martin Lel (Kalenjin) 7. Gilbert Okari (Kisii) 8.Hendrick Ramaala 9. John Yuda 10. Paul Tergat (Kalenjin-Tugen)

1. Paula Radcliffe 2. Birhane Adere 3. Lornah Kiplagat 4. Catherine Ndereba 5. SusanChepkemei 6. Derartu Tulu 7. Deena Drossin 8. Isabella Ochichi 9. Benita Johnson 10. Mizuki Noguchi

Source: Running Times Magazine

Appendix D

World Cross Country Championships (Men)

Team Championships

1980 ENGLAND
1981 ETHIOPIA
1982 ETHIOPIA
1983 ETHIOPIA
1984 ETHIOPIA
1985 ETHIOPIA
1986 KENYA

1987 KENYA	ENGLAND	
1988 KENYA	ETHIOPIA	FRANCE
1989 KENYA	GREAT BRITAIN	ETHIOPIA
1990 KENYA	ETHIOPIA	SPAIN
1991 KENYA	ETHIOPIA	SPAIN
1992 KENYA	FRANCE	GREAT BRITAIN
1993 KENYA	ETHIOPIA	PORTUGAL
1994 KENYA	MOROCCO	ETHIOPIA
1995 KENYA	MOROCCO	SPAIN
1996 KENYA	MOROCCO	ETHIOPIA
1997 KENYA	MOROCCO	ETHIOPIA
1998 KENYA	ETHIOPIA	MOROCCO
1999 KENYA	ETHIOPIA	TANZANI A
2000 KENYA	ETHIOPIA	PORTUGAL
2001 KENYA	FRANCE	USA
2002 KENYA	ETHIOPIA	MOROCCO
2003 KENYA	ETHIOPIA	MOROCCO

<http://sportsfacts.net/history/athletics/world_cross_country_championships/world_cros
s_country_championships.html>

Individual Championships

2003 Lausanne
Long Course

1.	Bekele Kenenisa	ETH	35:56
2.	Ivuti Patrick	KEN	36:09
3.	Gebremariam Gebre-egziabher	ETH	36:17
4.	Limo Richard	KEN	36:39
5.	Koech Paul	KEN	36:42
6.	Korir John Cheruiyot	KEN	36:50
7.	Sihine Sileshi	ETH	37:03
8.	Chatt Hicham	MAR	37:07
9.	Tadesse Zersenay	ERI	37:10
10.	El Amri Khalid	MAR	37:12

Short Course

1.	Bekele Kenenisa	ETH	11:01
2.	Kibowen John	KEN	11:04
3.	Limo Benjamin	KEN	11:06
4.	Kipyego Michael	KEN	11:18
5.	Kiplitany Thomas	KEN	11:20
6.	El Amri Khalid	MAR	11:22
7.	Tadesse Meba	ETH	11:24
8.	Kilel David	KEN	11:25
9.	Sghyr Ismaïl	FRA	11:27
10.	Goumri Abderrahim	MAR	11:28

2002 Dublin
Long Course

1.	Bekele Kenenisa	ETH	34:52
2.	Yuda John	TAN	34:58
3.	Talel Wilberforce	KEN	35:20
4.	Limo Richard	KEN	35:26
5.	Kamathi Charles	KEN	35:29
6.	Chepkurui Albert	KEN	35:32
7.	Goumri Abderrahim	MAR	35:43
8.	Kifle Yonas	ERI	35:47
9.	Mitei Enock	KEN	35:49
10.	Gharib Jaouad	MAR	35:57

Short Course

1.	Bekele Kenenisa	ETH	12:11
2.	Kipkosgei Luke	KEN	12:18
3.	Mekonnen Hailu	ETH	12:20
4.	Kipketer Sammy	KEN	12:26
5.	Mottram Craig	AUS	12:27
6.	Nyamu Julius	KEN	12:30
7.	Jiménez Antonio	ESP	12:30
8.	Kosgei Joseph	KEN	12:32
9.	El Amri Khalid	MAR	12:33
10.	Maazouzi Driss	FRA	12:34

2001 Ostend

Long Course

1.	Mourhit Mohammed	BEL	39:53
2.	Lebid Sergiy	UKR	40:03
3.	Kamathi Charles	KEN	40:05
4.	Guerra Paulo	POR	40:06
5.	Kosgei Paul	KEN	40:09
6.	El Himer Driss	FRA	40:13
7.	Ivuti Patrick	KEN	40:16
8.	Ornelas Hélder	POR	40:33
9.	Gómez Alejandro	ESP	40:37
10.	Stefko Róbert	SVK	40:41

Short Course

1.	Koech Enock	KEN	12:40
2.	Bekele Kenenisa	ETH	12:42
3.	Limo Benjamin	KEN	12:43
4.	Kipketer Sammy	KEN	12:44
5.	Kataron Cyrus	KEN	12:45
6.	Chepkurui Albert	KEN	12:46
7.	Kibowen John	KEN	12:49
8.	Mottram Craig	AUS	12:49
9.	Boulami Brahim	MAR	13:00
10.	Mekonnen Hailu	ETH	13:03

2000 Vilamoura

Long Course

1.	Mourhit Mohammed	BEL	35:00
2.	Mezgebu Assefa	ETH	35:01
3.	Tergat Paul	KEN	35:02
4.	Ivuti Patrick	KEN	35:03
5.	Kapkeny Talel Wilberforce	KEN	35:06
6.	Koech Paul	KEN	35:22
7.	Kamathi Charles	KEN	35:51
8.	Lebed Sergey	UKR	35:52
9.	Béhar Abdellah	FRA	35:55
10.	Henriques Eduardo	POR	35:56

Short Course

1.	Kibowen John	KEN	11:11
2.	Kipketer Sammy	KEN	11:12
3.	Kosgei Paul	KEN	11:15
4.	Maina Leonard Mucheru	KEN	11:21
5.	Chebii Abraham	KEN	11:25
6.	Mekonnen Hailu	ETH	11:27
7.	Mosima Philip	KEN	11:29
8.	El Wardi Mohamed Saïd	MAR	11:33
9.	Bessou Laïd	ALG	11:34
10.	Lebed Sergey	UKR	11:36

1999 Belfast

Long Course

1.	Tergat Paul	KEN	38:28
2.	Ivuti Patrick	KEN	38:32
3.	Guerra Paulo	POR	38:46
4.	Chelanga Joshua	KEN	39:05
5.	Rutto Evans	KEN	39:12
6.	Koech Paul	KEN	39:51
7.	Mourhit Mohammed	BEL	40:09
8.	Brown Jon	GBR	40:09
9.	Jifar Habte	ETH	40:21
10.	Castro Domingos	POR	40:25

Short Course

1.	LIMO Benjamin	KEN	12:28
2.	KOSGEI Paul	KEN	12:31

3. MEKONNEN Hailu	ETH	12:35
4. WOLDE Million	ETH	12:36
5. KOSKEI James	KEN	12:38
6. GACHARA Daniel	KEN	12:41
7. BEHAR Abdellah	FRA	12:44
8. KOSGEI John	KEN	12:45
9. LAHSSINI El Hassan	MAR	12:47
10. AMYN Mohammed	MAR	12:50

1998 Marrakech
Long Course

1. TERGAT Paul	KEN	34:01
2. KOECH Paul	KEN	34:06
3. MEZEGEBU Assefa	ETH	34:28
4. NYARIKI Thomas	KEN	34:37
5. KIPKETER Wilson Boit	KEN	34:38
6. KELONG Christopher	KEN	34:41
7. KIRUI Ismael	KEN	34:41
8. MOURHIT Mohammed	BEL	34:44
9. CASTRO Domingos	POR	34:46
10. RONCERO Fabian	ESP	34:50

Short Course

1. KIBOWEN John	KEN	10:43
2. KOMEN Daniel	KEN	10:46
3. KOSGEI Paul	KEN	10:50
4. LIMO Benjamin	KEN	10:59
5. KOSGEI John	KEN	11:04
6. BOULAMI Brahim	MAR	11:06
7. DAVIS Marc	USA	11:08
8. MISOI Kipkirui	KEN	11:10
9. BOUAOUICHE Hicham	MAR	11:11
10. DABA Maru	ETH	11:11

1997 Turin

1. Tergat	35:11
2. Hissou	35:13
3. Nyariki	35:20
4. P Koech	35:23
5. M Mourhit	35:35

6. B Barmasai	35:35
7. J Kibor	35:37
8. S Sghir	35:56
9. J Rey	35:57
10. K Boulami	35:59

1996 Cape Town

1. Tergat	33:44
2. Hissou	33:56
3. I Kirui	33:57
4. P Koech	34:10
5. Gebrselassie	34:28
6. J Kimani	34:30
7. Skah	34:34
8. I Sghir	34:34
9. Kiptum	34:35
10. Machuka	34:37

1995 Durham 12.02km

1. P Tergat	34:03
2. I Kirui	34:13
3. S Hissou	34:14
4. Gebrselassie	34:26
5. B Lahlafi	34:34
6. P Guerra	34:38
7. J Songok	34:41
8. S Chemoiywo	34:46
9. T Williams	34:47
10. M Fiz	34:50

1994 Budapest 12.06km

1. W Sigei	34:29
2. S Chemoiywo	34:30
3. H Gebrselassie	34:32
4. P Tergat	34:36
5. K Skah	34:56
6. J Songok	35:02
7. A Abebe	35:11
8. A Mezgebu	35:14
9. S Kororia	35:15
10. M Ntawulikura	35:19

1993 Amorebieta (11.75km)

1. W Sigei	32:51
2. D Kirui	32:56
3. I Kirui	32:59
4. M Tanui	33:14
5. E Bitok	33:21
6. K Skah	33:22
7. Gebrselassie	33:23
8. A Abebe	33:29
9. W Bikila	33:51
10. P Tergat	33:55

1992 Boston 12.53km

1. J Ngugi	37:05
2. W Mutwol	37:17
3. F Bayissa	37:18
4. K Skah	37:20
5. R Chelimo	37:21
6. S Moneghetti	37:23
7. D Kirui	37:26

1991 Antwerp 11.764km

1. K Skah	33:53
2. M Tanui	33:54
3. S Karori	33:54
4. R Chelimo	33:57
5. O Osoro	33:57
6. S Nyamu	34:01
7. C Kelele	34:06

1990 Aix-les-Bains 12km

1. K Skah	34:21
2. M Tanui	34:21
3. J Korir	34:22
4. H Bulbula	34:35
5. W Mutwol	34:26
6. I Kinuthia	34:30
7. Dom Castro	34:45

8. W Sigei	37:27	8. E Bitok	34:19	8. A Mekonnen	34:49
9. T Pantel	37:30	9. A Abebe	34:24	9. P Kipkoech	34:50
10. B Le Stum	37:33	10. H Boutayeb	34:28	10. A Prieto	34:52

1989 Stavanger 12km

1. J Ngugi   39:42
2. T Hutchings   40:10
3. W Korichi   40:21
4. S Moneghetti
5. Tesfaye
6. Gomez
7. Masai
8. Kipkemboi
9. Tanui
10. Halvorsen

1988 Auckland 12km

1. J Ngugi   34:32
2. P Kipkoech   34:54
3. K Koskei   35:07
4. B Merande   35:22
5. A Mekonnen   35:25
6. M Tanui   35:25
7. J Kiptum   35:46
8. K Rono   35:47
9. J Muge   35:48
10 H Bulbula   35:51

1987 Warsaw 11.95km

1. J Ngugi   36.07
2. P Kipkoech   36:07
3. P Aprin   36:51
4. A Mekonnen   36:53
5. S Muge   36:54
6. A Masai   37:01
7. P Porter   37:04
8. P McCloy   37:08
9. B Le Stum   37:09
10. D Clarke   37:10

1986 Neuchatel 12km

1. J Ngugi   35:33
2. A Mekonnen   35:35
3. Kiptum   35:40
4. Debele
5. Kipkoech
6. Porter
7. Koskei
8. Muge
9. Cova
10. Easker

1985 Lisbon

1. Lopes   33:33
2. Kipkoech   33:37
3. Bulti   33:38
4. Debele
5. Treacy
6. Balcha
7. Herle
8. Bounour
9. Levisse
10. Bickford

1984 New York

1. Lopes   33:25
2. Hutchings   33:30
3. S Jones   33:32
4. Porter
5. Waigwa
6. Eyestone
7. Levisse
8. Debele
9. Lema
10. Panetta

1983 Gateshead 12.55km

1. Debele   36:52
2. Lopes   36:52
3. Muge   36:52
4. Salazar
5. Prieto
6. De Castella
7. Clarke
8. Canario
9. Porter
10. Cova

1982 Rome 11.98km

1. Kedir   33:40
2. Salazar   33:45
3. Dixon   34:02
4. Kunze
5. McLeod
6. Tura
7. Cova
8. Schildhauer
9. Clarke
10. De Castella

1981 Madrid 12km

1. Virgin   35:05
2. Kedir   35:07
3. Mamede   35:09
4. Goater
5. Prieto
6. De Castella
7. Girma
8. Hunt
9. Hagelsteens
10. Levisee

1980 France

1. Virgin	37:01
2. Orthmann	37:02
3. Rose	37:05
4. Schots	
5. Robson	
6. Antipov	
7. Mosseyev	
8. Prieto	
9. S Jones	
10. Ford	

1979 Limerick 7.5 mile

1. Treacy	37:20
2. Malinowski	37:29
3. Antipov	37:30
4. Simmons	
5. Schots	
6. Zwiefelhofer	
7. S Jones	
8. Zimmerman	
9. Goater	
10. Muir	

1978 Glasgow 7.5 mile

1. Treacy	39:25
2. Antipov	39:28
3. Lismont	39:32
4. Simmons	
5. Arbogast	
6. Virgin	
7. Muir	
8 Fava	
9. Sellik	
10. Levisse	

1977 Dusseldorf 12km

1. Schots	37:43
2. Lopes	37:48
3. Uhlemann	37:52
4. Fava	
5. Ford	
6. Robertson	
7. Lismont	
8. Simmons	
9. Black	
10. Sellik	

1976 Wales 7.5 mile

1. Lopes	34:48
2. Simmons	35:04
3. Ford	35:07
4. Lismont	
5. Uhlemann	
6. Sellik	
7. Tuttle	
8. Fava	
9. Boxberger	
10. Kantanen	

1975 Rabat 12km

1. I Stewart	35:20
2. M Haro	35:21
3. B Rodgers	35:27
4. J Walker	
5. Robertson	
6. Fava	
7. Smedley	
8. Hildenbrand	
9. Orthmann	
10. Roelants	

1974 Italy 12km

1. De Beck	35:24
2. Haro	35:25
3. Lismont	35:27
4. Brown	
5. Uhlemann	
6. Scholz	
7. Smedley	
8. Tijou	
9. Black	
10. Fava	

1973 Belgium 12km

1. Paivarinta	35:46.4
2. Haro	35:46.5
3. Dixon	36:00
4. Kantanen	
5. Polleunis	
6. Clarke	
7. Hidalgo	
8. Roelants	
9. Sviridov	
10. Tijou	

Source: <http://ourworld.compuserve.com/homepages/K_Ken_Nakamura/wcrossm.htm>

Appendix E

World Championships Indoors

1987

800m
1.	Josè Luiz Barbosa (Bra)	1:47.49
2.	Vladimir GraudyÒ (SU)	1:47.68
3.	Faouzi Lahbi (Mor)	1:47.79
4.	Stanley Redwine (US)	1:47.81
5.	Dieudonnè Kwizèra (Bur)	1:47.87
6.	Slobodan Popovic (Yug)	1:48.07
7.	Babacar Niang (Sen)	1:48.33
8.	Rob Druppers (Hol)	1:48.89

1500m
1.	Marcus O'Sullivan (Ire)	3:39.04
2.	Josè Abascal (Spa)	3:39.13
3.	Han Kulker (Hol)	3:39.51
4.	Jim Spivey (US)	3:39.63
5.	Mike Hillardt (Aus)	3:39.77
6.	Dave Campbell (Can)	3:40.82
7.	Dieter Baumann (WG)	3:41.07
8.	Alessandro Lambruschini (Ita)	3:42.25

3000m
1.	Frank O'Mara (Ire)	8:03.32
2.	Paul Donovan (Ire)	8:03.89
3.	Terry Brahm (US)	8:03.92
4.	Mark Rowland (GB)	8:04.27
5.	Doug Padilla (US)	8:05.55
6.	Julius Kariuki (Ken)	8:06.77
7.	Pascal ThiÈbaut (Fra)	8:08.82
8.	Mogens Guldberg (Den)	8:10.25

1989

800m

1. Paul Ereng (Ken)	1:44.84 (WR)
2. Josè Luiz Barbosa (Bra)	1:45.55
3. Tonino Viali (Ita)	1:46.95
4. Stanley Redwine (US)	1:47.54
5. Ray Brown (US)	1:47.93
6. Ikem Billy (GB)	1:48.97

1500m

1. Marcus O'Sullivan (Ire)	3:36.64
2. Hauke Fuhlbrugge (EG)	3:37.80
3. Jeff Atkinson (US)	3:38.12
4. Sydney Maree (US)	3:38.14
5. Herve Phelippeau (Fra)	3:38.76
6. Radim Kuncicky (Cze)	3:39.97
7. Sergey Afanasyev (SU)	3:40.46
8. Manuel Pancorbo (Spa)	3:41.61

3000m

1. Said Aouita (Mor)	7:47.94
2. Josè Luis Gonz!lez (Spa)	7:48.66
3. Dieter Baumann (WG)	7:50.47
4. Doug Padilla (US)	7:50.93
5. Frank O'Mara (Ire)	7:52.21
6. Branko Zorko (Yug)	7:52.26
7. Josè Luis Carreira (Spa)	7:53.22
8. Stafano Mei (Ita)	7:53.73

1991

800m

1. Paul Ereng (Ken)	1:47.08
2. Tom!s de Teresa (Spa)	1:47.82
3. Simon Hoogewerf (Can)	1:47.88
4. Stanley Redwine (US)	1:47.98
5. Joachim Dehmel (Ger)	1:50.58
dq[1]—William Tanui (Ken)	(1:46.94)

1500m

1. Noureddine Morceli (Alg)	3:41.57
2. FermÌn Cacho (Spa)	3:42.68

3. M!rio Silva (Por)   3:43.85
4. Marcus O'Sullivan (Ire)   3:44.79
5. Han Kulker (Hol)   3:45.93
6. Jeff Atkinson (US)   3:46.25
7. Michael Busch (Ger)   3:46.72
8. Abdelaziz Sahere (Mor)   3:47.04

3000m
1. Frank O'Mara (Ire)   7:41.14
2. Brahim Boutayeb (Mor)   7:43.64
3. Rob Denmark (GB)   7:43.90
4. Mogens Guldberg (Den)   7:44.76
5. John Scherer (US)   7:45.12
6. Pascal ThiÈbaut (Fra)   7:47.51
7. JosÈ Luis Gonz!lez (Spa)   7:48.44
8. Matias Ntawulikura (Rwa)   7:48.92

1993

800m
1. Tom McKean (GB)   1:47.29
2. Charles Nkazamyampi (Bur)   1:47.62
3. Nico Motchebon (Ger)   1:48.15
4. Luc Bernaert (Bel)   1:48.30
5. Freddie Williams (Can)   1:51.26

1500m
1. Marcus O'Sullivan (Ire)   3:45.00
2. David Strang (GB)   3:45.30
3. Branko Zorko (Cro)   3:45.39
4. Steve Holman (US)   3:45.59
5. Michael Damian (Fra)   3:45.59
6. Bill Burke (US)   3:46.18
7. M!rio Silva (Por)   3:46.61
8. Marc Corstjens (Bel)   3:46.69

3000m
1. Genny Di Napoli (Ita)   7:50.26
2. Eric Dubus (Fra)   7:50.57
3. Enrique Molina (Spa)   7:51.10
4. Bob Kennedy (US)   7:51.27
5. Mogens Guldberg (Den)   7:52.60

6. John Mayock (GB)   7:54.41
7. Brendan Matthias (Can)   7:55.57
8. Mirko D'ring (Ger)   7:59.42
9. Joe Falcon (US)   8:01.94

1995

800m

1. Clive Terrelonge (Jam)   1:47.30
2. Benson Koech (Ken)   1:47.51
3. Pavel Soukup (Cze)   1:47.74
4. Tor-ÿyvind ÿdegÂrd (Nor) 1:48.34
5. Mahjoub Haida (Mor)   1:48.63
6. Joseph Tengelei (Ken)   1:49.22

1500m

1. Hicham El Guerrouj (Mor) 3:44.54
2. Mateo Caiellas (Spa)   3:44.85
3. ErickNedeau (US)   3:44.91
4. Niall Bruton (Ire)   3:45.05
5. Vyacheslav Shabunin (Rus) 3:45.40
6. Fermin Cacho (Spa)   3:45.46
7. R‚diger Stenzel (Ger)   3:45.64
8. Dominique L'ser (Ger)   3:46.09

3000m

1. Genny Di Napoli (Ita)   7:50.89
2. Anacleto JimÈnez (Spa)   7:50.98
3. Brahim Jabbour (Mor)   7:51.42
4. Mohamed Suleiman (Qat)   7:51.73
5. John Mayock (GB)   7:51.86
6. Reuben Reina (US)   7:53.86
7. Shaun Creighton (Aus)   7:54.46
8. Isaac Viciosa (Spa)   8:01.00

1997

800m

1. Wilson Kipketer (Den)   1:42.67 (WR)
2. Mahjoub Haida (Mor)   1:45.76
3. Rich Kenah (US)   1:46.16
4. Nico Motchebon (Ger)   1:46.19

5. Marko Koers (Hol)   1:46.43
6. Einars Tupuritis (Lat)   1:46.47

1500m
1. Hicham El Guerrouj (Mor)   3:35.31
2. Rudiger Stenzel (Ger)   3:37.24
3. William Tanui (Ken)   3:37.48
4. Branko Zorko (Cro)   3:39.25
5. Andrès Dìaz (Spa)   3:39.73
6. Ali Hakimi (Tun)   3:39.91
7. Jason Pyrah (US)   3:41.64
8. Niall Bruton (Ire)   3:42.65

3000m
1. Haile Gebrselassie (Eth)   7:34.71
2. Paul Bitok (Ken)   7:38.84
3. Smail Sghir (Mor)   7:40.01
4. Gennaro Di Napoli (Ita)   7:41.05 NR
5. Moses Kiptanui (Ken)   7:41.87
6. John Mayock (GB)   7:44.31
7. Fita Bayisa (Eth)   7:49.47
8. El Hassane Lahssini (Mor)   7:50.54

1999

800m
1. Johan Botha (SA)   1:45.47
2. Wilson Kipketer (Den)   1:45.49
3. Nico Motchebon (Ger)   1:45.74
4. Balizs Korinyi (Hun)   1:46.47
5. James Nolan (Ire)   1:47.77
6. Savieri Ngidhi (Zim)   1:47.79

1500m
1. Haile Gebrselassie (Eth)   3:33.77
2. Laban Rotich (Ken)   3:33.98
3. Andrès Dìaz (Spa)   3:34.46
4. William Tanui (Ken)   3:34.77
5. Rui Silva (Por)   3:34.99
6. Ali Hakimi (Tun)   3:37.88
7. Adil El Kaouche (Mor)   3:38.48

8. Richie Boulet (US)   3:39.93

3000m

1. Haile Gebrselassie (Eth)   7:53.57
2. Paul Bitok (Ken)   7:53.79
3. Million Wolde (Eth)   7:53.85
4. Gennaro Di Napoli (Ita)   7:55.60
5. Yousseff El Nasri (Spa)   7:56.70
6. Steve Holman (US)   7:56.96
7. Darren Lynch (Aus)   7:58.12
8. Marco Rufo (Spa)   7:58.24

2001

800m

1. Yuriy Borzakovskiy (Rus)   1:44.49
2. Johan Botha (SA)   1:46.42
3. AndrÈ Bucher (Swi)   1:46.46
4. David Lelei (Ken)   1:46.88
5. Glody Dube (Bot)   1:46.90
6. Pawel Czapiewski (Pol)   1:50.51

1500m

1. Rui Silva (Por)   3:51.06
2. Reyes EstÈvez (Spa)   3:51.24
3. Noah Ngeny (Ken)   3:51.63
4. Laban Rotich (Ken)   3:51.71
5. Adil Kaouch (Mor)   3:51.91
6. Seneca Lassiter (US)   3:52.39
7. Hailu Mekonnen (Eth)   3:52.72
8. Julius Achon (Uga)   3:53.03

3000m

1. Hicham El Guerrouj (Mor)   7:37.74
2. Mohammed Mourhit (Bel)   7:38.94
3. Alberto GarcÌa (Spa)   7:39.96
4. John Mayock (GB)   7:44.08
5. Million Wolde (Eth)   7:44.54
6. Bernard Lagat (Ken)   7:45.52
7. Mark Carroll (Ire)   7:46.79
8. Craig Mottram (Aus)   7:48.34

2003

800m

1. Krummenacker David USA   1:45.69
2. Kipketer Wilson DEN   1:45.87
3. Bungei Wilfred KEN   1:46.54
4. Reina Antonio Manuel ESP   1:46.58
5. Som Bram NED   1:47.00
6. Okken Arnoud NED   1:48.71

1500m

1. Maazouzi Driss FRA   3:42.59
2. Lagat Bernard KEN   3:42.62
3. Hachlaf Abdelkader MAR   3:42.71
4. Chirchir Cornelius KEN   3:43.03
5. Heshko Ivan UKR   3:44.56
6. Nolan James IRL   3:44.67
7. Zadorozhniy Andrey RUS   3:44.80
8. Higuero Juan Carlos ESP   3:44.81
9. Parra Roberto ESP   3:47.44

3000m

1. Gebrselassie Haile ETH   7:40.97
2. García Alberto ESP   7:42.08
3. Kipkosgei Luke KEN   7:42.56
4. España Jesús ESP   7:42.70
5. Abate Abiyote ETH   7:43.21
6. Liefers Gert-Jan NED   7:44.34
7. Leonard Mucheru KEN   7:44.83
8. Mayock John GBR   7:45.32
9. Goumri Abderrahim MAR   7:47.43
10. Weidlinger Günther AUT   7:53.59

Source: <www.trackandfieldnews.com>

Appendix F

World Championships

1983 Helsinki

800m

1. Wülbeck Willi FRG	1:43.65
2. Druppers Rob NED	1:44.20
3. Cruz Joaquim BRA	1:44.27
4. Elliott Peter GBR	1:44.87
5. Robinson James USA	1:45.12
6. Guimarães Agberto BRA	1:45.46
7. Ferner Hans-Peter FRG	1:45.74
8. Patrick David USA	1:46.56

1500m

1. Cram Steve GBR	3:41.59
2. Scott Steve USA	3:41.87
3. Aouita Saïd MAR	3:42.02
4. Ovett Steve GBR	3:42.34
5. Abascal José Manuel ESP	3:42.47
6. Délèze Pierre SUI	3:43.69
7. Busse Andreas GDR	3:43.72
8. Zdravkovic Dragan YUG	3:43.75
9. Walker John NZL	3:44.24
10. Kubista Jan TCH	3:44.30

3000m steeplechase

1. Ilg Patriz FRG	8:15.06
2. Maminski Boguslaw POL	8:17.03
3. Reitz Colin GBR	8:17.75
4. Mahmoud Joseph FRA	8:18.32
5. Hackney Roger GBR	8:19.38
6. Fell Graeme GBR	8:20.01
7. Korir Julius KEN	8:20.11

8. Marsh Henry USA   8:20.45
9. Scartezzini Mariano ITA   8:21.17
10. Ramón Domingo ESP   8:21.32

5000m
1. Coghlan Eamonn IRL   13:28.53
2. Schildhauer Werner GDR   13:30.20
3. Vainio Martti FIN   13:30.34
4. Dmitriyev Dmitriy URS   13:30.38
5. Padilla Doug USA   13:32.08
6. Wessinghage Thomas FRG   13:32.46
7. Bulti Wodajo ETH   13:34.03
8. Millonig Dietmar AUT   13:36.08
9. Kipkoech Paul KEN   13:37.44
10. Leitão António POR   13:38.55

10,000m
1. Cova Alberto ITA   28:01.04
2. Schildhauer Werner GDR   28:01.18
3. Kunze Hansjörg GDR   28:01.26
4. Vainio Martti FIN   28:01.37
5. Shahanga Gidamis TAN   28:01.93
6. Lopes Carlos POR   28:06.78
7. Rose Nick GBR   28:07.53
8. Herle Christoph FRG   28:09.05
9. Kedir Mohamed ETH   28:09.92
10. Debele Bekele ETH   28:11.13

Marathon
1. De Castella Robert AUS   2:10:03
2. Balcha Kebede ETH   2:10:27
3. Cierpinski Waldemar GDR   2:10:37
4. Ståhl Kjell-Erik SWE   2:10:38
5. Masong Agapius TAN   2:10:42
6. Parmentier Armand BEL   2:10:57
7. Poli Gianni ITA   2:11:05
8. Jones Hugh GBR   2:11:15
9. Lismont Karel BEL   2:11:24
10. Husby Stig Roar NOR   2:11:29

1987 Rome

800m

1. Konchellah Billy KEN   1:43.06 (CR)
2. Elliott Peter GBR   1:43.41
3. Barbosa José Luiz BRA   1:43.76
4. Ostrowski Ryszard POL   1:44.59
5. Lahbi Faouzi MAR   1:44.83
6. Ole Marai Stephen KEN   1:44.84
7. Popovic Slobodan YUG   1:45.07 (PB)
8. McKean Tom GBR   1:49.21

1500m

1. Bile Abdi SOM   3:36.80
2. Gonzalez José Luís ESP   3:38.03
3. Spivey Jim USA   3:38.82
4. Chesire Joseph KEN   3:39.36
5. Khalifa Omer SUD   3:39.81
6. Herold Jens-Peter GDR   3:40.14
7. Hillardt Mike AUS   3:40.23
8. Cram Steve GBR   3:41.19
9. Kulker Han NED   3:42.16
10. Geoffroy Rémy FRA   3:43.03
11. Cheruiyot Kipkoech KEN   3:44.54
12. Scott Steve USA   3:45.92

3000m steeplechase

1. Panetta Francesco ITA   8:08.57 (CR)
2. Melzer Hagen GDR   8:10.32
3. Van Dijck William BEL   8:12.18
4. Diemer Brian USA   8:14.46
5. Fell Graeme CAN   8:16.46
6. Marsh Henry USA   8:17.78
7. Koech Peter KEN   8:20.08
8. Sang Patrick KEN   8:20.45
9. Lambruschini Alessandro ITA 8:24.25
10. Pannier Raymond FRA   8:26.50

5000m

1. Aouita Saïd MAR   13:26.44
2. Castro Domingos POR   13:27.59
3. Buckner Jack GBR   13:27.74
4. Délèze Pierre SUI   13:28.06

5. Rousseau Vincent BEL   13:28.56
6. Ignatov Evgeni BUL   13:29.68
7. Hutchings Tim GBR   13:30.01
8. Castro Dionisio POR   13:30.94
9. O'Mara Frank IRL   13:32.04
10. Ovett Steve GBR   13:33.49

10,000m
1. Kipkoech Paul KEN   27:38.63 (CR)
2. Panetta Francesco ITA   27:48.98
3. Kunze Hansjörg GDR   27:50.37
4. Barrios Arturo MEX   27:59.66
5. Binns Steve GBR   28:03.08
6. Vrabel Martin TCH   28:05.59
7. Andriopoulos Spyros GRE   28:07.17 (NR)
8. Plasencia Steve USA   28:11.38
9. Prianon Jean-Louis FRA   28:19.47
10. Vera Rolando ECU   28:20.24

Marathon
1. Wakiihuri Douglas KEN   2:11:48
2. Salah Ahmed DJI   2:12:30
3. Bordin Gelindo ITA   2:12:40
4. Moneghetti Steve AUS   2:12:49
5. Jones Hugh GBR   2:12:54
6. Ikangaa Juma TAN   2:13:43
7. Pizzolato Orlando ITA   2:14:03
8. Kashapov Ravil URS   2:14:41
9. Jørgensen Henrik DEN   2:14:58
10. Vanderherten Dirk BEL   2:16:42

1991 Tokyo

800m
1. Konchellah Billy KEN   1:43.99
2. Barbosa José Luiz BRA   1:44.24
3. Everett Mark USA   1:44.67
4. Ereng Paul KEN   1:44.75
5. Piekarski Piotr POL   1:45.44
6. Gray Johnny USA   1:45.67
7. Sudnik Andrey URS   1:46.36
8. de Teresa Tomás ESP   1:47.65

1500m
1. Morceli Noureddine ALG   3:32.84 (CR)
2. Kirochi Wilfred KEN   3:34.84
3. Fuhlbrügge Hauke GER   3:35.28
4. Herold Jens-Peter GER   3:35.37
5. Cacho Fermín ESP   3:35.62
6. Silva Mário POR   3:35.76
7. Kibet David KEN   3:36.03
8. Di Napoli Gennaro ITA   3:36.56
9. Suleiman Mohamed QAT   3:38.12
10. Yates Matthew GBR   3:38.71

3000m steeplechase
1. Kiptanui Moses KEN   8:12.59
2. Sang Patrick KEN   8:13.44
3. Brahmi Azzedine ALG   8:15.54
4. Kariuki Julius KEN   8:16.81
5. Diemer Brian USA   8:17.76
6. Sahere Abdelaziz MAR   8:19.40
7. Carosi Angelo ITA   8:20.80
8. Panetta Francesco ITA   8:26.79
9. Van Dijck William BEL   8:30.46
10. Mahmoud Joseph FRA   8:37.09

5000m
1. Ondieki Yobes KEN   13:14.45 (CR)
2. Bayissa Fita ETH   13:16.64
3. Boutayeb Brahim MAR   13:22.70
4. Baumann Dieter GER   13:28.67
5. Castro Domingos POR   13:28.88
6. Skah Khalid MAR   13:32.90
7. Ulmala Risto FIN   13:33.46
8. Castro Dionisio POR   13:35.39
9. Denmark Robert GBR   13:36.24
10. Kinuthia Ibrahim KEN   13:38.96

10,000m
1. Tanui Moses KEN   27:38.74
2. Chelimo Richard KEN   27:39.41
3. Skah Khalid MAR   27:41.74
4. Osano Thomas KEN   27:53.66

 5. Nerurkar Richard GBR   27:57.14
 6. Nizigama Aloÿs BUR   28:03.03
 7. Ntawulikura Mathias RWA   28:10.38
 8. Boutayeb Hammou MAR   28:12.77
 9. Gómez Alejandro ESP   28:13.14
10. Morishita Koichi JPN   28:13.71

Marathon
 1. Taniguchi Hiromi JPN   2:14:57
 2. Salah Ahmed DJI   2:15:26
 3. Spence Steve USA   2:15:36
 4. Huruk Jan POL   2:15:47
 5. Shinohara Futoshi JPN   2:15:52
 6. Bettiol Salvatore ITA   2:15:58
 7. Castillo Maurilio MEX   2:16:15
 8. Bordin Gelindo ITA   2:17:03
 9. Gebrselassie Tekeye ETH   2:18:37
10. Dobler Konrad GER   2:19:01

1993 Stuttgart

800m
 1. Ruto Paul KEN   1:44.71
 2. D'Urso Giuseppe ITA   1:44.86
 3. Konchellah Billy KEN   1:44.89
 4. Robb Curtis GBR   1:45.54
 5. Sepeng Hezekiél RSA   1:45.64
 6. Williams Freddie CAN   1:45.79
 7. Tanui William KEN   1:45.80
 8. McKean Tom GBR   1:46.17

1500m
 1. Morceli Noureddine ALG   3:34.24
 2. Cacho Fermín ESP   3:35.56
 3. Bile Abdi SOM   3:35.96
 4. Suleiman Mohamed QAT   3:36.87
 5. Spivey Jim USA   3:37.42
 6. Yates Matthew GBR   3:37.61
 7. El Basir Rachid MAR   3:37.68
 8. Taki Mohamed MAR   3:37.76
 9. Doyle Simon AUS   3:38.04

10. Stenzel Rüdiger GER   3:38.66

3000m steeplechase
 1. Kiptanui Moses KEN   8:06.36 (CR)
 2. Sang Patrick KEN   8:07.53
 3. Lambruschini Alessandro ITA   8:08.78
 4. Birir Matthew KEN   8:09.42
 5. Croghan Mark USA   8:09.76
 6. Brand Steffen GER   8:15.33
 7. Khattabi Elarbi MAR   8:17.96
 8. Carosi Angelo ITA   8:23.42
 9. Creighton Shaun AUS   8:23.45
10. Buchleitner Michael AUT   8:25.88

5000m
 1. Kirui Ismael KEN   13:02.75 (WJ)
 2. Gebrselassie Haile ETH   13:03.17
 3. Bayissa Fita ETH   13:05.40
 4. Bikila Worku ETH   13:06.64
 5. Skah Khalid MAR   13:07.18
 6. Jabbour Brahim MAR   13:18.87
 7. Nizigama Aloÿs BUR   13:20.59
 8. Bitok Paul KEN   13:23.41
 9. Denmark Robert GBR   13:27.09
10. Ntawulikura Mathias RWA   13:28.58

10,000m
 1. Gebrselassie Haile ETH   27:46.02
 2. Tanui Moses KEN   27:46.54
 3. Chelimo Richard KEN   28:06.02
 4. Franke Stéphane GER   28:10.69
 5. Nizigama Aloÿs BUR   28:13.43
 6. Panetta Francesco ITA   28:27.05
 7. Williams Todd USA   28:30.49
 8. Silio Antonio Fabian ARG   28:36.88
 9. Silva Gérman MEX   28:39.47
10. Sigei William KEN   28:54.39

Marathon
 1. Plaatjes Mark USA   2:13:57
 2. Swartbooi Luketz NAM   2:14:11
 3. Van Vlaanderen Bert NED   2:15:12

4. Kim Jae-Ryong KOR   2:17:14
5. Uchikoshi Tadao JPN   2:17:54
6. Dobler Konrad GER   2:18:28
7. Merande Boniface KEN   2:18:52
8. Zhelonkin Aleksey RUS   2:18:52
9. Mansouri Tahar TUN   2:18:54
10. Maher Peter CAN   2:19:26

1995 Göteborg

800m
1. Kipketer Wilson DEN   1:45.08
2. Hatungimana Arthémon BUR   1:45.64
3. Rodal Vebjørn NOR   1:45.68
4. Motchebon Nico GER   1:45.97
5. Rock Brandon USA   1:46.42
6. Parrilla Jose USA   1:46.44
7. Giocondi Andrea ITA   1:47.78
8. Everett Mark USA   1:53.12

1500m
1. Morceli Noureddine ALG   3:33.73
2. El Guerrouj Hicham MAR   3:35.28
3. Niyongabo Vénuste BUR   3:35.56
4. El Basir Rachid MAR   3:35.96
5. Sullivan Kevin CAN   3:36.73
6. Chékhémani Abdelkader FRA   3:36.90
7. Suleiman Mohamed QAT   3:36.96
8. Cacho Fermín ESP   3:37.02
9. Lough Gary GBR   3:37.59
10. McMullen Paul USA   3:38.23

3000m steeplechase
1. Kiptanui Moses KEN   8:04.16 (CR)
2. Koskei Christopher KEN   8:09.30
3. Al-Asmari Saad Shaddad KSA   8:12.95 (AR)
4. Brand Steffen GER   8:14.37
5. Carosi Angelo ITA   8:14.85
6. Ionescu Florin ROM   8:15.44
7. Pronin Vladimir RUS   8:16.59
8. Strege Martin GER   8:18.57

9. Birir Matthew KEN   8:21.15
10. Lambruschini Alessandro ITA   8:22.64

5000m
1. Kirui Ismael KEN   13:16.77
2. Boulami Khalid MAR   13:17.15
3. Kororia Shem KEN   13:17.59
4. Sghyr Ismaïl MAR   13:17.86
5. Lahlafi Brahim MAR   13:18.89
6. Bikila Worku ETH   13:20.12
7. Kennedy Bob USA   13:32.10
8. Bayissa Fita ETH   13:34.52
9. Baumann Dieter GER   13:39.98
10. Hanneck Philemon ZIM   13:41.28

10.000m
1. Gebrselassie Haile ETH   27:12.95 (CR)
2. Skah Khalid MAR   27:14.53
3. Tergat Paul KEN   27:14.70
4. Hissou Salah MAR   27:19.30
5. Machuka Josephat KEN   27:23.72
6. Kimani Joseph KEN   27:30.02
7. Franke Stéphane GER   27:48.88
8. Guerra Paulo POR   27:52.55
9. Williams Todd USA   27:52.87
10. Hayata Toshiyuki JPN   27:53.12

Marathon
1. Fiz Martín ESP   2:11:41
2. Cerón Dionicio MEX   2:12:13
3. Dos Santos Luíz Antônio BRA   2:12:49
4. Whitehead Peter GBR   2:14:08
5. Juzdado Alberto ESP   2:15:29
6. Garcia Diego ESP   2:15:34
7. Nerurkar Richard GBR   2:15:47
8. Moneghetti Steve AUS   2:16:13
9. Pérez Espinosa Andrés MEX   2:16:44
10. Plasencia Steve USA   2:16:56

1997 Athens

800m

1. Kipketer Wilson DEN	1:43.38
2. Téllez Norberto CUB	1:44.00 (SB)
3. Kenah Rich USA	1:44.25 (PB)
4. Konchellah Patrick KEN	1:44.26
5. Rodal Vebjørn NOR	1:44.53
6. Koers Marko NED	1:44.85
7. Ndururi Patrick KEN	1:45.24
8. Everett Mark USA	1:49.02

1500m

1. El Guerrouj Hicham MAR	3:35.83
2. Cacho Fermín ESP	3:36.63
3. Estévez Reyes ESP	3:37.26
4. Morceli Noureddine ALG	3:37.37
5 Hakimi Alí TUN	3:37.51
6. Suleiman Mohamed QAT	3:37.53
7. Hood Graham CAN	3:37.55
8. Andersen Robert DEN	3:37.66
9. Mayock John GBR	3:38.67
10. Stenzel Rüdiger GER	3:38.82

3000m steeplechase

1. Boit Kipketer Wilson KEN	8:05.84
2. Kiptanui Moses KEN	8:06.04
3. Barmasai Bernard KEN	8:06.04
4. Al-Asmari Saad Shaddad KSA	8:13.87
5. Bouaouiche Hicham MAR	8:14.04
6. Croghan Mark USA	8:14.09
7. Svenøy Jim NOR	8:14.80
8. Carosi Angelo ITA	8:16.01
9. Ostendarp Mark GER	8:18.49
10. Boulami Brahim MAR	8:23.34

5000m

1. Komen Daniel KEN	13:07.38
2. Boulami Khalid MAR	13:09.34
3. Nyariki Tom KEN	13:11.09
4. Sghyr Ismaïl MAR	13:17.45
5. Baumann Dieter GER	13:17.64

6. Kennedy Bob USA   13:19.45
7. Lahssini El Hassan MAR   13:20.52
8. Molina Enrique ESP   13:24.54
9. Pancorbo Manuel ESP   13:25.78
10. Bayissa Fita ETH   13:25.98

10,000m
1. Gebrselassie Haile ETH   27:24.58
2. Tergat Paul KEN   27:25.62 (SB)
3. Hissou Salah MAR   27:28.67 (SB)
4. Koech Paul KEN   27:30.39 (SB)
5. Mezgebu Assefa ETH   27:32.48
6. Castro Domingos POR   27:36.52
7. Jifar Habte ETH   28:00.29
8. Rey Julio ESP   28:07.06
9. Baldini Stefano ITA   28:11.97
10. Wilson Darren AUS   28:20.16

Marathon
1. Antón Abel ESP   2:13:16
2. Fiz Martín ESP   2:13:21
3. Moneghetti Steve AUS   2:14:16
4. Goffi Danilo ITA   2:14:47
5. Dos Santos Luíz Antônio BRA   2:15:31
6. Roncero Fabián ESP   2:16:53
7. Leone Giacomo ITA   2:17:16
8. Sakhri Azzedine ALG   2:17:44
9. Tukhbatullin Eduard RUS   2:17:44
10. Rodrigues Antonio POR   2:17:54

1999 Sevilla

800m
1. Kipketer Wilson DEN   1:43.30
2. Sepeng Hezekiél RSA   1:43.32
3. Saïd-Guerni Djabir ALG   1:44.18
4. Téllez Norberto CUB   1:45.03
5. Kimutai Japheth KEN   1:45.18
6. Longo Andrea ITA   1:45.33
7. Kimwetich Kennedy KEN   1:46.27
8. Schumann Nils GER   1:46.79

1500m

1. El Guerrouj Hicham MAR	3:27.65
2. Ngeny Noah KEN	3:28.73
3. Estévez Reyes ESP	3:30.57
4. Cacho Fermín ESP	3:31.34
5. Díaz Andrés ESP	3:31.83
6. Rotich Laban KEN	3:33.32
7. Lelei David KEN	3:33.82
8. Maazouzi Driss FRA	3:34.02
9. Holman Steve USA	3:34.32
10. Hood Graham CAN	3:35.35

3000m steeplechase

1. Koskei Christopher KEN	8:11.76
2. Boit Kipketer Wilson KEN	8:12.09
3. Ezzine Ali MAR	8:12.73
4. Kallabis Damian GER	8:13.11
5. Barmasai Bernard KEN	8:13.51
6. Martín Eliseo ESP	8:16.09
7. Kosgei Paul KEN	8:17.55
8. Ionescu Florin ROM	8:18.17
9. Weidlinger Günther AUT	8:19.02
10. Maffei Giuseppe ITA	8:22.65

5000m

1. Hissou Salah MAR	12:58.13
2. Limo Benjamin KEN	12:58.72
3. Mourhit Mohammed BEL	12:58.80
4. Lahlafi Brahim MAR	12:59.09
5. Komen Daniel KEN	13:04.71
6. Bayissa Fita ETH	13:13.86
7. Mekonnen Hailu ETH	13:18.97
8. Wolde Million ETH	13:20.81
9. Kennedy Bob USA	13:23.52
10. Olmedo Pablo MEX	13:27.74

10,000m

1. Gebrselassie Haile ETH	27:57.27
2. Tergat Paul KEN	27:58.56
3. Mezgebu Assefa ETH	27:59.15
4. Tolla Girma ETH	28:02.08
5. Pinto António POR	28:03.42

6. Jifar Habte ETH   28:08.82
7. Maiyo Benjamin KEN   28:14.98
8. Maase Kamiel NED   28:15.58
9. Chelule David KEN   28:17.77
10. Skah Khalid MAR   28:25.10

Marathon

1. Antón Abel ESP   2:13:36
2. Modica Vincenzo ITA   2:14:03
3. Sato Nobuyuki JPN   2:14:07
4. Novo Luis POR   2:14:27
5. Goffi Danilo ITA   2:14:50
6. Fujita Atsushi JPN   2:15:45
7. Shimizu Koji JPN   2:15:50
8. Fiz Martín ESP   2:16:17
9. Biwott Simon KEN   2:16:20
10. Caimmi Daniele ITA   2:16:23

2001 Edmonton

800m

1. Bucher André SUI   1:43.70
2. Bungei Wilfred KEN   1:44.55
3. Czapiewski Pawel POL   1:44.63
4. Yiampoy William KEN   1:44.96
5. Schumann Nils GER   1:45.00
6. Mulaudzi Mbulaeni RSA   1:45.01
7. Tighazouine Khalid MAR   1:45.58
8. Sepeng Hezekiél RSA   1:46.68

1500m

1. El Guerrouj Hicham MAR   3:30.68
2. Lagat Bernard KEN   3:31.10
3. Maazouzi Driss FRA   3:31.54
4. Chirchir William KEN   3:31.91
5. Estévez Reyes ESP   3:32.34
6. Redolat José Antonio ESP   3:34.29
7. Silva Rui POR   3:35.74
8. Hachlaf Abdelkader MAR   3:36.54
9. Liefers Gert-Jan NED   3:36.99
10. McMullen Paul USA   3:39.35

3000m steeplechase
1.	Kosgei Reuben KEN	8:15.16
2.	Ezzine Ali MAR	8:16.21
3.	Barmasai Bernard KEN	8:16.59
4.	Martín Luis Miguel ESP	8:18.87
5.	Tahri Bouabdallah FRA	8:19.56
6.	Jiménez Antonio ESP	8:19.82
7.	Saifeldin Khamis Abdullah QAT	8:20.01
8.	Yator Raymond KEN	8:20.87
9.	Assmus Ralf GER	8:21.73
10.	Boulami Brahim MAR	8:21.95

5000m
1.	Limo Richard KEN	13:00.77
2.	Wolde Million ETH	13:03.47
3.	Kibowen John KEN	13:05.20
4.	García Alberto ESP	13:05.60
5.	Sghyr Ismaïl FRA	13:07.71
6.	Kipketer Sammy KEN	13:08.46
7.	Abate Abiyote ETH	13:14.07
8.	Mekonnen Hailu ETH	13:20.24
9.	Bakken Marius NOR	13:22.07
10.	Goucher Adam USA	13:24.00

10,000m
1.	Kamathi Charles KEN	27:53.25
2.	Mezgebu Assefa ETH	27:53.97
3.	Gebrselassie Haile ETH	27:54.41
4.	Admassu Yibeltal ETH	27:55.24
5.	Roncero Fabián ESP	27:56.07
6.	Rios José ESP	27:56.58
7.	Kosgei Paul KEN	27:57.56
8.	Korir John Cheruiyot KEN	27:58.06
9.	Jifar Habte ETH	28:02.71
10.	Maase Kamiel NED	28:05.41

Marathon
1.	Abera Gezahegne ETH	2:12:42
2.	Biwott Simon KEN	2:12:43
3.	Baldini Stefano ITA	2:13:18
4.	Tola Tesfaye ETH	2:13:
5.	Aburaya Shigeru JPN	2:14:

6. El Mouaziz Abdelkader MAR   2:15:41
7. Jifar Tesfaye ETH   2:16:
8. Morishita Yoshiteru JPN   2:17:
9. Nishida Takayuki JPN   2:17:
10. Alemayehu Simretu ETH   2:17:35

2003 Paris

800m
1. Saïd-Guerni Djabir ALG   1:44.81
2. Borzakovskiy Yuriy RUS   1:44.84
3. Mulaudzi Mbulaeni RSA   1:44.90
4. Kipketer Wilson DEN   1:45.23
5. Longo Andrea ITA   1:45.43
6. Koech Justus KEN   1:45.63
7. Sepeng Hezekiél RSA   1:45.74
8. dos Santos Osmar Barbosa BRA   1:46.28

1500m
1. El Guerrouj Hicham MAR   3:31.77
2. Baala Mehdi FRA   3:32.31
3. Heshko Ivan UKR   3:33.17
4. Korir Paul KEN   3:33.47
5. Silva Rui POR   3:33.68
6. Estévez Reyes ESP   3:33.84
7. Liefers Gert-Jan NED   3:33.99
8. Chouki Fouad FRA   3:34.05
9. Shabunin Vyacheslav RUS   3:34.37
10. Songok Isaac KEN   3:34.39

3000m steeplechase
1. Shaheen Saif Saaeed QAT   8:04.39
2. Kemboi Ezekiel KEN   8:05.11
3. Martín Eliseo ESP   8:09.09
4. Tahri Bouabdallah FRA   8:10.65
5. Cherono Abraham KEN   8:13.37
6. Martín Luis Miguel ESP   8:13.52
7. Vroemen Simon NED   8:13.71
8. Blanco José Luis ESP   8:17.16
9. Keskisalo Jukka FIN   8:17.72
10. Ezzine Ali MAR   8:19.15

5000m

1. Kipchoge Eliud KEN	12:52.79
2. El Guerrouj Hicham MAR	12:52.83
3. Bekele Kenenisa ETH	12:53.12
4. Kibowen John KEN	12:54.07
5. Chebii Abraham KEN	12:57.74
6. Gebremariam Gebre-egziabher ETH	12:58.08
7. Limo Richard KEN	13:01.13
8. Tadesse Zersenay ERI	13:05.57
9. de la Ossa Juan Carlos ESP	13:21.04
10. Goumri Abderrahim MAR	13:23.67

10,000m

1. Bekele Kenenisa ETH	26:49.57
2. Gebrselassie Haile ETH	26:50.77
3. Sihine Sileshi ETH	27:01.44
4. Hassan Abdullah Ahmad QAT	27:18.28
5. Korir John Cheruiyot KEN	27:19.94
6. Talel Wilberforce KEN	27:33.60
7. Kamathi Charles KEN	27:45.05
8. Maase Kamiel NED	27:45.46
9. Keska Karl GBR	27:47.89
10. Sghyr Ismaïl FRA	27:54.87

Marathon

1. Gharib Jaouad MAR	2:08:31
2. Rey Julio ESP	2:08:38
3. Baldini Stefano ITA	2:09:14
4. Chaíça Alberto POR	2:09:25
5. Aburaya Shigeru JPN	2:09:26
6. Caimmi Daniele ITA	2:09:29
7. Syster Ian RSA	2:10:17
8. Rotich Michael KEN	2:10:35
9. Ramaala Hendrick RSA	2:10:37
10. Sato Atsushi JPN	2:10:38

Source: <www.iaaf.org>

Appendix G

Olympics

1960

5000m
1. M Halberg   13:43.4
2. H Grodotzki   13:44.6
3. K Zimny   13:44.8

10,000m
1. P Bolotnikov   28:32.2 OR
2. H Grodotzki   28:37.0
3. D Power   28:38.2

Marathon
1. Abebe Bikila (Eth)   2:15:17 WR
2. Rhadi Ben Abdesselem (Mor)   2:15:42
3. Barry Magee (NZ)   2:17:19

1964 Tokyo

5000m
1. Bob Schul (US)   13:48.8
2. Harald Norpoth (WG)   13:49.6
3. Bill Dellinger (US)   13:49.8

10,000m
1. Billy Mills (US)   28:24.4
2. Mohamed Gammoudi (Tun)   28:24.8
3. Ron Clarke (Aus)   28:25.8

Marathon
1. Abebe Bikila (Eth)   2:12:12 WR
2. Basil Heatley (GB)   2:16:20
3. Kokichi Tsuburaya (Jpn)   2:16:23

1968 Mexico

1500m
1. Kip Keino (Ken)   3:34.9(A)
2. Jim Ryun (US)   3:37.8
3. Bodo Tümmler (WG)   3:39.0

3000m st
1. Amos Biwott (Ken)   8:51.0(A)
2. Ben Kogo (Ken)   8:51.6
3. George Young (US)   8:51.8

5000m
1. Mohamed Gammoudi (Tun)   14:05.0(A)
2. Kip Keino (Ken)   14:05.2
3. Naftali Temu (Ken)   14:06.4

10,000m
1. Naftali Temu (Ken)   29:27.4(A)
2. Mamo Wolde (Eth)   29:28.0
3. Mohamed Gammoudi (Tun)   29:34.2

Marathon
1. Mamo Wolde (Eth)   2:20:27(A)
2. Kenji Kimihara (Jpn)   2:23:31
3. Mike Ryan (NZ)   2:23:45

1972 Munich

1500m
1. Pekka Vasala (Fin)   3:36.33
2. Kip Keino (Ken)   3:36.81
3. Rod Dixon (NZ)   3:37.46

3000m st
1. Kip Keino (Ken)   8:23.64
2. Ben Jipcho (Ken)   8:24.62
3. Tapio Kantanen (Fin)   8:24.66

5000m
1. Lasse Viren (Fin)   13:26.42
2. Mohamed Gammoudi (Tun)   13:27.33
3. Ian Stewart (GB)   13:27.61

10,000m
1. Lasse Viren (Fin)   27:38.35 WR
2. Emiel Puttemans (Bel)   27:39.58
3. Miruts Yifter (Eth)   27:40.96

Marathon
1. Frank Shorter (US)   2:12:20
2. Karel Lismont (Bel)   2:14:32
3. Mamo Wolde (Eth)   2:15:09

1976 Montreal (Kenyan boycott)

1500m
1. John Walker (NZ)   3:39.17
2. Ivo Van Damme (Bel)   3:39.27
3. Paul-Heinz Wellmann (WG)   3:39.33

3000m st
1. Anders Gärderud (Swe)   8:08.02 WR
2. Bronislaw Malinowski (Pol)   8:09.11
3. Frank Baumgartl (EG)   8:10.36

5000m
1. Lasse Viren (Fin)   13:24.76
2. Dick Quax (NZ)   13:25.16
3. Klaus-Peter Hildenbrand (WG)   13:25.38

10,000m
1. Lasse Viren (Fin)   27:40.38
2. Carlos Lopes (Por)   27:45.17
3. Brendan Foster (GB)   27:54.92

Marathon
1. Waldemar Cierpinski (EG)   2:09:55
2. Frank Shorter (US)   2:10:46
3. Karel Lismont (Bel)   2:11:13

1980 Moscow (Kenyan boycott)

1500m
1. Seb Coe (GB)   3:38.40
2. Jurgen Straub (EG)   3:38.80
3. Steve Ovett (GB)   3:38.99

3000m st
1. Bronislaw Malinowski (Pol)   8:09.70
2. Filbert Bayi (Tan)   8:12.48
3. Eshetu Tura (Eth)   8:13.57

5000m
1. Miruts Yifter (Eth)   13:20.91
2. Suleiman Nyambui (Tan)   13:21.60
3. Kaarlo Maaninka (Fin)   13:22.00

10,000m
1. Miruts Yifter (Eth)   27:42.69
2. Kaarlo Maaninka (Fin)   27:44.28
3. Mohammed Kedir (Eth)   27:44.64

Marathon
1. Waldemar Cierpinski (EG)   2:11:03
2. Gerard Nijboer (Hol)   2:11:20
3. Satymkul Dzhumanazarov (SU)   2:11:35

1984 Los Angeles

1500m
1. Seb Coe (GB)   3:32.52
2. Steve Cram (GB)   3:33.40
3. José Abascal (Spa)   3:34.30

3000m st
1. Julius Korir (Ken)   8:11.80
2. Joseph Mahmoud (Fra)   8:13.31
3. Brian Diemer (US)   8:14.06

5000m
1. Saïd Aouita (Mor)   13:05.59
2. Markus Ryffel (Swi)   13:07.54
3. Antonio Leitao (Por)   13:09.20

10,000m
1. Alberto Cova (Ita)   27:47.54
2. Mike McLeod (GB)   28:06.22
3. Mike Musyoki (Ken)   28:06.46

Marathon
1. Carlos Lopes (Por)   2:09:21
2. John Treacy (Ire)   2:09:56
3. Charlie Spedding (GB)   2:09:58

1988 Seoul

800m

1. Paul Ereng (Ken)	1:43.45
2. Joaquim Cruz (Bra)	1:43.90
3. Saïd Aouita (Mor)	1:44.06

1500m

1. Peter Rono (Ken)	3:35.96
2. Peter Elliott (GB)	3:36.15
3. Jens-Peter Herold (EG)	3:36.21

3000m st

1. Julius Kariuki (Ken)	8:05.51
2. Peter Koech (Ken)	8:06.79
3. Mark Rowland (GB)	8:07.96

5000m

1. John Ngugi (Ken)	13:11.70
2. Dieter Baumann (WG)	13:15.52
3. Hansjörg Kunze (EG)	13:15.73

10,000m

1. Brahim Boutaïb (Mor)	27:21.46
2. Salvatore Antibo (Ita)	27:23.55
3. Kipkemboi Kimeli (Ken)	27:53.16

Marathon

1. Gelindo Bordin (Ita)	2:10:32
2. Douglas Wakiihuri (Ken)	2:10:47
3. Ahmed Salah (Dji)	2:10:59

1992 Barcelona

800m

1. William Tanui (Ken)	1:43.66
2. Nixon Kiprotich (Ken)	1:43.70
3. Johnny Gray (US)	1:43.97

1500m

1. Fermin Cacho (Spa)	3:40.12
2. Rachid El Basir (Mor)	3:36.48
3. Mohamed Suleiman (Qua)	3:40.69

3000m st
1. Matthew Birir (Ken)   8:08.84
2. Patrick Sang (Ken)   8:09.55
3. William Mutwol (Ken)   8:10.74

5000m
1. Dieter Baumann (Ger)   13:12.52
2. Paul Bitok (Ken)   13:12.71
3. Fita Bayissa (Eth)   13:13.03

10,000m
1. Khalid Skah (Mor)   27:46.70
2. Richard Chelimo (Ken)   27:47.72
3. Addis Abebe (Eth)   28:00.07

Marathon
1. Hwang Young-Jo (SK)   2:13:23
2. Koichi Morishita (Jpn)   2:13:45
3. Stephan Freigang (Ger)   2:14:00

1996 Atlanta

800m
1. Vebjørn Rodal (Nor)   1:42.58
2. Hezekiel Sepeng (SA)   1:42.74
3. Fred Onyancha (Ken)   1:42.79

1500m
1. Noureddine Morceli (Alg)   3:35.78
2. Fermín Cacho (Spa)   3:36.40
3. Stephen Kipkorir (Ken)   3:36.72

3000m st
1. Joseph Keter (Ken)   8:07.12
2. Moses Kiptanui (Ken)   8:08.33
3. Alessandro Lambruschini (Ita)   8:11.28

5000m
1. Vénuste Niyongabo (Bur)   13:07.96
2. Paul Bitok (Ken)   13:08.16
3. Khalid Boulami (Mor)   13:08.37

10,000m
1. Haile Gebrselassie (Eth)   27:07.34
2. Paul Tergat (Ken)   27:08.17
3. Salah Hissou (Mor)   27:24.67

Marathon
1. Josia Thugwane (SA)   2:12:36
2. Lee Bong-ju (SK)   2:12:39
3. Eric Wainaina (Ken)   2:12:44

2000 Sydney

800m
1. Nils Schumann (Ger)   1:45.08
2. Wilson Kipketer (Den)   1:45.14
3. Djabir Saïd Guerni (Alg)   1:45.16

1500m
1. Noah Ngeny (Ken)   3:32.07
2. Hicham El Guerrouj (Mor)   3:32.32
3. Bernard Lagat (Ken) 3:32.44

3000m st
1. Reuben Kosgei (Ken)   8:21.43
2. Wilson Boit (Ken)   8:21.77
3. Ali Ezzine (Mor)   8:22.15

5000m
1. Million Wolde (Eth)   13:35.49
2. Ali Saïdi Sief (Alg)   13:36.20
3. Brahim Lahlafi (Mor)   13:36.47

10,000m
1. Haile Gebrselassie (Eth)   27:18.20
2. Paul Tergat (Ken)   27:18.29
3. Assefa Mezegebu (Eth)   27:19.75

Marathon
1. Gezahegne Abera (Eth)   2:10:11
2. Eric Wainaina (Ken)   2:10:31
3. Tesfaye Tola (Eth)   2:11:10

Source: <http://ourworld.compuserve.com/homepages/K_Ken_Nakamura/olympic.htm>

APPENDIX H

WORLD HALF MARATHON CHAMPIONSHIPS

1997

1.	KORORIA Shem	KEN	59:56 CB
2.	TANUI Moses	KEN	59:58
3.	CHERUIYOT Kenneth	KEN	1:00:00
4.	RAMAALA Hendrick	RSA	1:00:07
5.	MOURHIT Mohammed	BEL	1:00:18
6.	THYS Gert	RSA	1:00:23
7.	ASSEFA Abraham	ETH	1:00:52
8.	JESUS Luis	POR	1:00:56
9.	BALDINI Stefano	ITA	1:01:01
10.	CHEGE Laban	KEN	1:01:13

1998

1.	KOECH Paul	KEN	1:00:01
2.	RAMAALA Hendrick	RSA	1:00:24
3.	SKAH Khalid	MAR	1:00:24
4.	IBRAHIM Seid	ETH	1:00:31
5.	THYS Gert	RSA	1:00:37
6.	SILIO Antonio	ARG	1:00:45
7.	JESUS Luis	POR	1:01:10
8.	CHIMUSASA Tendai	ZIM	1:01:14
9.	CHIPU Abner	RSA	1:01:20
10.	KORORIA Shem	KEN	1:01:30

1999

1.	Tergat Paul	KEN	1:01:50
2.	Ramaala Hendrick	RSA	1:01:50

3. Jifar Tesfaye	ETH	1:01:51
4. Bihar Abdellah	FRA	1:01:53
5. Henriques Eduardo	POR	1:01:53
6. Chipu Abner	RSA	1:01:54
7. Chege Laban	KEN	1:01:54
8. Tola Tesfaye	ETH	1:01:56
9. Degefu Fekadu	ETH	1:02:16
10. Nobanda Mluleki	RSA	1:02:17

2000

1. Tergat Paul	Kenya	1:03:47
2. Phaustin Baha Sulle	Tanzania	1:03:48
3. Tesfaye Jifar	Ethiopia	1:03:50
4. Joseph Kimani	Kenya	1:03:52
5. David Ruto	Kenya	1:03:59
6. John Gwako	Kenya	1:04:16
7. Zebedayo Bayo	Tanzania	1:04:25
8. Oscar Fernandez	Spain	1:04:25
9. Marco Mazza	Italy	1:04:26
10. Noureddine Betim	Algeria	1:04:40

2001

1. Gebrselassie Haile	ETH	1:00:03
2. Jifar Tesfaye	ETH	1:00:04
3. Yuda John	TAN	1:00:12
4. Ramaala Hendrick	RSA	1:00:15
5. Tola Tesfaye	ETH	1:00:24
6. Rutto Evans	KEN	1:00:43
7. Chebet Peter	KEN	1:00:56
8. Cheboiboch Christopher	KEN	1:01:14
9. Gharib Jaouad	MAR	1:01:41
10. Skah Khalid	MAR	1:01:41

2002

1. Kosgei Paul	KEN	1:00:39
2. Gharib Jaouad	MAR	1:00:42
3. Yuda John	TAN	1:00:57
4. Kifle Yonas	ERI	1:01:05
5. Jifar Tesfaye	ETH	1:01:11

6.	Hoff Shadrack	RSA	1:01:23
7.	Berradi Rachid	ITA	1:01:32
8.	Sato Atsushi	JPN	1:01:37
9.	Kamathi Charles	KEN	1:02:01
10.	Kirui Paul	KEN	1:02:02

2003

1.	Lel Martin	KEN	1:00:49
2.	Joseph Fabiano	TAN	1:00:52
3.	Sulle Martin Hhaway	TAN	1:00:56
4.	Korir John Cheruiyot	KEN	1:01:02
5.	Yuda John	TAN	1:01:13
6.	Songoka Yusuf	KEN	1:01:18
7.	Tadesse Zersenay	ERI	1:01:26
8.	Koech Jackson	KEN	1:01:28
9.	Tola Tesfaye	ETH	1:01:35
10.	Harroufi Ridouane	MAR	1:02:46

Source: <www.iaaf.org>

Appendix I

World Track Rankings

1500m/mile

2002
1. Hicham El Guerrouj (Mor) 2. Bernard Lagat (Ken) 3. Rui Silva (Por) 4. Cornelius Chirchir (Ken) 5. William Chirchir (Ken) 6. Mehdi Baala (Fra) 7. Robert Rono (Ken) 8. Laban Rotich (Ken) 9. Vyacheslav Shabunin (Rus) 10. Reyes Estevez (Spa)

2001
1. Hicham El Guerrouj (Mor) 2. Bernard Lagat (Ken) 3. William Chirchir (Ken) 4. Noah Ngeny (Ken) 5. Laban Rotich (Ken) 6. Driss Maazouzi (Fra) 7. Jose Antonio Redolat (Spa) 8. Enock Koech (Ken) 9. Benjamin Kipkurui (Ken) 10. Reyes Estevez (Spa)

2000
1. Hicham El Guerrouj (Mor) 2. Noah Ngeny (Ken) 3. Bernard Lagat (Ken) 4. William Chirchir (Ken) 5. Kevin Sullivan (Can) 6. Andres Diaz (Spa) 7. Driss Maazouzi (Fra) 8. Benjamin Kipkurui (Ken) 9. Mehdi Baala (Fra) 10. Vyacheslav Shabunin (Rus)

1999
1. Hicham El Guerrouj (Mor) 2. Noah Ngeny (Ken) 3. Laban Rotich (Ken) 4. Bernard Lagat (Ken) 5. Noureddine Morceli (Alg) 6. Andres Diaz (Spa) 7. Reyes Estevez (Spa) 8. Rui Silva (Por) 9. Driss Maazouzi (Fra) 10. Ali Saldi Sief (Alg)

1998
1. Hicham El Guerrouj (Mor) 2. Laban Rotich (Ken) 3. John Kibowen (Ken) 4. Noureddine Morceli (Alg) 5. Daniel Komen (Ken) 6. Noah Ngeny (Ken) 7. Reyes Estevez (Spa) 8. William Tanui (Ken) 9. Rui Silva (Por) 10. Andres Diaz (Spa)

1997

1. Hicham El Guerrouj (Mor) 2. Daniel Komen (Ken) 3. Venuste Niyongabo (Bur) 4. Fermin Cacho (Spa) 5. Noureddine Morceli (Alg) 6. Robert Andersen (Den) 7. Laban Rotich (Ken) 8. William Tanui (Ken) 9. John Kibowen (Ken) 10. Steve Holman (US)

1996

1. Noureddine Morceli (Alg) 2. Hicham El Guerrouj (Mor) 3. Venuste Niyongabo (Bur) 4. William Tanui (Ken) 5. Laban Rotich (Ken) 6. Fermin Cacho (Spa) 7. Stephen Kipkorir (Ken) 8. Elijah Maru (Ken) 9. Marko Koers (Hol) 10. Isaac Viciosa (Spa)

1995

1. Noureddine Morceli (Alg) 2. Venuste Niyongabo (Bur) 3. Hicham El Guerrouj (Mor) 4. Steve Holman (US) 5. Rashid El Basir (Mor) 6. Kevin Sullivan (Can) 7. Abdelkader Chekhemani (Fra) 8. Mohamed Suleiman (Qat) 9. William Kemei (Ken) 10. Eric Dubus (Fra)

1994

1. Noureddine Morceli (Alg) 2. Venuste Niyongabo (Bur) 3. Abdi Bile (Som) 4. Mohamed Suleiman (Qat) 5. Steve Holman (US) 6. Benson Koech (Ken) 7. Azzedine Sediki (Mor) 8. Matthew Yates (GB) 9. Atoi Boru (Ken) 10. Fermin Cacho (Spa)

1993

1. Noureddine Morceli (Alg) 2. Fermin Cacho (Spa) 3. Abdi Bile (Som) 4. Mohamed Suleiman (Qat) 5. Jim Spivey (US) 6. Matthew Yates (GB) 7. Rashid El Basir (Mor) 8. Simon Doyle (Aus) 9. Marcus O'Sullivan (Ire) 10. Jonah Birir (Ken)

1992

1. Noureddine Morceli (Alg) 2. Wilfred Kirochi (Ken) 3. William Kemei (Ken) 4. Fermin Cacho (Spa) 5. Rashid El Basir (Mor) 6. Mohamed Suleiman (Qat) 7. Joseph Chesire (Ken) 8. Jens-Peter Herold (Ger) 9. Jim Spivey (US) 10. Jonah Birir (Ken)

1991

1. Noureddine Morceli (Alg) 2. Peter Elliott (GB) 3. Wilfred Kirochi (Ken) 4. Hauke Fuhlbrügge (Ger) 5. Jens-Peter Herold (Ger) 6. Fermin Cacho (Spa) 7. Said Aouita (Mor) 8. David Kibet (Ken) 9. Simon Doyle (Aus) 10. Jim Spivey (US)

1990

1. Noureddine Morceli (Alg) 2. Simon Doyle (Aus) 3. Joe Falcon (US) 4. Jens-Peter Herold (EG) 5. Peter Elliott (GB) 6. Abdi Bile (Som) 7. Wilfred Kirochi (Ken) 8. Genny Di Napoli (Ita) 9. Tony Morrell (GB) 10. Jose Luis González (Spa)

1989

1. Abdi Bile (Som) 2. Said Aouita (Mor) 3. Wilfred Kirochi (Ken) 4. Kip Cheruiyot (Ken) 5. Seb Coe (GB) 6. Genny Di Napoli (Ita) 7. Joseph Chesire (Ken) 8. Jens-Peter Herold (EG) 9. Herve Phelippeau (Fra) 10. Pascal Thiebaut (Fra)

1988

1. Steve Cram (GB) 2. Said Aouita (Mor) 3. Peter Elliott (GB) 4. Jens-Peter Herold (EG) 5. Peter Rono (Ken) 6. Steve Scott (US) 7. Jim Spivey (US) 8. Kip Cheruiyot (Ken) 9. Dieter Baumann (WG) 10. Joaquim Cruz (Bra)

1987

1. Said Aouita (Mor) 2. Abdi Bile (Som) 3. Jose Luis González (Spa) 4. Steve Cram (GB) 5. Jim Spivey (US) 6. Joseph Chesire (Ken) 7. Jens-Peter Herold (EG) 8. Markus Hacksteiner (Swi) 9. Steve Crabb (GB) 10. Peter Elliott (GB)

1986

1. Steve Cram (GB) 2. Seb Coe (GB) 3. Steve Scott (US) 4. Said Aouita (Mor) 5. Jose Luis González (Spa) 6. Jose Abascal (Spa) 7. Steve Ovett (GB) 8. Sydney Maree (US) 9. Jim Spivey (US) 10. John Walker (NZ)

1985

1. Steve Cram (GB) 2. Said Aouita (Mor) 3. Sydney Maree (US) 4. Jose Luis González (Spa) 5. Jose Abascal (Spa) 6. Seb Coe (GB) 7. Steve Scott (US) 8. Pierre Deleze (Swi) 9. Omer Khalifa (Sud) 10. Mike Hillardt (Aus)

1984

1. Said Aouita (Mor) 2. Seb Coe (GB) 3. Steve Cram (GB) 4. Jose Abascal (Spa) 5. Omer Khalifa (Sud) 6. John Walker (NZ) 7. Joseph Chesire (Ken) 8. Steve Scott (US) 9. Jim Spivey (US) 10. Pierre Deleze (Swi)

1983

1. Steve Cram (GB) 2. Steve Scott (US) 3. Steve Ovett (GB) 4. Said Aouita (Mor) 5. Jose Luis González (Spa) 6. Jose Abascal (Spa) 7. Sydney Maree (US) 8. Pierre Deleze (Swi) 9. John Walker (NZ) 10. Thomas Wessinghage (WG)

1982
1. Steve Cram (GB) 2. Steve Scott (US) 3. Sydney Maree (US) 4. John Walker (NZ) 5. Thomas Wessinghage (WG) 6. Dave Moorcroft (GB) 7. Tom Byers (US) 8. Nikolay Kirov (SU) 9. Todd Harbour (US) 10. Jose Abascal (Spa)

1981
1. Seb Coe (GB) 2. Steve Ovett (GB) 3. Mike Boit (Ken) 4. Steve Scott (US) 5. Sydney Maree (SA) 6. John Walker (NZ) 7. Olaf Beyer (EG) 8. Jose Luis Gonzälez (Spa) 9. Steve Cram (GB) 10. Thomas Wessinghage (WG)

1980
1. Steve Ovett (GB) 2. Seb Coe (GB) 3. Thomas Wessinghage (WG) 4. Steve Scott (US) 5. John Walker (NZ) 6. Jürgen Straub (EG) 7. Andreas Busse (EG) 8. Pierre Deleze (Swi) 9. Harald Hudak (WG) 10. Omer Khalifa (Sud)

1979
1. Seb Coe (GB) 2. Steve Ovett (GB) 3. Steve Scott (US) 4. Thomas Wessinghage (WG) 5. Jürgen Straub (EG) 6. Eamonn Coghlan (Ire) 7. Don Paige (US) 8. Suleiman Nyambui (Tan) 9. John Robson (GB) 10. Willi Wülbeck (WG)

3000m

2002
1. Benjamin Limo (Ken) 2. Abraham Chebii (Ken) 3. Abderrahim Goumri (Mor) 4. Paul Bitok (Ken) 5. Sammy Kipketer (Ken) 6. Luke Kipkosgei (Ken) 7. Salah El Ghazi (Mor) 8. Richard Limo (Ken) 9. Mark Bett (Ken) 10. Sergey Lebed (Ukr)

2001
1. Paul Bitok (Ken) 2. Kenenisa Bekele (Eth) 3. Hailu Mekonnen (Eth) 4. Luke Kipkosgei (Ken) 5. Hicham El Guerrouj (Mor) 6. Abiyote Abate (Mor) 7. John Kibowen (Ken) 8. Sammy Kipketer (Ken) 9. Richard Limo (Ken) 10. Benjamin Limo (Ken)

2000
1. Ali Saldi Sief (Alg) 2. Daniel Komen (Ken) 3. Brahim Lahlafi (Mor) 4. Luke Kipkosgei (Ken) 5. Million Wolde (Eth) 6. Mohammed Mourit (Bel) 7. Mohamed Säid El Wardi (Mor) 8. Small Sghir (Fra) 9. Noah Ngeny (Ken) 10. Benjamin Limo (Ken)

1999

1. Haile Gebrselassie (Eth) 2. Hicham El Guerrouj (Mor) 3. Benjamin Limo (Ken) 4 Salah Hissou (Mor) 5. Brahim Lahlafi (Mor) 6. Daniel Komen (Ken) 7. Paul Bitok (Ken) 8. Mohammed Mourit (Bel) 9. Richard Limo (Ken) 10. Sammy Kipketer (Ken)

1998

1. Haile Gebrselassie (Eth) 2. Daniel Komen (Ken) 3. Luke Kipkosgei (Ken) 4. Julius Gitahi (Ken) 5. Assefa Mezegebu (Eth)

1997

1 Haile Gebrselassie (Eth) 2 Daniel Komen (Ken) 3 Khalid Boulami (Mor) 4 Paul Bitok (Ken) 5 Thomas Nyariki (Ken)

1996

1. Daniel Komen (Ken) 2. Khalid Boulami (Mor) 3. Paul Bitok (Ken) 4. Thomas Nyariki (Ken) 5. Paul Tergat (Ken)

1995

1. Moses Kiptanui (Ken) 2. Noureddine Morceli (Alg) 3. Haile Gebrselassie (Eth) 4. Venuste Niyongabo (Bur) 5. Khalid Boulami (Mor)

1994

1. Noureddine Morceli (Alg) 2. Dieter Baumann (Ger) 3. Paul Bitok (Ken) 4. Moses Kiptanui (Ken) 5. Aloys Nizigama (Bur)

1993

1. Noureddine Morceli (Alg) 2. Brahim Jabbour (Mor) 3. Paul Bitok (Ken) 4. Mohamed Issangar (Mor) 5. Moses Kiptanui (Ken)

1992

1. Moses Kiptanui (Ken) 2. Paul Bitok (Ken) 3. Yobes Ondieki (Ken) 4. Dieter Baumann (Ger) 5. William Sigei (Ken)

1991

1. Noureddine Morceli (Alg) 2. Dieter Baumann (Ger) 3. Brahim Boutaib (Mor) 4. Khalid Skah (Mor) 5. Yobes Ondieki (Ken)

1990

1. Khalid Skah (Mor) 2. Mohamed Issangar (Mor) 3. Yobes Ondieki (Ken) 4. Brahim Boutaib (Mor) 5. Cyrille Laventure (Fra)

1989

1. Said Aouita (Mor) 2. Yobes Ondieki (Ken) 3. Arturo Barrios (Mex) 4. Dieter Baumann (WG) 5. Brahim Boutaib (Mor)

3000m steeplechase

2002

1. Stephen Cherono (Ken) 2. Wilson Boit (Ken) 3. Ezekiel Kemboi (Ken) 4. Paul Koech II (Ken) 5. Reuben Kosgei (Ken) 6. Sa'ad Al-Asmari (Sau) 7. Julius Nyamu (Ken) 8. Antonio Jimenez (Spa) 9. Luis Miguel Martin (Spa) 10. Simon Vroemen (Hol)

2001

1. Brahim Boulami (Mor) 2. Reuben Kosgei (Ken) 3. Bernard Barmasai (Ken) 4. Wilson Boit (Ken) 5. Stephen Cherono (Ken) 6. Kipkirui Misoi (Ken) 7. Ali Ezzine (Mor) 8. Luis Miguel Martin (Spa) 9. Bouabdallah Tahri (Fra) 10. Julius Nyamu (Ken)

2000

1. Reuben Kosgei (Ken) 2. Wilson Boit (Ken) 3. Ali Ezzine (Mor) 4. Bernard Barmasai (Ken) 5. Brahim Boulami (Mor) 6. Kipkirui Misoi (Ken) 7. Raymond Yator (Ken) 8. Luis Miguel Martin (Spa) 9. Eliseo Martin (Spa) 10. Günther Weidlinger (Aut)

1999

1. Bernard Barmasai (Ken) 2. Christopher Kosgei (Ken) 3. Wilson Boit (Ken) 4. Ali Ezzine (Mor) 5. Paul Kosgei (Ken) 6. Kipkirui Misoi (Ken) 7. Damian Kallabis (Ger) 8. Moses Kiptanui (Ken) 9. Elarbi Khattabi (Mor) 10. Bouabdallah Tahri (Fra)

1998

1. Bernard Barmasai (Ken) 2. Wilson Boit (Ken) 3. Moses Kiptanui (Ken) 4. Patrick Sang (Ken) 5. Paul Kosgei (Ken) 6. Kipkirui Misoi (Ken) 7. Eliud Barngetuny (Ken) 8. Elarbi Khattabi (Mor) 9. Brahim Boulami (Mor) 10. Jonathan Kandie (Ken)

1997

1. Moses Kiptanui (Ken) 2. Wilson Boit (Ken) 3. Bernard Barmasai (Ken) 4. Eliud Barngetuny (Ken) 5. Patrick Sang (Ken) 6. Joseph Keter (Ken) 7. John Kosgei (Ken) 8. Paul Kosgei (Ken) 9. Sa'ad Shaddad Al-Asmari (Sau) 10. Matthew Birir (Ken)

1996

1. Joseph Keter (Ken) 2. Moses Kiptanui (Ken) 3. Gideon Chirchir (Ken) 4. Patrick Sang (Ken) 5. John Kosgei (Ken) 6. Bernard Barmasai (Ken) 7. Alessandro Lambruschini (Ita) 8. Christopher Kosgei (Ken) 9. Matthew Birir (Ken) 10. Richard Kosgei (Ken)

1995

1. Moses Kiptanui (Ken) 2. Eliud Barngetuny (Ken) 3. Christopher Kosgei (Ken) 4. Patrick Sang (Ken) 5. Richard Kosgei (Ken) 6. Gideon Chirchir (Ken) 7. Bernard Barmasai (Ken) 8. Sa'ad Shaddad Al-Asmari (Sau) 9. Johnstone Kipkoech (Ken) 10. Steffen Brand (Ger)

1994

1. Moses Kiptanui (Ken) 2. Richard Kosgei (Ken) 3. Eliud Barngetuny (Ken) 4. Mark Croghan (US) 5. Matthew Birir (Ken) 6. Alessandro Lambruschini (Ita) 7. Johnstone Kipkoech (Ken) 8. Patrick Sang (Ken) 9. Abdelaziz Sahere (Mor) 10. William Mutwol (Ken)

1993

1. Moses Kiptanui (Ken) 2. Patrick Sang (Ken) 3. Alessandro Lambruschini (Ita) 4. Mark Croghan (US) 5. Richard Kosgei (Ken) 6. Julius Kariuki (Ken) 7. Steffen Brand (Ger) 8. Elarbi Khattabi (Mor) 9. Matthew Birir (Ken) 10. Shaun Creighton (Aus)

1992

1. Moses Kiptanui (Ken) 2. Matthew Birir (Ken) 3. Patrick Sang (Ken) 4. Philip Barkutwo (Ken) 5. William Mutwol (Ken) 6. Micah Boinett (Ken) 7. Alessandro Lambruschini (Ita) 8. Steffen Brand (Ger) 9. Tom Hanlon (GB) 10. Brian Diemer (US)

1991

1. Moses Kiptanui (Ken) 2. Patrick Sang (Ken) 3. Julius Kariuki (Ken) 4. William Mutwol (Ken) 5. Abdelaziz Sahere (Mor) 6. Philip Barkutwo (Ken) 7. Azzedine Brahmi (Alg) 8. Brian Diemer (US) 9. Johnstone Kipkoech (Ken) 10. William van Dijck (Bel)

1990

1. Julius Kariuki (Ken) 2. Peter Koech (Ken) 3. Patrick Sang (Ken) 4. Francesco Panetta (Ita) 5. William Mutwol (Ken) 6. Graeme Fell (Can) 7. Mark Rowland (GB) 8. Julius Korir (Ken) 9. Alessandro Lambruschini (Ita) 10. Angelo Carosi (Ita)

1989

1. Peter Koech (Ken) 2. Julius Kariuki (Ken) 3. Patrick Sang (Ken) 4. Alessandro Lambruschini (Ita) 5. Hagen Melzer (EG) 6. Graeme Fell (Can) 7. Joseph Mahmoud (Fra) 8. Bruno LeStum (Fra) 9. Brian Diemer (US) 10. Mark Rowland (GB)

1988

1. Julius Kariuki (Ken) 2. Peter Koech (Ken) 3. Mark Rowland (GB) 4. Patrick Sang (Ken) 5. Francesco Panetta (Ita) 6. Alessandro Lambruschini (Ita) 7. William van Dijck (Bel) 8. Henry Marsh (US) 9. Boguslaw Maminski (Pol) 10. Hagen Melzer (EG)

1987

1. Francesco Panetta (Ita) 2. Hagen Melzer (EG) 3. Julius Korir (Ken) 4. William van Dijck (Bel) 5. Brian Diemer (US) 6. Peter Koech (Ken) 7. Graeme Fell (Can) 8. Henry Marsh (US) 9. Patrick Sang (Ken) 10. Raymond Pannier (Fra)

1986

1. William van Dijck (Bel) 2. Hagen Melzer (EG) 3. Henry Marsh (US) 4. Julius Kariuki (Ken) 5. Julius Korir (Ken) 6. Graeme Fell (Can) 7. Colin Reitz (GB) 8. Francesco Panetta (Ita) 9. Patriz Ilg (WG) 10. Ivan Huff (US)

1985

1. Henry Marsh (US) 2. Patriz Ilg (WG) 3. Boguslaw Maminski (Pol) 4. Joseph Mahmoud (Fra) 5. Graeme Fell (Can) 6. Krzysztof Wesolowski (Pol) 7. Julius Kariuki (Ken) 8. Peter Koech (Ken) 9. William van Dijck (Bel) 10. Ivan Konovalov (SU)

1984

1. Julius Korir (Ken) 2. Joseph Mahmoud (Fra) 3. Boguslaw Maminski (Pol) 4. Brian Diemer (US) 5. Henry Marsh (US) 6. Colin Reitz (GB) 7. Krzysztof Wesolowski (Pol) 8. Peter Renner (NZ) 9. William van Dijck (Bel) 10. Domingo Ramön (Spa)

1983

1. Patriz Ilg (WG) 2. Henry Marsh (US) 3. Boguslaw Maminski (Pol) 4. Colin Reitz (GB) 5. Joseph Mahmoud (Fra) 6. Graeme Fell (GB) 7. Francisco Sänchez (Spa) 8. Roger Hackney (GB) 9. Julius Korir (Ken) 10. Domingo Ramön (Spa)

1982

1. Henry Marsh (US) 2. Patriz Ilg (WG) 3. Boguslaw Maminski (Pol) 4. Domingo Ramön (Spa) 5. Hagen Melzer (EG) 6. Wolfgang Konrad (Aut) 7. Ilkka Ayravainen (Fin) 8. Julius Korir (Ken) 9. Colin Reitz (GB) 10. Greg Duhaime (Can)

1981

1. Henry Marsh (US) 2. Boguslaw Maminski (Pol) 3. Mariano Scartezzini (Ita) 4. John Gregorek (US) 5. Patriz Ilg (WG) 6. Domingo Ramön (Spa) 7. Ralf Pönitzsch (EG) 8. Amos Korir (Ken) 9. Solomon Chebor (Ken) 10. Ken Martin (US)

1980

1. Bronislaw Malinowski (Pol) 2. Kiprotich Rono (Ken) 3. Filbert Bayi (Tan) 4. Mariano Scartezzini (Ita) 5. Eshetu Tura (Eth) 6. Domingo Ramön (Spa) 7. Henry Marsh (US) 8. Francisco Sänchez (Spa) 9. Boguslaw Maminski (Pol) 10. Giuseppe Gerbi (Ita)

1979

1. Bronislaw Malinowski (Pol) 2. Henry Rono (Ken) 3. Kiprotich Rono (Ken) 4. Mariano Scartezzini (Ita) 5. Paul Copu (Rom) 6. Henry Marsh (US) 7. Ralf Pönitzsch (EG) 8. Michael Karst (WG) 9. Hillary Tuwei (Ken) 10. Boguslaw Maminski (Pol)

5000m

2002

1. Benjamin Limo (Ken) 2. Sammy Kipketer (Ken) 3. Richard Limo (Ken) 4. Abraham Chebii (Ken) 5. Salah Hissou (Mor) 6. John Kibowen (Ken) 7. Paul Bitok (Ken) 8. Abderrahim Goumri (Mor) 9. Mohammed Amyn (Mor) 10. Mark Bett (Ken)

2001

1. Richard Limo (Ken) 2. Paul Bitok (Ken) 3. John Kibowen (Ken) 4. Million Wolde (Eth) 5. Sammy Kipketer (Ken) 6. Hailu Mekonnen (Eth) 7. Benjamin Limo (Ken) 8. Luke Kipkosgei (Ken) 9. Mark Bett (Ken) 10. Abiyote Abate (Eth)

2000

1. Haile Gebrselassie (Eth) 2. Sammy Kipketer (Ken) 3. Brahim Lahlafi (Mor) 4. Paul Tergat (Ken) 5. Mohammed Mourhit (Bel) 6. Ali Saldi Sief (Alg) 7. Million Wolde (Eth) 8. Richard Limo (Ken) 9. Benjamin Limo (Ken) 10. Daniel Komen (Ken)

1999

1. Haile Gebrselassie (Eth) 2. Salah Hissou (Mor) 3. Benjamin Limo (Ken) 4. Daniel Komen (Ken) 5. Sammy Kipketer (Ken) 6. Mohammed Mourhit (Bel) 7. Brahim Lahlafi (Mor) 8. Paul Tergat (Ken) 9. Richard Limo (Ken) 10. Luke Kipkosgei (Ken)

1998

1. Haile Gebrselassie (Eth) 2. Luke Kipkosgei (Ken) 3. Daniel Komen (Ken) 4. Assefa Mezgebu (Eth) 5. Tom Nyariki (Ken) 6. Paul Tergat (Ken) 7. Brahim Lahlafi (Mor) 8. Salah Hissou (Mor) 9. Khalid Boulami (Mor) 10. Million Wolde (Eth)

1997

1. Haile Gebrselassie (Eth) 2. Daniel Komen (Ken) 3. Khalid Boulami (Mor) 4. Tom Nyariki (Ken) 5. Paul Koech (Ken) 6. Smail Sghir (Mor) 7. Salah Hissou (Mor) 8. Dieter Baumann (Ger) 9. Paul Tergat (Ken) 10. Mohammed Mourhit (Bel)

1996

1 Daniel Komen (Ken) 2 Salah Hissou (Mor) 3 Venuste Niyongabo (Bur) 4 Khalid Boulami (Mor) 5 Haile Gebrselassie (Eth) 6 Bob Kennedy (US) 7 Paul Koech (Ken) 8 Tom Nyariki (Ken) 9 Paul Bitok (Ken) 10 Paul Tergat (Ken)

1995

1. Haile Gebrselassie (Eth) 2. Moses Kiptanui (Ken) 3. Ismael Kirui (Ken) 4. Khalid Boulami (Mor) 5. Smail Sghir (Mor) 6. Dieter Baumann (Ger) 7. Shem Kororia (Ken) 8. Daniel Komen (Ken) 9. Worku Bikila (Eth) 10. Salah Hissou (Mor)

1994

1. Noureddine Morceli (Alg) 2. Khalid Skah (Mor) 3. Brahim Lahlafi (Mor) 4. Bob Kennedy (US) 5. Haile Gebrselassie (Eth) 6. Dieter Baumann (Ger) 7. Khalid Boulami (Mor) 8. Salah Hissou (Mor) 9. Worku Bikila (Eth) 10. Moses Kiptanui (Ken)

1993

1. Ismael Kirui (Ken) 2. Khalid Skah (Mor) 3. Haile Gebrselassie (Eth) 4. Yobes Ondieki (Ken) 5. Fita Bayissa (Eth) 6. Richard Chelimo (Ken) 7. Worku Bikila (Eth) 8. Paul Bitok (Ken) 9. William Sigei (Ken) 10. Brahim Jabbour (Mor)

1992

1. Dieter Baumann (Ger) 2. Paul Bitok (Ken) 3. Yobes Ondieki (Ken) 4. Moses Kiptanui (Ken) 5. Khalid Skah (Mor) 6. Fita Bayissa (Eth) 7. Brahim Boutaib (Mor) 8. Richard Chelimo (Ken) 9. Arturo Barrios (Mex) 10. Mathias Ntawulikura (Rwa)

1991

1. Yobes Ondieki (Ken) 2. Fita Bayissa (Eth) 3. Salvatore Antibo (Ita) 4. Brahim Boutaib (Mor) 5. Khalid Skah (Mor) 6. Ibrahim Kinuthia (Ken) 7. Richard Chelimo (Ken) 8. Julius Korir II (Ken) 9. Mathias Ntawulikura (Rwa) 10. Mikhail Dasko (SU)

1990

1. Salvatore Antibo (Ita) 2. Khalid Skah (Mor) 3. Arturo Barrios (Mex) 4. Yobes Ondieki (Ken) 5. John Ngugi (Ken) 6. Hammou Boutayeb (Mor) 7. Brahim Boutaib (Mor) 8. Mohamed Issangar (Mor) 9. Gary Staines (GB) 10. Dionisio Castro (Por)

1989

1. Said Aouita (Mor) 2. Arturo Barrios (Mex) 3. Brahim Boutaib (Mor) 4. Yobes Ondieki (Ken) 5. Sydney Maree (US) 6. John Ngugi (Ken) 7. Domingos Castro (Por) 8. Salvatore Antibo (Ita) 9. John Doherty (Ire) 10. Dionisio Castro (Por)

1988

1. John Ngugi (Ken) 2. Jose Regalo (Por) 3. Dieter Baumann (WG) 4. Hansjörg Kunze (EG) 5. Domingos Castro (Por) 6. Sydney Maree (US) 7. John Doherty (Ire) 8. Pascal Thiebaut (Fra) 9. Arturo Barrios (Mex) 10. Eamonn Martin (GB)

1987

1. Said Aouita (Mor) 2. Jack Buckner (GB) 3. Domingos Castro (Por) 4. Arturo Barrios (Mex) 5. Pierre Deleze (Swi) 6. Evgeni Ignatov (Bul) 7. Jose Luis Gonzälez (Spa) 8. Dionisio Castro (Por) 9. Sydney Maree (US) 10. Vincent Rousseau (Bel)

1986

1. Said Aouita (Mor) 2. Stefano Mei (Ita) 3. Jack Buckner (GB) 4. Tim Hutchings (GB) 5. Antonio Leitão (Por) 6. Pierre Deleze (Swi) 7. Alberto Cova (Ita) 8. Vincent Rousseau (Bel) 9. Paul Kipkoech (Ken) 10. Sydney Maree (US)

1985

1. Said Aouita (Mor) 2. Doug Padilla (US) 3. Sydney Maree (US) 4. Alberto Cova (Ita) 5. Vincent Rousseau (Bel) 6. Stefano Mei (Ita) 7. Dietmar Millonig (Aut) 8. Nat Muir (GB) 9. Antonio Leitão (Por) 10. Bruce Bickford (US)

1984

1. Said Aouita (Mor) 2. Fernando Mamede (Por) 3. Markus Ryffel (Swi) 4. Antonio Leitão (Por) 5. Tim Hutchings (GB) 6. Paul Kipkoech (Ken) 7. Charles Cheruiyot (Ken) 8. Martti Vainio (Fin) 9. Doug Padilla (US) 10. Evgeni Ignatov (Bul)

1983

1. Fernando Mamede (Por) 2. Eamonn Coghlan (Ire) 3. Dmitriy Dmitriyev (SU) 4. Martti Vainio (Fin) 5. Doug Padilla (US) 6. Antonio Leitão (Por) 7. Thomas Wessinghage (WG) 8. Werner Schildhauer (EG) 9. Markus Ryffel (Swi) 10. Dietmar Millonig (Aut)

1982

1. Dave Moorcroft (GB) 2. Thomas Wessinghage (WG) 3. Werner Schildhauer (EG) 4. Hansjörg Kunze (EG) 5. Fernando Mamede (Por) 6. Henry Rono (Ken) 7. Peter Koech (Ken) 8. Alberto Salazar (US) 9. Dietmar Millonig (Aut) 10. Wodajo Bulti (Eth)

1981

1. Eamonn Coghlan (Ire) 2. Henry Rono (Ken) 3. Hansjörg Kunze (EG) 4. Bill McChesney (US) 5. Dave Moorcroft (GB) 6. Valeriy Abramov (SU) 7. Fernando Mamede (Por) 8. Thomas Wessinghage (WG) 9. Barry Smith (GB) 10. Julian Goater (GB)

1980

1. Miruts Yifter (Eth) 2. Thomas Wessinghage (WG) 3. Suleiman Nyambui (Tan) 4. Kaarlo Maaninka (Fin) 5. Eamonn Coghlan (Ire) 6. John Treacy (Ire) 7. Markus Ryffel (Swi) 8. Aleksandr Fyedotkin (SU) 9. Wilson Waigwa (Ken) 10. Dietmar Millonig (Aut)

1979

1. Miruts Yifter (Eth) 2. Valeriy Abramov (SU) 3. Thomas Wessinghage (WG) 4. Suleiman Nyambui (Tan) 5. Aleksandr Fyedotkin (SU) 6. Rod Dixon (NZ)

7. Henry Rono (Ken) 8. Markus Ryffel (Swi) 9. Mike McLeod (GB) 10. Sydney Maree (SA)

10,000m

2002

1. Sammy Kipketer (Ken) 2. Assefa Mezgebu (Eth) 3. Richard Limo (Ken) 4. Albert Chepkurui (Ken) 5. Paul Kosgei (Ken) 6. Wilberforce Talel (Ken) 7. John Cheruiyot Korir (Ken) 8. John Yuda (Tan) 9. Meb Keflezighi (US) 10. Jose Martinez (Spa)

2001

1. Charles Kamathi (Ken) 2. Assefa Mezgebu (Eth) 3. Haile Gebrselassie (Eth) 4. Mark Bett (Ken) 5. Robert Kipchumba (Ken) 6. Yibeltal Admassu (Eth) 7. Fabián Roncero (Spa) 8. Jose Rios (Spa) 9. Paul Kosgei (Ken) 10. Abraham Chebii (Ken)

2000

1. Haile Gebrselassie (Eth) 2. Paul Tergat (Ken) 3. Assefa Mezegebu (Eth) 4. Patrick Ivuti (Ken) 5. John Cheruiyot Korir (Ken) 6. Felix Limo (Ken) 7. Simon Maina (Ken) 8. Said Berioui (Mor) 9. Girma Tolla (Eth) 10. William Kalya (Ken)

1999

1. Haile Gebrselassie (Eth) 2. Paul Tergat (Ken) 3. Assefa Mezgebu (Eth) 4. Charles Kamathi (Ken) 5. Mohammed Mourhit (Bel) 6 Habte Jifar (Eth) 7. Girma Tolla (Eth) 8. Antonio Pinto (Por) 9. David Chelule (Ken) 10. Paul Koech (Ken)

1998

1. Haile Gebrselassie (Eth) 2. Paul Tergat (Ken) 3. Paul Koech (Ken) 4. Julius Gitahi (Ken) 5. Antonio Pinto (Por) 6. Simon Maina (Ken) 7. Fabián Roncero (Spa) 8. Mark Bett (Ken) 9. Dieter Baumann (Ger) 10. Jon Brown (GB)

1997

1. Haile Gebrselassie (Eth) 2. Paul Tergat (Ken) 3. Paul Koech (Ken) 4. Salah Hissou (Mor) 5. Assefa Mezgebu (Eth) 6. Mohammed Mourhit (Bel) 7. Dieter Baumann (Ger) 8. Domingos Castro (Por) 9. Dominic Kirui (Ken) 10. Elijah Korir (Ken)

1996

1. Haile Gebrselassie (Eth) 2.. Salah Hissou (Mor) 3. Paul Tergat (Ken) 4. Josephat Machuka (Ken) 5. Paul Koech (Ken) 6. William Kiptum (Ken) 7. Aloys Nizigama (Bur) 8. Khalid Skah (Mor) 9. Mathias Ntawulikura (Rwa) 10. Stephane Franke (Ger)

1995

1. Haile Gebrselassie (Eth) 2. Khalid Skah (Mor) 3. Paul Tergat (Ken) 4. Salah Hissou (Mor) 5. Josephat Machuka (Ken) 6. Worku Bikila (Eth) 7. Ismael Kirui (Ken) 8. Joseph Kimani (Ken) 9. Shem Kororia (Ken) 10. William Sigei (Ken)

1994

1. William Sigei (Ken) 2. Haile Gebrselassie (Eth) 3. Aloys Nizigama (Bur) 4. William Kiptum (Ken) 5. Paul Tergat (Ken) 6. Armando Quintanilla (Mex) 7. Salah Hissou (Mor) 8. Khalid Skah (Mor) 9. Ondoro Osoro (Ken) 10. Mathias Ntawulikura (Rwa)

1993

1. Yobes Ondieki (Ken) 2. Haile Gebrselassie (Eth) 3. Khalid Skah (Mor) 4. Moses Tanui (Ken) 5. Richard Chelimo (Ken) 6. William Sigei (Ken) 7. Ismael Kirui (Ken) 8. Fita Bayissa (Eth) 9. Todd Williams (US) 10. Antonio Silio (Arg)

1992

1. Khalid Skah (Mor) 2. Richard Chelimo (Ken) 3. Addis Abebe (Eth) 4. Fita Bayissa (Eth) 5. Arturo Barrios (Mex) 6. Tony Martins (Fra) 7. Salvatore Antibo (Ita) 8. Joseph Keino (Ken) 9. Paul Evans (GB) 10. Francesco Panetta (Ita)

1991

1. Moses Tanui (Ken) 2. Richard Chelimo (Ken) 3. Khalid Skah (Mor) 4. Thomas Osano (Ken) 5. John Ngugi (Ken) 6. Salvatore Antibo (Ita) 7. Julius Korir II (Ken) 8. Arturo Barrios (Mex) 9. Richard Nerurkar (GB) 10. Hammou Boutayeb (Mor)

1990

1. Salvatore Antibo (Ita) 2. Hammou Boutayeb (Mor) 3. Arturo Barrios (Mex) 4. Khalid Skah (Mor) 5. John Ngugi (Ken) 6. Are Nakkim (Nor) 7. Antonio Prieto (Spa) 8. Addis Abebe (Eth) 9. Stefano Mei (Ita) 10. Thierry Pantel (Fra)

1989

1. Arturo Barrios (Mex) 2. Salvatore Antibo (Ita) 3. Addis Abebe (Eth) 4. Kipkemboi Kimeli (Ken) 5. Francesco Panetta (Ita) 6. John Ngugi (Ken) 7. Domingos Castro (Por) 8. Brahim Boutayeb (Mor) 9. Hammou Boutayeb (Mor) 10. Mark Nenow (US)

1988

1. Brahim Boutayeb (Mor) 2. Salvatore Antibo (Ita) 3. Kipkemboi Kimeli (Ken) 4. Arturo Barrios (Mex) 5. Hansjörg Kunze (EG) 6. Eamonn Martin (GB) 7. Francesco Panetta (Ita) 8. Jean-Louis Prianon (Fra) 9. Moses Tanui (Ken) 10. Paul Arpin (Fra)

1987

1. Paul Kipkoech (Ken) 2. Francesco Panetta (Ita) 3. Hansjörg Kunze (EG) 4. Arturo Barrios (Mex) 5. Wodajo Bulti (Eth) 6. Mark Nenow (US) 7. Martti Vainio (Fin) 8. Xolile Yawa (SA) 9. Jean-Louis Prianon (Fra)10. Takeyuki Nakayama (Jpn)

1986

1. Said Aouita (Mor) 2. Mark Nenow (US) 3. Stefano Mei (Ita) 4. Alberto Cova (Ita) 5. Salvatore Antibo (Ita) 6. Martti Vainio (Fin) 7. Domingos Castro (Por) 8. Jon Solly (GB) 9. Hansjörg Kunze (EG) 10. Paul Kipkoech (Ken)

1985

1. Bruce Bickford (US) 2. Alberto Cova (Ita) 3. Mark Nenow (US) 4. Toshihiko Seko (Jpn) 5. Fernando Mamede (Por) 6. Francesco Panetta (Ita) 7. Yutaka Kanai (Jpn) 8. Hisatoshi Shintaku (Jpn) 9. Wodajo Bulti (Eth) 10. Ed Eyestone (US)

1984

1. Alberto Cova (Ita) 2. Fernando Mamede (Por) 3. Carlos Lopes (Por) 4. Martti Vainio (Fin) 5. Mike Musyoki (Ken) 6. Salvatore Antibo (Ita) 7. Mike McLeod (GB) 8. Sosthenes Bitok (Ken) 9. Paul Cummings (US) 10. Bruce Bickford (US)

1983

1. Werner Schildhauer (EG) 2. Alberto Cova (Ita) 3. Hansjörg Kunze (EG) 4. Carlos Lopes (Por) 5. Fernando Mamede (Por) 6. Gidamis Shahanga (Tan) 7. Martti Vainio (Fin) 8. Nick Rose (GB) 9. Steve Jones (GB) 10. Antonio Prieto (Spa)

1982

1. Fernando Mamede (Por) 2. Alberto Salazar (US) 3. Werner Schildhauer (EG) 4. Alberto Cova (Ita) 5. Carlos Lopes (Por) 6 .Henry Rono (Ken) 7. Martti Vainio (Fin) 8. Julian Goater (GB) 9. Gidamis Shahanga (Tan) 10. Alex Hagelsteens (Bel)

1981

1. Werner Schildhauer (EG) 2. Geoff Smith (GB) 3. Mohamed Kedir (Eth) 4. Martti Vainio (Fin) 5. Suleiman Nyambui (Tan) 6. Alberto Salazar (US) 7. Fernando Mamede (Por) 8. Venanzio Ortis (Ita) 9. Bill McChesney (US) 10. Henry Rono (Ken)

1980

1. Miruts Yifter (Eth) 2. Craig Virgin (US) 3. Henry Rono (Ken) 4. Toshihiko Seko (Jpn) 5. Kaarlo Maaninka (Fin) 6. Mohamed Kedir (Eth) 7. Tolossa Kotu (Eth) 8. Lasse Viren (Fin) 9. Aleksandr Antipov (SU) 10. Jörg Peter (EG)

1979

1. Miruts Yifter (Eth) 2. Craig Virgin (US) 3. Mike McLeod (GB) 4. Brendan Foster (GB) 5. Leon Schots (Bel) 6. Aleksandr Antipov (SU) 7. Aleksandr Fyedotkin (SU) 8. Karl Fleschen (WG) 9. Matthews Motshwarateu (SA) 10. Frank Zimmermann (WG)

Marathon

2002

1. Khalid Khannouchi (US) 2. Paul Tergat (Ken) 3. Daniel Njenga (Ken) 4. Toshinari Takaoka (Jpn) 5. Abdelkader El Mouaziz (Mor) 6. Rodgers Rop (Ken) 7. Haile Gebrselassie (Eth) 8. Raymond Kipkoech (Ken) 9. Simon Biwott (Ken) 10. Christopher Cheboiboch (Ken)

2001

1. Gezahegne Abera (Eth) 2. Abdelkader El Mouaziz (Mor) 3. Simon Biwott (Ken) 4. Josephat Kiprono (Ken) 5. Tesfaye Jifar (Eth) 6. Stefano Baldini (Ita) 7. Driss El Himer (Fra) 8. Paul Tergat (Ken) 9. Shigeru Aburaya (Jpn) 10. Tesfaye Tolla (Eth)

2000

1. Gezahegne Abera (Eth) 2. Abdelkader El Mouaziz (Mor) 3. Khalid Khannouchi (US) 4. Antonio Pinto (Por) 5. Atsushi Fujita (Jpn) 6. Japhet Kosgei

(Ken) 7. Elijah Lagat (Ken) 8. Eric Wainaina (Ken) 9. Bong-ju Lee (SK) 10. Simon Biwott (Ken)

1999

1. Joseph Chebet (Ken) 2. Khalid Khannouchi (Mor) 3. Abdelkader El Mouaziz (Mor) 4. Abel Anton (Spa) 5. Josephat Kiprono (Ken) 6. Gert Thys (SA) 7. Japhet Kosgei (Ken) 8. Julius Rutto (Ken) 9. Fred Kiprop (Ken) 10. Moses Tanui (Ken)

1998

1. Ondoro Osoro (Ken) 2. Ronaldo da Costa (Bra) 3. Moses Tanui (Ken) 4. Joseph Chebet (Ken) 5. Fabiän Roncero (Spa) 6. John Kagwe (Ken) 7. Gert Thys (SA) 8. Khalid Khannouchi (Mor) 9. Jackson Kabiga (Ken) 10. Abel Anton (Spa)

1997

1. Abel Anton (Spa)m 2. Josiah Thugwane (SA) 3. Martin Fiz (Spa) 4. John Kagwe (Ken) 5. Stefano Baldini (Ita) 6. Antonio Pinto (Por) 7. Khalid Khannouchi (Mor) 8. Joseph Chebet (Ken) 9. Elijah Lagat (Ken) 10. Eric Kimaiyo (Ken)

1996

1. Bong-ju Lee (SK) 2. Josiah Thugwane (SA) 3. Martin Fiz (Spa) 4. Eric Wainaina (Ken) 5. Paul Evans (GB) 6. Moses Tanui (Ken) 7. Alberto Juzdado (Spa) 8. Antonio Pinto (Por) 9. Vanderlei de Lima (Bra) 10. Dionicio Ceron (Mex)

1995

1. Martin Fiz (Spa) 2. Dionicio Ceron (Mex) 3. Luiz dos Santos (Bra) 4. Sammy Lelei (Ken) 5. Vincent Rousseau (Bel) 6. Cosmas Ndeti (Ken) 7. Antonio Pinto (Por) 8. Steve Moneghetti (Aus) 9. Moses Tanui (Ken) 10. Domingos Castro (Por)

1994

1. Steve Moneghetti (Aus) 2. Vincent Rousseau (Bel) 3. Cosmas Ndeti (Ken) 4. Andres Espinosa (Mex) 5. Boay Akonay (Tur) 6. Manuel Matias (Por) 7. German Silva (Mex) 8. Dionicio Ceron (Mex) 9. Antonio Pinto (Por) 10. Martin Fiz (Spa)

1993

1. Dionicio Ceron (Mex) 2. Mark Plaatjes (US) 3. Lucketz Swartbooi (Nam) 4. Kim Jae-ryong (SK) 5. Cosmas Ndeti (Ken) 6. Richard Nerurkar (GB) 7.

Sevarino Bernardini (Ita) 8. Andres Espinosa (Mex) 9. Vincent Rousseau (Bel) 10. Bert van Vlaanderen (Hol)

1992

1. Young-cho Hwang (SK) 2. Koichi Morishita (Jpn) 3. Stephan Freigang (Ger) 4. Takeyuki Nakayama (Jpn) 5. Jan Huruk (Pol) 6. Tena Negere (Eth) 7. Dionicio Ceron (Mex) 8. Willie Mtolo (SA) 9. Ibrahim Hussein (Ken) 10. Salvatore Bettiol (Ita)

1991

1. Hiromi Taniguchi (Jpn) 2. Abebe Mekonnen (Eth) 3. Jan Huruk (Pol) 4. Ahmed Salah (Dji) 5. Steve Spence (US) 6. Shuichi Morita (Jpn) 7. Salvador Garcia (Mex) 8. Ibrahim Hussein (Ken) 9. Rob de Castella (Aus) 10. Koichi Morishita (Jpn)

1990

1. Gelindo Bordin (Ita) 2. Douglas Wakiihuri (Ken) 3. Steve Moneghetti (Aus) 4. Gidamis Shahanga (Tan) 5. Simon Robert (Tan) 6. Juma Ikangaa (Tan) 7. Martin Pitayo (Mex) 8. Antoni Niemczak (Pol) 9. Belayneh Dinsamo (Eth) 10. Jörg Peter (EG)

1989

1. Juma Ikangaa (Tan) 2. Abebe Mekonnen (Eth) 3. Douglas Wakiihuri (Ken) 4. Belayneh Dinsamo (Eth) 5. Steve Moneghetti (Aus) 6. Alfredo Shahanga (Tan) 7. Ahmed Salah (Dji) 8. Manuel Matias (Por) 9. Ravil Kashapov (SU) 10. Zeleke Metafaria (Eth)

1988

1. Belayneh Dinsamo (Eth) 2. Gelindo Bordin (Ita) 3. Ahmed Salah (Dji) 4. Abebe Mekonnen (Eth) 5. Juma Ikangaa (Tan) 6. Douglas Wakiihuri (Ken) 7. Steve Jones (GB) 8. Takeyuki Nakayama (Jpn) 9. Ibrahim Hussein (Ken) 10. Toshihiro Shibutani (Jpn)

1987

1. Takeyuki Nakayama (Jpn) 2. Hiromi Taniguchi (Jpn) 3. Douglas Wakiihuri (Ken) 4. Ahmed Salah (Dji) 5. Toshihiko Seko (Jpn) 6. Hisatoshi Shintaku (Jpn) 7. Gelindo Bordin (Ita) 8. Ibrahim Hussein (Ken) 9. Jörg Peter (EG) 10. Steve Moneghetti (Aus)

1986

1. Juma Ikangaa (Tan) 2. Rob de Castella (Aus) 3. Taisuke Kodama (Jpn) 4. Toshihiko Seko (Jpn) 5. Kunimitsu Itoh (Jpn) 6. Belayneh Dinsamo (Eth) 7.

Abebe Mekonnen (Eth) 8. Takeyuki Nakayama (Jpn) 9. Gelindo Bordin (Ita) 10. Gianni Poli (Ita)

1985

1. Steve Jones (GB) 2. Carlos Lopes (Por) 3. Ahmed Salah (Dji) 4. Takeyuki Nakayama (Jpn) 5. Djama Robleh (Dji) 6. Charlie Spedding (GB) 7. Rob de Castella (Aus) 8. Michael Heilmann (EG) 9. Orlando Pizzolato (Ita) 10. Shigeru Soh (Jpn)

1984

1. Carlos Lopes (Por) 2. Steve Jones (GB) 3. John Treacy (Ire) 4. Charlie Spedding (GB) 5. Takeshi Soh (Jpn) 6. Rob de Castella (Aus) 7. Juma Ikangaa (Tan) 8. Joseph Nzau (Ken) 9. Dereje Nedi (Eth) 10. Takeyuki Nakayama (Jpn)

1983

1. Rob de Castella (Aus) 2. Toshihiko Seko (Jpn) 3. Carlos Lopes (Por) 4. Takeshi Soh (Jpn) 5. Rodolfo Gomez (Mex) 6. Kebede Balcha (Eth) 7. Juma Ikangaa (Tan) 8. Waldemar Cierpinski (EG) 9. Joseph Nzau (Ken) 10. Hugh Jones (GB)

1982

1. Alberto Salazar (US) 2. Rob de Castella (Aus) 3. Rodolfo Gomez (Mex) 4. Gerard Nijboer (Hol) 5. Juma Ikangaa (Tan) 6. Paul Ballinger (NZ) 7. Benji Durden (US) 8. Dick Beardsley (US) 9. Hugh Jones (GB) 10. Armand Parmentier (Bel)

1981

1. Alberto Salazar (US) 2. Rob de Castella (Aus) 3. Toshihiko Seko (Jpn) 4. Kunimitsu Itoh (Jpn) 5. Shigeru Soh (Jpn) 6. Craig Virgin (US) 7. Bill Rodgers (US) 8. Takeshi Soh (Jpn) 9. Dick Beardsley (US) 10. Jukka Toivola (Fin)

1980

1. Waldemar Cierpinski (EG) 2. Gerard Nijboer (Hol) 3. Toshihiko Seko (Jpn) 4. Alberto Salazar (US) 5. Vladimir Kotov (SU) 6. Satymkul Dzhumanazarov (SU) 7. Rodolfo Gomez (Mex) 8. Tony Sandoval (US) 9. Takeshi Soh (Jpn) 10. Kunimitsu Itoh (Jpn)

1979

1. Bill Rodgers (US) 2. Toshihiko Seko (Jpn) 3. Leonid Moseyev (SU) 4. Shigeru Soh Jpn) 5. Kebede Balcha (Eth) 6. Takeshi Soh (Jpn) 7. Bernie Ford (GB) 8. Sop Choe Chang (NK) 9. Bill Scott (Aus) 10. Kirk Pfeffer (U1987

Source: Track & Field News, Mountain View, CA

BIBLIOGRAPHY

Amin, M., and P. Moll. 1972. *Kenya's World-Beating Athletes*. East African Publishing House. p. 16.

Ajani ya Azibo, D. 2003. *African-Centered Psychology*. Carolina Academic Press.

Angier, N. 1999. *Woman: An Intimate Geography*. Anchor Books. pp. 149–50.

Anshel, M. H. 1994. *Sport Psychology from Theory to Practice*. Gorsuch Scarlsbrick Publishers. pp. 42–43.

Appadurai, A. 1996. *Modernity at Large, Decolonization of Indian Cricket*. University of Minnesota Press.

Azevedo, M. 1993. *Kenya: The Land, the People, and the Nation*. Carolina Academic Press. p. 29.

Bale, J., and J. Sang. 1996. *Kenyan Running*. Frank Cass & Co. Ltd. pp. 51–52, 94.

Bellafante, G. 2003. At Gender's Last Frontier. *The New York Times* (June 8): 9.

Bloom, M. 2000. Olympic Hopeful: Inger Miller. *Runner's World* (June): 56.

Brooks, G. A., T. D. Fahey, and T. P. White. 2000. *Exercise Physiology: Human Bioenergetics and its Applications*. Mayfield Publishing.

Chalmers, D. J. 1996. *The Conscious Mind*. Oxford University Press.

Clifford, J. 1988. *The Predicament of Culture, On Ethnographic Authority*. Harvard University Press. pp. 30-34.

Cox, R. H. 1990. *Sport Psychology Concepts and Applications*. Wm. C. Brown Publishers. pp. 10–11, 37–41, 107.

Farred, G. 1996. *Rethinking CLR James*. Blackwell Publishers.

Hoberman, J. 1997. *Darwin's Athletes*. Houghton Mifflin. p. 228.

Hochachka, P. W., and G. N. Somero. 2002. *Biochemical Adaptation: Mechanism and Process in Physiological Evolution.* Oxford University Press. pp. 75, 206, 382.

Holdstock, T. L. 2000. *Re-examining Psychology—Critical Perspectives and African Insights.* Taylor & Francis Group. pp. 74, 166, 201.

Hoppeler, H., and M. Fluck. 2003. Plasticity of Skeletal Muscle Mitochondria: Structure and Function. *Medicine and Science in Sports and Exercise* 35(1): 97–98.

Huffington, A. 1994. *The Fourth Instinct.* Simon & Schuster. pp. 79.

Imbo, S. 1998. *Introduction to African Philosophy.* Rowman & Littlefield Publishers.

July, R. 1970. *The History of the African People.* Charles Scribner & Sons. pp. 85, 237.

Kennedy, T. 1996. Waiting for Machuka: The Pre-Olympic Drama of the World's Best Distance Runners. *Running Times* (November): 30–32.

Kennedy, T. 1998. Developing Nation: How Long Can the Kenyans Keep Command of Distance Running? *Running Times* (May): 58–62.

Klein, A. M. 1991. *Sugarball: The American Game, the Dominican Dream.* Yale University Press. pp. 107–11

Kornblum, W. 1994. *Sociology in a Changing Society.* Harcourt Brace. Pp. 115, 141, 374, 487.

Larsen, N. 1998. The Riddle about the African Runners. *Djembe Magazine* (January) 23: 5.

Layton, R. 1997. *An Introduction to Theory in Anthropology.* Cambridge University Press. pp. 159, 215.

Lee, B. 1975. *The Tao of Jeet Kune Do.* Ohara Publications. pp. 5–7, 202.

LeVine, R. A. 1994. *Child Care and Culture—Lessons from Africa.* Cambridge University Press. p. 81.

Masolo, D. 1994. *African Philosophy in Search of Identity.* Indiana University Press. pp. 182.

Mayes, R. 2000. Mental Preparations for Racing. *Washington Running Report* (January/February). pp. 44–45.

McArdle, W. D., Frank I. K., and V. L. Katch. 2001. *Exercise Physiology.* Lippincott, Williams & Wilkins. pp. 604–5, 612–13.

Menon, J. 1999. Why Americans Chase Kenyans. *Track and Field News* (July). p. 51.

Mudimbe, V. Y. 1988. *The Invention of Africa.* Indiana University Press. pp. 44, 169.

Mudimbe, V. Y. 1991. *Parables and Fables.* University of Wisconsin Press. pp. 4, 32.

Mudimbe, V. Y. 1994. *The Idea of Africa.* Indiana University Press.

Naidoo, A. V. 1996. Challenging the Hegemony of Eurocentric Psychology. *Journal of Community Health Sciences* 2(2): 2.

Noblit, G. W., R. D. Hare. 1988. *Meta-Ethnography: Synthesizing Qualitative Studies.* Sage Publications. p. 9.

Oldham, J. M., MD, and L. B. Morris. 1991. *Personality Self Portrait.* Bantam Books. pp. 359–60.

Oniang'o, C. M. P. 1995. The Foundations of African Philosophy. *Lock Haven International Review* Issue 9: 1–2.

Pinker, S., and J. Mehler. 1989. *Connections and Symbols.* MIT Press. p. 74.

Plog, F., and D. G. Bates. 1976. *Cultural Anthropology.* Knopf Publishers. p. 125.

Powers, S. K., and E. T. Howley. 1997. *Exercise Physiology.* McGraw-Hill. pp. 27, 56–57.

Rigby, P. 1992. *Cattle, Capitalism, and Class.* Temple University Press.

Rodgers, B. 1980. *Marathoning.* Simon & Schuster. p. 111.

Shipley, A. 1998. Living Small, Winning Big. *The Washington Post* (October 30).

Strauss, C., and N. Quinn. 1997. *A Cognitive Theory of Cultural Meaning.* Cambridge University Press. pp. 8–11, 45, 50, 57, 83–86, 213.

Tanser, T. 1997. *Train Hard, Win Easy.* TAFNEWS Press. p. 96.

Thomas, R. M. 2001. *Folk Psychologies across Cultures.* Sage Publications. p. 57.

Umpleby, S. A. 1989. The Science of Cybernetics and the Cybernetics of Science. *Cybernetics and Systems* 21 (1): 113.

Umpleby, S. A. 1994. Cybernetics of Conceptual Systems. *Cybernetics and Systems* 28(8): 641–43.

Van Bottenburg, M. 2001. *Global Games.* University of Illinois Press. pp. 72–76.

Walton, S., and J. Huey. 1992. *Sam Walton: Made in America.* Doubleday. pp. 207, 213, 249.

Wells, S. 2002. *The Journey of Man: A Genetic Odyssey.* Princeton University Press. pp. 4, 30–31.

Wilson, E. O. 1980. *Sociobiology: The New Synthesis.* Boston, MA: Harvard University Press. p. 159.

Wiredu, K. 1995. *Conceptual Decolonization in African Philosophy.* Hope Publications. p. 9.

Wiredu, K. 1996. *Cultural Universal and Particulars: An African Perspective.* Indiana University Press. p. 45.

Wright, R. 1979. *African Philosophy: An Introduction.* University Press of America. p. 141.

Index